DISCARDED

D0919106

THE DEMAND FOR MONEY
Theoretical and Empirical Approaches

THE DEMAND FOR MONEY
Theoretical and Empirical Approaches

by

Apostolos Serletis
University of Calgary

Kluwer Academic Publishers
Boston/Dordrecht/London

Distributors for North, Central and South America:
Kluwer Academic Publishers
101 Philip Drive
Assinippi Park
Norwell, Massachusetts 02061 USA
Telephone (781) 871-6600
Fax (781) 871-6528
E-Mail <kluwer@wkap.com>

Distributors for all other countries:
Kluwer Academic Publishers Group
Distribution Centre
Post Office Box 322
3300 AH Dordrecht, THE NETHERLANDS
Telephone 31 78 6392 392
Fax 31 78 6546 474
E-Mail <orderdept@wkap.nl>

 Electronic Services <http://www.wkap.nl>

Library of Congress Cataloging-in-Publication Data

A C.I.P. Catalogue record for this book is available from the Library of Congress.

Copyright © 2001 by Kluwer Academic Publishers.

All rights reserved. No part of this publication may be reproduced, stored in a retrieval system or transmitted in any form or by any means, mechanical, photo-copying, recording, or otherwise, without the prior written permission of the publisher, Kluwer Academic Publishers, 101 Philip Drive, Assinippi Park, Norwell, Massachusetts 02061

Printed on acid-free paper.

Printed in the United States of America

To Anna and Demitre

Contents

Part 1: Static Monetary Macroeconomics

List of Tables

Acknowledgments

My intellectual debt to William Barnett, Erwin Diewert, Douglas Fisher, and David Laidler, some of the pioneers of the discipline, should be obvious. Their work provided the framework for my own work and shaped the contents of this textbook.

I am also grateful to Adrian Fleissig, Jim Swofford, and Gerald Whitney who provided great advice and comments on critical issues over the years. My recent work with Adrian on flexible functional forms and demand systems is also marked in the study.

Thanks are also due to my students Periklis Gogas, Terence Molik, and Ricardo Rangel-Ruiz, who provided significant help in the development of the material for this book. I also thank Joanne Longworth for a thoroughly professional job of preparing the camera-ready copy of this book. It is no exaggeration to say that this work would not have been possible without her help.

Finally, I want to thank my wife Aglaia, my son Demitre, and my daughter Anna, for their love and support, and my parents, who long ago put me on the 'high road' that led to this book.

Apostolos Serletis

Foreword

Almost half a century has elapsed since the demand for money began to attract widespread attention from economists and econometricians, and it has been a topic of ongoing controversy and research ever since. Interest in the topic stemmed from three principal sources.

First of all, there was the matter of the internal dynamics of macroeconomics, to which Harry Johnson drew attention in his 1971 Ely Lecture on "The Keynesian Revolution and the Monetarist Counter-Revolution," *American Economic Review* 61 (May 1971). The main lesson about money that had been drawn from the so-called "Keynesian Revolution" was — rightly or wrongly — that it didn't matter all that much. The inherited wisdom that undergraduates absorbed in the 1950s was that macroeconomics was above all about the determination of income and employment, that the critical factors here were saving and investment decisions, and that monetary factors, to the extent that they mattered at all, only had an influence on these all important variables through a rather narrow range of market interest rates. Conventional wisdom never goes unchallenged in economics, except where its creators manage to control access to graduate schools and the journals, and it is with no cynical intent that I confirm Johnson's suggestion that those of us who embarked on academic careers in the '60s found in this wisdom a ready-made target. University faculties were expanding at that time, so rewards for hitting that target cleanly were both visible before the event, and quickly available after it, particularly when the weapons employed were those provided by then rapidly developing computer technology. Seldom can a novel hypothesis — in this case that the demand for money is a stable function of a few arguments — have been better calculated simultaneously to undermine established beliefs and to exploit newly available technology. Small wonder that studies of the demand for money flourished in the academic journals.

But second, in the late '50s - early '60s there was a new audience for monetary research outside of the academic community. The relaxation

Introduction

A stable demand function for money is a necessary condition for money to exert a predictable influence on the economy so that control of the money supply can be a useful instrument of economic policy. As such, the notion of a stable money demand function appears to require that money holdings, as observed in the real world, should be predictably related to a small set of variables representing significant links to spending and economic activity in the real sector of the economy.

Prior to 1973, both the theoretical derivation and the econometric form of the money demand function were considered settled, and the evidence was interpreted as showing that the money demand function was stable. This evidence, occurring as it did in a climate of worsening inflation, convinced the Federal Reserve to give emphasis to monetary aggregates targeting. After 1973, however, the standard money demand formulation performed poorly, showing inaccurate forecasting ability and parameter instability — both of which remain largely unexplained today despite extensive research devoted to determining the reasons for this poor performance.

In trying to explain what happened, economists in addition to re-opening the pre-1973 agenda of empirical issues (mainly concerned with the inappropriate specification of the original function and the choice of dependent and explanatory variables), pointed to financial innovations (and to a lesser extent regulatory changes) which have led to the emergence of new assets and the changing of the relative degrees of 'moneyness' possessed by the various assets. A review of the vast literature devoted to these issues [see Edgar Feige and Douglas Pearce (1977) and John Judd and John Scadding (1992)] reveals that these studies were largely unsuccessful in explaining the instability in money demand after 1973.

There is another problem with this literature, and this is that the many studies of the demand for money (and of the influence of money on the economy in general) are based on official simple-sum monetary

Part 1:
Static Monetary
Macroeconomics

Overview of Part 1

Chapters 1 and 2 concern macroeconomic analysis with a strong emphasis on monetary aspects, in the context of static 'classical' and 'Keynesian' models. These models, as Bennett McCallum (1989, p. 13) puts it, " ... have been extremely important in macroeconomic analysis and teaching over the last 40 years."

An important feature of these models is that they each incorporate a demand for money function, but make different assumptions about the flexibility of some prices. Our purpose, then, is to investigate the implications for monetary macroeconomics of different assumptions about the money demand function, in different economic environments.

of this model is its assumption that prices and nominal wages are fully flexible, in the sense that they continuously adjust to clear markets; the implications of introducing some inflexibility of prices are discussed in the next chapter.

Another important feature of the classical model is that it incorporates a money demand function, a function that explains people's willingness to hold money. Our task is to make as clear as possible what the implications are for monetary macroeconomics of different assumptions about the demand for money function. In describing the model, we follow Chapter 1 of Thomas Sargent's 1979 book, *Macroeconomic Theory*.

1.1 The Complete Classical Model

The classical model can be summarized as consisting of the following seven equations, potentially able to determine seven endogenous variables,

$$\frac{w}{P} = F_L \tag{1.1}$$

$$L = L(\frac{w}{P}) \tag{1.2}$$

$$Y = F(K, L) \tag{1.3}$$

$$C = C(R - \pi^e) \tag{1.4}$$

$$I = I\left(q(K, L, R - \pi^e, \delta)\right) \tag{1.5}$$

$$Y = C + I + G \tag{1.6}$$

$$\frac{M}{P} = \Phi(Y, R). \tag{1.7}$$

Equation (1.1) is the demand function for labor, derived by maximizing economy wide profits with respect to employment. The basic hypothesis is that firms maximize profits (that is, gross revenue less factor costs). Formally, the firms' problem is

$$\max_{L} PF(K, L) - wL - (R - \pi^e + \delta)PK$$

where P the price of the economy's single good, w the money wage rate, and $(R - \pi^e + \delta)$ the cost of capital. The reader should note that R is the nominal interest rate on bonds, π^e the expected inflation rate, and δ the rate of depreciation of capital. Taking the stock of capital as given, the first-order condition for profit maximization with respect to L is

$$PF_L - w = 0,$$

which can be rewritten as in equation (1.1), and states that firms maximize profits by equating the marginal product of labor, F_L, to the real wage rate, w/P.

Equation (1.2) is the labor supply function and describes the labor-leisure preferences of workers. It is assumed that the supply of labor is an increasing function of w/P (that is, $L' > 0$) and that the labor market is in equilibrium (that is, actual employment, L, equals labor supply, L^s). Equation (1.3) is the aggregate production function where Y is output of the economy's single good, with K and L denoting capital and labor inputs. We assume that both marginal products are positive but diminishing, that is,

$$F_L > 0, \ F_K > 0, \ F_{LL} < 0, \ F_{KK} < 0,$$

where subscripts stand for partial derivatives. We also assume that capital and labor are complements, that is,

$$F_{LK} = F_{KL} > 0.$$

Equation (1.4) is the consumption function relating real consumption spending, C, to the real interest rate on bonds, $R - \pi^e$, which is the difference between the nominal interest rate, R, and the expected inflation rate, π^e. It is assumed that $C' < 0$, because of the intertemporal substitution effect arising from changes in the rate of interest — see Robert Barro (1997, Chapter 3). Equation (1.5) is the investment function that relates real investment spending by firms, I, to the relative price q, defined by

$$q(K, L, R - \pi^e, \delta) = \frac{F_K - \delta}{R - \pi^e}.$$

The assumption is that investment demand is a function of the gap between the real rate of return to physical capital, $F_K - \delta$, and the real rate of return to financial capital, $R - \pi^e$. In particular, investment demand is higher the higher is the marginal product of capital and the lower is the real interest rate, $R - \pi^e$ — that is, $I' > 0$.[1] Notice that the derivatives of q with respect to K, L, and $R - \pi^e$ are

---

[1] See Barro (1997, Chapter 9) for more details regarding a theoretical analysis of investment.

$$q_K = \frac{F_{KK}}{R - \pi^e} < 0, \quad q_L = \frac{F_{KL}}{R - \pi^e} > 0, \quad q_{R-\pi^e} = -\frac{q}{R - \pi^e} < 0,$$

so q is an increasing function of L and a decreasing function of K and $R - \pi^e$.

Equation (1.6) is the national income identity linking aggregate real output, Y, and its components — real consumption, C, real investment, I, and real government purchases, G. Finally, equation (1.7) character-izes portfolio equilibrium by equating the real money supply, M/P — which is the ratio of the nominal money supply, M, to the price level, P — and the real money demand, $\Phi(Y, R)$. Notice that real output, Y, enters the $\Phi(\cdot)$ function as a proxy for the rate of transactions in the economy and also that the nominal interest rate, R, enters the $\Phi(\cdot)$ function as a proxy for the opportunity cost of holding money — which is the real interest rate on bonds, $R - \pi^e$, less the real interest rate on money, $-\pi^e$. We assume that

$$\Phi_Y > 0 \quad \text{and} \quad \Phi_R < 0,$$

that is, the demand for money depends positively on real income and negatively on the nominal interest rate.

Assuming that at any moment the stock of capital is fixed, equations (1.1)-(1.7) determine seven endogenous variables

$$L, \frac{w}{P}, Y, C, I, R, \text{ and } P.$$

The exogenous variables are

$$G, K, M, \text{ and } \pi^e.$$

The parameters of the model,

$$F_K, F_{KK}, F_L, F_{LL}, F_{KL}, L', C', I', q_L, q_K, q_{R-\pi^e}, \Phi_Y, \Phi_R, \text{ and } \delta,$$

determine the shapes of the underlying functions. Notice that we assume that the expected inflation rate, π^e, is exogenously determined.

1.2   The Classical Dichotomy

The hallmark of classical macroeconomic theory is its separation of real and nominal variables, known as the *classical dichotomy*. This classical dichotomy arises because in the classical model changes in the money supply do not influence real variables and allows us to study first how the values of the real variables are determined in isolation. Given the equilibrium values of the real variables, the equilibrium in the money market then determines the price level and, as a result, all other nominal variables.

It is easy to verify that the classical model we have been studying dichotomizes. Consider the model formed by equations (1.1)- (1.7) and assume that an initial equilibrium exists. Write the model in change form to obtain the following linear system (assuming, for simplicity, that δ is always constant, so $d\delta = 0$)

$$d\left(w/P\right) = F_{LL}dL + F_{LK}dK \tag{1.8}$$
$$dL = L'd\left(w/P\right) \tag{1.9}$$
$$dY = F_K dK + F_L dL \tag{1.10}$$
$$dC = C'\left(dR - d\pi^e\right) \tag{1.11}$$
$$dI = I'q_K dK + I'q_L dL + I'q_{R-\pi^e}\left(dR - d\pi^e\right) \tag{1.12}$$
$$dY = dC + dI + dG \tag{1.13}$$
$$\frac{dM}{P} - \frac{M}{P}\frac{dP}{P} = \Phi_Y dY + \Phi_R dR \tag{1.14}$$

Notice that this system is not fully simultaneous. In particular, only two endogenous variables, $d(w/P)$ and dL, appear in the first two equations, implying that these two equations form an independent subset that can determine employment and the real wage rate. Similarly, only three endogenous variables, $d(w/P)$, dL, and dY, appear in the first three equations. As a consequence, these equations form an independent subset that determines employment, the real wage, and output. This very important property of the classical model is known as *block recursiveness* and is what yields the dichotomy. That is, the key real variables (output and employment) are determined solely in a subsystem involving only production considerations, and are independent of the level of the money supply and the general price level. In such a system *money is a veil*.

1.3 The Classical AD-AS Model

In order to solve the classical model, we utilize the aggregate demand (AD)-aggregate supply (AS) apparatus. That is, we collapse equations (1.8)-(1.14) into a system of two equations in dR and dY. This is accomplished by eliminating $d(w/P)$, dL, dC, dI, and dP by substitution.

First we obtain the total differential of the aggregate supply schedule. Substituting (1.9) into (1.8) to eliminate dL yields

$$d\left(\frac{w}{P}\right) = \frac{F_{LK}}{1 - F_{LL}L'}dK,$$ (1.15)

which implies that an increase in the capital stock increases the real wage, since

$$F_{LK} > 0, \ F_{LL} < 0, \ L' > 0, \quad \text{and hence} \quad \frac{F_{LK}}{(1 - F_{LL}L')} > 0.$$

Also, substituting (1.15) into (1.9), to eliminate $d(w/P)$, yields

$$dL = L'\frac{F_{LK}}{1 - F_{LL}L'}dK,$$ (1.16)

which implies that an increase in the capital stock also increases employment.

The total differential of the aggregate supply curve can be obtained by substituting (1.16) into (1.10), to eliminate dL

$$dY = \left(F_K + \frac{F_{LL}L'F_{LK}}{1 - F_{LL}L'}\right)dK.$$ (1.17)

Equation (1.17) implies that an increase in the capital stock would increase output. In fact, the increase in capital increases output, both because the marginal product of capital is positive as well as because the increase in capital increases the marginal product of labor.

Clearly, equations (1.15)-(1.17) completely determine the values of the only three endogenous variables involved and show that K is the only exogenous variable that enters into the determination of Y, L, and w/P — in this model, there is no interaction with other variables. Thus output, Y, is determined independently of the price level. In what follows we assume that capital can be accumulated only by investing, thus ruling out once-and-for-all changes in the stock of capital. This implies that, at a point in time, output, employment, and the real wage are constants, independent of fiscal and monetary variables and the public's expectations.

We now turn our attention to deriving the total differential of the aggregate demand schedule. Assuming that $dK = 0$ [which implies, from solving (1.8)-(1.10), that $dY = dL = 0$] and substituting (1.11) and (1.12) into (1.13) yields the total differential of the AD schedule or, equivalently, the total differential of the reduced form of R (after solving for dR)

$$dR = -\frac{1}{C' + I'q_{R-\pi^e}}dG + d\pi^e,$$ (1.18)

where $C' + I'q_{R-\pi^e}$ — the total derivative of aggregate demand with respect to the interest rate — is negative since $C' < 0$, $I' > 0$, and $q_{R-\pi^e} < 0$.

Manipulation of the reduced form for R, equation (1.18), implies that

$$\frac{\partial R}{\partial G} = -\frac{1}{C' + I'q_{R-\pi^e}} > 0, \qquad \frac{\partial R}{\partial \pi^e} = 1.$$

Thus the nominal interest rate rises in response to an increase in government spending. Also, a change in π^e produces an equivalent change in R, with no change in $R - \pi^e$ — the *Fisher effect*. Notice that in this version of the model, the interest rate bears the entire burden of adjusting the level of aggregate demand, so that it equals the level of aggregate supply determined by equations (1.1)-(1.3), given the capital stock.

To determine the effect of changes in G and π^e on consumption and net investment we substitute (1.18) into (1.11) and (1.12), respectively, and solve for the reduced form partial derivatives with respect to these exogenous variables, keeping $dK = dL = dY = 0$. The effects on consumption and investment are

$$\frac{\partial C}{\partial G} = C'\frac{\partial R}{\partial G} < 0, \qquad \frac{\partial I}{\partial G} = I'q_{R-\pi^e}\frac{\partial R}{\partial G} < 0,$$

$$\frac{\partial C}{\partial \pi^e} = C'\frac{\partial R}{\partial \pi^e} - C' = 0, \qquad \frac{\partial I}{\partial \pi^e} = I'q_{R-\pi^e}\frac{\partial R}{\partial \pi^e} - I'q_{R-\pi^e} = 0.$$

Thus, an increase in government expenditures tends to increase the interest rate, which in turn, through equations (1.11) and (1.12) induces changes in consumption and rates of capital accumulation. In fact, the rise in the interest rate *crowds out* both forms of private spending, C and I. However, changes in π^e do not affect consumption and investment. This is so because of the Fisherian link, according to which a change in π^e leads to an equivalent change in R, leaving $R - \pi^e$ unchanged.

Once the differentials for R and Y are determined, equation (1.14) has only one free variable in it — the differential of the price level, dP. In fact, the role of equation (1.14) is to determine dP/P to equate the nominal demand for money to the given nominal quantity of money.

1.4   The Neutrality of Money

So far we have dealt with changes in the demand for money while holding fixed the aggregate supply of nominal money. We have shown

Chapter 2

Keynesian Macroeconomic Theory

In Chapter 1 we began our discussion of macroeconomic theory with a view of nominal wages and prices as fully flexible. This approach ensures that markets are always in equilibrium, in the sense that there is continual balance between the quantities demanded and the quantities supplied. The classical model was the dominant macroeconomic theory until the Great Depression in the 1930s. The prolonged unemployment, however, in the United Kingdom and the United States during the 1930s prompted John Maynard Keynes to significantly depart from the classical assumption of perfectly flexible prices and develop models based on the assumption that there are constraints on the flexibility of some prices.

The crucial assumption in the Keynesian models is that some prices are sticky — i.e., do not adjust promptly to ensure continual balance between the quantities supplied and demanded. Hence, unlike the classical model, some markets do not always clear and output and employment typically end up below the optimal amounts. Although Keynes's analysis and some subsequent treatments — see, for example, Don Patinkin (1965, Chapter 13) and Barro and Herschel Grossman (1976) — focused on sticky money wages, the price level is sometimes assumed to be perfectly flexible (leading to the so-called *complete Keynesian model*),

$$\frac{d\overline{w}}{\overline{w}} - \frac{dP}{P} = \frac{F_{LL}}{F_L} dL, \tag{2.7}$$

$$dY = F_L dL, \tag{2.8}$$
$$dC = C_1 dY - C_1 dT + C_2(dR - d\pi^e), \tag{2.9}$$
$$dI = I' q_L dL + I' q_{R-\pi^e}(dR - d\pi^e), \tag{2.10}$$
$$dY = dC + dI + dG, \tag{2.11}$$

$$\frac{dM}{P} - \frac{M}{P}\frac{dP}{P} = \Phi_Y dY + \Phi_R dR. \tag{2.12}$$

Notice that this system, unlike the classical system, is not block recursive, in the sense that it is impossible to find an independent subset of equations that determine a subset of variables. That means, of course, that output is not determined solely on the basis of aggregate supply considerations, as it is in the classical model. In other words, the Keynesian model does not dichotomize.

In what follows, we shall generate the basic Keynesian results in the context of three different versions of the Keynesian model. In particular, the Keynesian-cross, the IS-LM, and the AD-AS Keynesian models are developed.

2.3   The Keynesian-Cross Model

An extreme version of the Keynesian model is the Keynesian-cross. In addition to assuming that there is perpetual excess supply in the goods market, the Keynesian-cross model also assumes that the nominal interest rate is fixed. This allows it to ignore the money market and focus exclusively on the goods market to determine the level of output, which is demand determined.

We can summarize the main aspects of this simple Keynesian model using equations (2.8), (2.9), (2.10), and (2.11) to obtain the total differential of the reduced form of Y (assuming that $dR = d\pi^e = 0$)

$$(1 - C_1 - I'\frac{q_L}{F_L})dY = dG - C_1 dT. \tag{2.13}$$

Assuming that the marginal propensity to save out of disposable income, $1 - C_1$, exceeds the marginal propensity to invest out of income, $I' q_L / F_L$, the coefficient on dY in (2.13) is positive.[2] Then the reduced form partial derivatives of Y with respect to G and T are given by

$$\frac{\partial Y}{\partial G} = \frac{1}{1 - C_1 - I'q_L/F_L}, \quad \frac{\partial Y}{\partial T} = -\frac{C_1}{1 - C_1 - I'q_L/F_L},$$

where the expression for $\partial Y/\partial G$ is the *government purchases multiplier* — the amount output changes in response to a unit change in government purchases. The expression for $\partial Y/\partial T$ is the *tax multiplier* — the amount output changes in response to a unit change in taxes. Notice that if investment does not respond to changes in income, that is if I' equals zero, the above expressions reduce to the standard simple Keynesian multiplier formulas.

Finally, if $I' = 0$, the effect on output of a change in G matched by an equal change in T is given by

$$\left.\frac{\partial Y}{\partial G}\right|_{dG=dT} = 1,$$

which is the so-called *balanced budget multiplier*.

2.4   The IS-LM Model

The Keynesian-cross model shows how to determine the level of output for a given interest rate. The assumption, however, that the interest rate is given means that the analysis is seriously incomplete. Therefore, we now want to go further to determine simultaneously the interest rate and the level of output. To carry this analysis we use John Hick's (1937) IS-LM curve apparatus. That is, we collapse equations (2.7), (2.8), (2.9), (2.10), (2.11), and (2.12) into a system of two equations in dY and dR, this being accomplished by eliminating the other endogenous variables by substitution.

First we obtain the total differential of the IS curve, the locus of the combinations of R and Y that satisfy (2.5), the aggregate demand-aggregate supply equality. Substituting (2.8), (2.9), and (2.10) into (2.11) and rearranging yields the total differential of the IS curve

---

[2]To see that $I'q_L/F_L$ is the marginal propensity to invest out of income, differentiate the investment schedule partially with respect to Y to obtain

$$\frac{\partial I}{\partial Y} = \frac{\partial I}{\partial q}\frac{\partial q}{\partial L}\frac{\partial L}{\partial Y} = I'\frac{q_L}{F_L}.$$

$$(1 - C_1 - I'q_L/F_L)dY = -C_1 dT + dG$$

$$+ (C_2 + I'q_{R-\pi^e})(dR - d\pi^e).$$

(2.14)

The slope of the IS curve in the $R - Y$ plane is thus given by

$$\frac{dR}{dY} = \frac{1 - C_1 - I'q_L/F_L}{C_2 + I'q_{R-\pi^e}},$$

which is negative, since $C_2 + I'q_{R-\pi^e} < 0$ and $1 - C_1$ has been assumed to be greater than $I'q_L/F_L$. Notice that the smaller the government purchases multiplier and the smaller the sensitivity of aggregate demand to the interest rate, $C_2 + I'q_{R-\pi^e}$, the steeper the IS curve.

To determine how the IS curve shifts when the exogenous variables, T, G, and π^e, change, we can use (2.14) to determine the horizontal shift in the IS curve by evaluating the partial derivatives of Y with respect to each exogenous variable, dR being set equal to zero. Alternatively, we can use (2.14) to determine the vertical shift in the IS curve by evaluating the partial derivatives of R with respect to each exogenous variable, dY being set equal to zero. So we have

$$\frac{\partial Y}{\partial T} = \frac{-C_1}{1 - C_1 - I'q_L/F_L} < 0, \quad \frac{\partial Y}{\partial G} = \frac{1}{1 - C_1 - I'q_L/F_L} > 0, \quad \frac{\partial R}{\partial \pi^e} = 1.$$

An increase in government purchases or a decrease in taxes will shift the IS curve out to the right, the extent of the shift depending on the size of the relevant (Keynesian-cross model) multiplier. Also, when the expected inflation rate changes, the IS curve shifts upward by the amount of the increase in π^e.

The IS curve does not determine either R or Y. It only provides the combinations of nominal interest rates and income (output) that clear the goods market. To determine the equilibrium of the economy, we need another relationship between these two variables, to which we now turn.

By using (2.7) and (2.8) to eliminate dP/P from (2.12) yields the total differential of the LM curve, a schedule that shows all combinations of interest rates and levels of income that clear the market for money balances

$$\left(\frac{F_{LL}}{F_L^2}\frac{M}{P} - \Phi_Y\right)dY = -\frac{dM}{P} + \frac{M}{P}\frac{d\overline{w}}{\overline{w}} + \Phi_R dR.$$

(2.15)

The slope of the LM curve is

$$\frac{dR}{dY} = \frac{1}{\Phi_R} \left(\frac{F_{LL}}{F_L^2} \frac{M}{P} - \Phi_Y \right) > 0.$$

Notice that the smaller the interest sensitivity and the smaller the income sensitivity of the demand for money, the steeper the LM curve. In fact, as $\Phi_R \to 0$, the LM curve approaches a vertical position while as $\Phi_R \to -\infty$, as is supposed in the case of the *liquidity trap*, the LM curve approaches a horizontal position.

To determine how the LM curve shifts when the exogenous variables, M and $\overline{w}$ change, we use equation (2.15) to evaluate the partial derivatives of R with respect to each of the exogenous variables, dY being set equal to zero. Thus

$$\frac{\partial R}{\partial M} = \frac{1}{\Phi_R P}, \quad \frac{\partial R}{\partial \overline{w}} = -\frac{M}{\Phi_R P \overline{w}}.$$

The expression $\partial R/\partial M$ is zero when $\Phi_R \to -\infty$ and negative when $\Phi_R > -\infty$. Also, the expression $\partial R/\partial \overline{w}$ is zero when $\Phi_R \to -\infty$ and positive as long as $\Phi_R > -\infty$. Hence, the LM curve shifts down and to the right when the nominal money supply rises or the money wage falls.

We now have all the components of the IS-LM model. Given that the two equations of this model are (2.14) and (2.15) we can solve the system analytically to analyze the (short run) effects of policy changes and other events on national income.[3] Substituting (2.15) into (2.14) to eliminate dR yields the total differential of the reduced form of Y

$$H dY = -C_1 dT + dG - (C_2 + I'q_{R-\pi^e}) d\pi^e$$

$$+ \frac{C_2 + I'q_{R-\pi^e}}{\Phi_R} \left(\frac{dM}{P} - \frac{M}{P} \frac{d\overline{w}}{\overline{w}} \right),$$

where the coefficient on dY, H, is given by

$$H = 1 - C_1 - I' \frac{q_L}{F_L} - \frac{C_2 + I'q_{R-\pi^e}}{\Phi_R} \left(\frac{F_{LL}}{F_L^2} \frac{M}{P} - \Phi_Y \right).$$

---

[3] Alternatively, using our knowledge of how changes in the various exogenous variables of the model shift the IS and LM curves, we can make use of a graphical device — see, for example, Barro (1997, Chapter 20).

Under the assumption that $1 - C_1$ exceeds $I'q_L/F_L$, H is positive and the reduced form partial derivatives of Y with respect to the exogenous variables of the model are given by

$$\frac{\partial Y}{\partial T} = -\frac{C_1}{H} \leq 0, \quad \frac{\partial Y}{\partial G} = \frac{1}{H} \geq 0,$$

$$\frac{\partial Y}{\partial \pi^e} = -\frac{C_2 + I'q_{R-\pi^e}}{H} \geq 0, \quad \frac{\partial Y}{\partial M} = \frac{C_2 + I'q_{R-\pi^e}}{\Phi_R PH} \geq 0,$$

$$\frac{\partial Y}{\partial \overline{w}} = -\frac{(C_2 + I'q_{R-\pi^e})M}{\Phi_R P\overline{w}H} \leq 0.$$

Thus, except in limiting cases, increases in G, π^e, and M and decreases in T and $\overline{w}$ will in general increase the level of real income. Therefore, money is not neutral in this model.

Notice that if money demand is insensitive to the interest rate ($\Phi_R \to$ 0 and the LM curve is vertical), $H \to \infty$ and the effect on output from a disturbance that shifts the IS curve is nil, that is, $\partial Y/\partial T$, $\partial Y/\partial G$, and $\partial Y/\partial \pi^e$ all approach zero. Under those circumstances, a fiscal expansion raises the interest rate and crowds out interest sensitive private spending. However, any shift in the (vertical) LM curve has a maximal effect on the level of income.

On the other hand, in the liquidity trap ($\Phi_R \to -\infty$ and the LM curve is horizontal), monetary policy has no impact on the equilibrium of the economy, since $\partial Y/\partial M$ and $\partial Y/\partial \overline{w}$ both approach zero. Fiscal policy, however, has its full multiplier effect on the level of income, since $\partial Y/\partial T$ and $\partial Y/\partial G$ reduce to the tax multiplier and government purchases multiplier, respectively, of the Keynesian cross model.

Finally, if the interest rate has a negligible effect on aggregate demand ($C_2 = I' = 0$), the IS curve is vertical and changes in the money supply and the money wage have no effect on output, that is, $\partial Y/\partial M = \partial Y/\partial \overline{w} = 0$. On the other hand, if aggregate demand is extremely sensitive to the interest rate, the IS curve is very flat and shifts in the LM have a large effect on output.

2.5   The Keynesian AD-AS Model

In the previous section we solved the Keynesian model [equations (2.7), (2.8), (2.9), (2.10), (2.11), and (2.12)] by collapsing it into two equations in a pair of variables, dR and dY. We can also solve the same model by collapsing it into two equations in another pair of variables,

dP and dY, thereby obtaining the Keynesian version of the aggregate demand (AD)-aggregate supply (AS) model.

Solving (2.7) and (2.8) for dY yields the total differential of the aggregate supply function in the $P - Y$ plane

$$dY = \frac{F_L^2}{F_{LL}} \frac{d\overline{w}}{\overline{w}} - \frac{F_L^2}{F_{LL}} \frac{dP}{P}. \tag{2.16}$$

Since $F_{LL} < 0$, equation (2.16) implies that aggregate supply increases in response to an increase in the price level or (for a given price level) a decline in the money wage. The slope of the aggregate supply schedule is

$$\frac{dP}{dY} = -\frac{PF_{LL}}{F_L^2} > 0.$$

This expression equals zero if the marginal product of labor is constant — that is, if $F_{LL} = 0$ — as it happens, for example, when capital and labor are combined in fixed proportions.

The total differential of the aggregate demand curve in the $P - Y$ plane, a schedule that, in the present context, represents all those combinations of P and Y that satisfy the demands for goods and assets, comes from equations (2.9), (2.10), (2.11), and (2.12) and is given by

$$\widehat{H}dY = -C_1 dT + dG - (C_2 + I'q_{R-\pi^e})d\pi^e \tag{2.17}$$

$$+ \frac{C_2 + I'q_{R-\pi^e}}{\Phi_R} \frac{dM}{P} - \frac{C_2 + I'q_{R-\pi^e}}{\Phi_R} \frac{M}{P^2} dP,$$

where the coefficient on dY, $\widehat{H}$, is

$$\widehat{H} = 1 - C_1 - I'\frac{q_L}{F_L} + \frac{C_2 + I'q_{R-\pi^e}}{\Phi_R} \Phi_Y.$$

The slope of the aggregate demand schedule is thus given (substituting back for $\widehat{H}$) by

$$\frac{dP}{dY} = \frac{-\left[\left(1 - C_1 - I'\frac{q_L}{F_L}\right)\Phi_R + (C_2 + I'q_{R-\pi^e})\Phi_Y\right]P^2}{(C_2 + I'q_{R-\pi^e})M},$$

which, under the assumption that $1 - C_1 > I'_q L / F_L$, is negative.

Notice that the AD curve is flatter the smaller the interest sensitivity of the demand for money, Φ_R, the smaller the income sensitivity of money demand, Φ_Y, and the larger the interest sensitivity of aggregate demand, $C_2 + I'_{qR-\pi^e}$. Also, the larger the marginal propensity to consume out of disposable income, C_1, (or, equivalently, the smaller the marginal propensity to save out of disposable income, $1 - C_1$), and the larger the sensitivity of investment demand to income, that is, the larger I'_qL / F_L, the flatter the AD curve. It is also interesting to note that as $C_2 + I'_{qR-\pi^e} \to 0$ or $\Phi_R \to -\infty$, the aggregate demand curve becomes vertical in the $P - Y$ plane.

To determine how the aggregate demand curve shifts when the exogenous variables, T, G, π^e, and M change, we use equation (2.17) to evaluate the partial derivatives of Y with respect to each exogenous variable, dP being set equal to zero. Letting $\widehat{H}$ stand for the coefficient on dY in equation (2.17) we obtain

$$\frac{\partial Y}{\partial T} = -\frac{C_1}{\widehat{H}} < 0, \quad \frac{\partial Y}{\partial G} = \frac{1}{\widehat{H}} > 0,$$

$$\frac{\partial Y}{\partial \pi^e} = -\frac{C_2 + I'_{qR-\pi^e}}{\widehat{H}} > 0, \quad \frac{\partial Y}{\partial M} = \frac{C_2 + I'_{qR-\pi^e}}{\widehat{H}\Phi_R P} > 0.$$

Thus, increases in G, π^e, and M and decreases in T will in general shift the aggregate demand curve outward and/or upward in the $P - Y$ plane.

We now have all the components of the Keynesian AD-AS model. It consists of equations (2.16) and (2.17), which we can solve to analyze the effects of policy actions on national income.[4] In particular, substituting (2.16) into (2.17) to eliminate dP/P yields the total differential of the reduced form of Y

$$\widetilde{H} dY = -C_1 dT + dG - (C_2 + I'_{qR-\pi^e}) d\pi^e$$

$$+ \frac{C_2 + I'_{qR-\pi^e}}{\Phi_R} \left(\frac{dM}{P} - \frac{M}{P} \frac{d\overline{w}}{\overline{w}} \right),$$

where the coefficient on dY, now $\widetilde{H}$, is given by

---

[4] Alternatively, we can make use of a graphical device as, for example, in Barro (1997, Chapter 20).

$$\tilde{H} = 1 - C_1 - I'\frac{q_L}{F_L} - \frac{C_2 + I'q_{R-\pi^e}}{\Phi_R}\left(2\frac{F_{LL}}{F_L^2}\frac{M}{P} - \Phi_Y\right).$$

Again, under the assumption that $1 - C_1$ exceeds $I'q_L/F_L$, $\tilde{H}$ is positive and the reduced form partial derivatives of Y with respect to the exogenous variables are

$$\frac{\partial Y}{\partial T} = -\frac{C_1}{\tilde{H}} \le 0, \quad \frac{\partial Y}{\partial G} = \frac{1}{\tilde{H}} \ge 0,$$

$$\frac{\partial Y}{\partial \pi^e} = -\frac{C_2 + I'q_{R-\pi^e}}{\tilde{H}} \ge 0, \quad \frac{\partial Y}{\partial M} = \frac{C_2 + I'q_{R-\pi^e}}{\Phi_R P\tilde{H}} \ge 0,$$

$$\frac{\partial Y}{\partial \overline{w}} = -\frac{(C_2 + I'q_{R-\pi^e})\,M}{\Phi_R P\overline{w}\tilde{H}} \le 0.$$

Hence, this model produces the same qualitative results as the IS-LM model. The reader should also notice that the AD-AS Keynesian model does not dichotomize as the classical model does, as presented in Chapter 1.

2.6 Conclusion

In this chapter, we have summarized a great deal of traditional Keynesian macroeconomic theory. We have seen that if there are constraints on the flexibility of some prices, then the financial market and the money demand function play a crucial role in determining the effects not only of monetary policy, but also of fiscal policy. In fact, the relationship between the demand for money and the level of real income and the nominal rate of interest is of crucial importance in these Keynesian models.

In particular, with sticky prices knowledge of the various functions and of the values of their parameters is particularly useful in evaluating the effects of policy actions on the macroeconomy. In the case, for example, of the money demand function, if the interest elasticity of the demand for money balances is high, then fluctuations in the level of income are not likely to be caused by variations in the money supply. If it is low, then exactly the converse is true.

Of course, the theories of macroeconomic behavior that we have so far discussed in Chapters 1 and 2 are static in specification. As Bennett McCallum (1989, p. 77-78) puts it "[o]ne way in which these models are static is that they treat the economy's capital stock — its collection of productive machines, plants, highways, and so on — as *fixed* in quantity. As a result of that simplification, the models are not well designed for the analysis of policy actions or other events that would tend to induce substantial changes in the stock of capital within the relevant time frame."

Although this weakness of the classical and Keynesian models can be remedied, the current fashion is to explore short-run and long-run phenomena in the context of nonlinear dynamical models. Models of this type have displaced the IS-LM and AD-AS frameworks in mainstream macroeconomic theory and dominate current research in almost all areas in economics. In the light of these developments, we now turn to these models.

Part 2:
Dynamic Monetary
Macroeconomics

Overview of Part 2

In Chapter 3, we begin developing the framework for dynamic monetary macroeconomics, using the tools of neoclassical growth theory and related dynamical approaches. As Costas Azariadis (1993, p. xii) puts it "[d]ynamical systems have spread so widely into macroeconomics that vector fields and phase diagrams are on the verge of displacing the familiar supply-demand schedules and Hicksian crosses of static macroeconomics."

In Chapter 4, we discuss monetary versions of neoclassical growth theory. Among monetary growth models, three that have seen wide and expanding use in the last two decades are the Tobin model, the Sidrauski model, and the overlapping generations model. Chapter 4 covers the Tobin and Sidrauski models in detail, leaving a discussion of the overlapping generations model for Chapter 7.

Chapter 3

Neoclassical Growth Theory

In Chapters 1 and 2 we considered the role of the money demand function in comparative static models. These models were the dominant macroeconomic paradigm up until thirty years ago. Recently, however, neoclassical growth theory and related dynamical approaches have widely spread into both macroeconomics and monetary economics and are now routinely used in exploring fiscal and monetary policy issues.

Among dynamic macroeconomic models, three that have seen wide and expanding use in the last twenty years are the neoclassical growth model of Robert Solow (1956), the *optimal growth model* originated by Frank Ramsey (1928), and further developed by David Cass (1965) and Tjalling Koopmans (1965), and the *overlapping generations model* of Peter Diamond (1965). In what follows, we briefly discuss non-monetary versions of neoclassical growth theory, leaving monetary versions of the theory for the next chapter. In doing so, we focus on discrete time systems, given that economic data are available in discrete form.

3.1 The Solow Model

With the publication of Solow's (1956) seminal article on growth theory, entitled "A Contribution to the Theory of Economic Growth," macroeconomics and monetary economics started developing a central theoretical core. The Solow model is the cornerstone of that core.

The model consists of two equations, a production function and a capital accumulation equation. The production function describes how private factor inputs of capital, K_t, and labor, L_t, combine to produce output, Y_t. It takes the form

$$Y_t = F(K_t, L_t),$$

and is assumed to exhibit constant returns to scale, so that

$$F(\psi K_t, \psi L_t) = \psi Y_t,$$

for $\psi > 0$. Choosing $\psi = 1/L_t$ for $L_t > 0$, we can write the production function as

$$Y_t = F(K_t, L_t) = L_t F\left(\frac{K_t}{L_t}, 1\right) = L_t F(k_t, 1) = L_t f(k_t),$$

or in per capita (that is, per worker) terms,

$$y_t = f(k_t), \tag{3.1}$$

where y_t is output per person, Y_t/L_t, and k_t is capital per person, K_t/L_t. Writing the production function as in equation (3.1), has the advantage of focusing attention on per capita output, y_t, which is a better measure of living standards than total output, Y_t. The production function is also assumed to satisfy the conditions

$$f' > 0, \ f'' < 0, \ f'(0) = \infty, \ \text{and} \ f'(\infty) = 0.$$

It is assumed that there are many firms in the economy, so that perfect competition prevails, and that the firms are price-takers. Each firm maximizes profits, Π_t, by solving the following problem

$$\max_{K_t, L_t} \ \Pi_t = L_t f(k_t) - w_t L_t - r_t K_t, \tag{3.2}$$

where w_t is the real wage rate, r_t is the real rental price of capital, and $L_t f(k_t) = Y_t$ — the latter obtained by rearranging (3.1). The first-order conditions for profit maximization are

$$f(k_t) - k_t f'(k_t) = w_t \tag{3.3}$$

$$f'(k_t) = r_t. \tag{3.4}$$

Equation (3.3) states that firms will hire labor until the marginal product of labor, $f(k_t) - k_t f'(k_t)$, equals the real wage rate, w_t, and equation (3.4) states that firms will hire capital until the marginal product of capital, $f'(k_t)$, equals the real rental price of capital, r_t. In other words, under perfect competition and profit maximization, markets clear when the real return to each factor equals its marginal product.

Notice also that, with constant returns to scale, payments to capital and labor sum to equal national income — that is, $r_t K_t + w_t L_t = Y_t$. We can show this (in per capita terms) by combining the results from (3.3) and (3.4) as follows

$$r_t k_t + w_t = f'(k_t)k_t + f(k_t) - k_t f'(k_t)$$

$$= f(k_t),$$

which when multiplied by L_t becomes

$$r_t K_t + w_t L_t = Y_t.$$

The second key equation of the Solow model is the capital accumulation equation. Assuming that capital depreciates at the constant rate $\delta > 0$, the capital accumulation equation is given by

$$K_{t+1} = I_t + (1 - \delta)K_t$$

$$= sY_t + (1 - \delta)K_t,$$

where I_t is gross investment and s $(0 \leq s \leq 1)$ is the *saving rate* — the fraction of output that is saved and invested.

Under the assumption that the rate of population growth is ν, that is $L_{t+1} = (1 + \nu)L_t$, we have

$$k_{t+1} = \frac{K_{t+1}}{L_{t+1}} = \frac{sY_t + (1 - \delta)K_t}{(1 + \nu)L_t},$$

which implies the following first-order difference equation

$$(1 + \nu)k_{t+1} = sf(k_t) + (1 - \delta)k_t. \tag{3.5}$$

maximizing behavior by economic agents — the optimal growth model of Ramsey (1928) and the overlapping generations model of Diamond (1965). In this section we discuss the Ramsey model, leaving the Diamond model for the next section.

Consider an economy populated by a large number of infinite-lived households each of which has preferences (at an arbitrary time, denoted $t = 0$) given by

$$\mathcal{U}(c_0, c_1, c_2, \cdots) = \sum_{t=0}^{\infty} \beta^t u(c_t), \tag{3.8}$$

or, written out in full,

$$\mathcal{U} = u(c_0) + \beta u(c_1) + \beta^2 u(c_2) + \cdots,$$

where c_t is per capita consumption at time t. The discount factor β equals $1/(1 + \rho)$, where ρ $(0 < \rho < \infty)$ is a *time preference* parameter. Notice that a positive ρ implies that $\beta < 1$ and therefore a positive time preference — i.e., a preference for current over future consumption. The within-period utility function, $u(c_t)$, satisfies the following conditions

$$u'(c_t) > 0, \ u''(c_t) < 0, \ u'(0) = \infty, \ \text{and} \ u'(\infty) = 0.$$

We also assume that the household supplies inelastically one unit of labor each period — in other words, leisure is not valued.

The household operates a production function with constant returns to scale in capital and labor, given by (3.1). The household's budget constraint (in per capita terms) for period t can be written as[2]

---

[2] The budget constraint is derived as follows. We start with the national income accounts identity

$$f(k_t) = c_t + i_t,$$

and the capital accumulation equation

$$K_{t+1} = I_t + (1 - \delta)K_t.$$

Dividing the capital accumulation equation by L_t (to express the equation in per capita terms) and rearranging gives

$$(1 + \nu)k_{t+1} = i_t + (1 - \delta)k_t,$$

where ν is the population growth rate, defined by $(1+\nu) = L_{t+1}/L_t$. Finally, solving the last expression for i_t and substituting into the national income accounts identity to eliminate i_t, yields the household's budget constraint (3.9).

$$f(k_t) = c_t + i_t$$

$$= c_t + (1+\nu)k_{t+1} - (1-\delta)k_t. \tag{3.9}$$

As of time 0, the household chooses c_t and k_{t+1} (for $t = 0, 1, 2, ...$) to maximize (3.8) subject to (3.9), taking the initial stock of capital, k_0, as given. Formally, the household's problem in period 0 is

$$\max_{\{c_t,\ k_{t+1}\}_{t=0}^{\infty}} \sum_{t=0}^{\infty} \beta^t u\left(c_t\right)$$

subject to

$$f(k_t) = c_t + (1+\nu)k_{t+1} - (1-\delta)k_t,$$

for $t = 0, 1, 2, \cdots$, with k_0 given.

The Lagrangian function for this problem is

$$\mathcal{L} = \sum_{t=0}^{\infty} \beta^t u\left(c_t\right) + \sum_{t=0}^{\infty} \beta^t \lambda_t \left[f(k_t) - c_t - (1+\nu)k_{t+1} + (1-\delta)k_t \right].$$

As c_t is subject to the control of the economic agent it is called a *control* variable. k_{t+1} is called a *state* variable. λ is the Lagrange multiplier associated with the household's period t budget constraint.

The first-order conditions necessary for optimality can be obtained by differentiating $\mathcal{L}$ with respect to c_t and k_{t+1}. They are (for all t)

$$u'(c_t) = \lambda_t, \tag{3.10}$$

$$-(1+\nu)\lambda_t + \beta\lambda_{t+1}\left[f'(k_{t+1}) + 1 - \delta\right] = 0. \tag{3.11}$$

Conditions (3.9)-(3.11) are necessary for a maximum. In addition, there is a transversality condition,

$$\lim_{t\to\infty} k_{t+1}\beta^t u'(c_t) = 0, \tag{3.12}$$

stating that the present value of the stock of capital, k_{t+1}, in marginal utility units, must approach zero as $t \to \infty$. Notice that (3.12) does not require that $k_{t+1} \to 0$, since $\beta^t \to 0$ as $t \to \infty$.

In this setting, (3.9)-(3.11) are necessary for a maximum, while (3.9)-(3.12) are jointly sufficient. In other words, if (3.12) is satisfied, the household's choices of c_t and k_{t+1} will be described by (3.9)-(3.11).

Consider an individual born at time t. His (constrained) maximization problem is

$$\max_{c_{1t},\ c_{2t+1}} u(c_{1t}) + \beta u(c_{2t+1})$$

subject to

$$c_{1t} + s_t = w_t \quad \text{and} \quad c_{2t+1} = (1 + r_{t+1})s_t.$$

By substituting the budget constraints into the objective function, the individual's optimization problem can be written (in unconstrained form) as

$$\max_{s_t} u(w_t - s_t) + \beta u\left((1 + r_{t+1})s_t\right).$$

The first-order condition for choice of s_t is

$$\frac{u'(c_{1t})}{\beta u'(c_{2t+1})} = (1 + r_{t+1}). \tag{3.15}$$

This is the Euler equation, saying that the marginal rate of intertemporal substitution equals the gross real rate of interest.[5]

Equation (3.15) implies that the quantity saved can be expressed as a function of the wage rate and interest rate,

$$s_t = s(w_t, r_{t+1}).$$

We assume that s is a differentiable function with $0 < s_w < 1$. However, s_r may be positive, negative, or zero, because of the income and intertemporal substitution effects. For example, an increase in the interest rate reduces the price of second period consumption, leading individuals to substitute second- for first-period consumption — this is the *intertemporal substitution effect*. But it also increases the feasible consumption

---

[5] Alternatively, we can solve the individual's problem by obtaining the intertemporal budget constraint, by eliminating s_t from the two, one-period budget constraints to get

$$c_{2t+1} - (1 + r_{t+1})(w_t - c_{1t}) = 0.$$

Setting up the Lagrangian

$$\mathcal{L} = u(c_{1t}) + \beta u(c_{2t+1}) + \lambda \left[c_{2t+1} - (1 + r_{t+1})(w_t - c_{1t}) \right],$$

the first-order conditions for choice of c_{1t} and c_{2t+1} are

$$u'(c_{1t}) + \lambda(1 + r_{t+1}) = 0$$

$$\beta u'(c_{2t+1}) + \lambda = 0,$$

which when combined give the Euler equation (3.15).

set, making it possible to increase consumption in both periods — this is the *income effect*. The net effect of these substitution and income effects is ambiguous.[6]

Turning now to firms, it is assumed that they act competitively using a constant returns to scale production function, (3.1). Each firm is assumed to maximize profits, taking the real wage rate, w_t, and the rental rate on capital, r_t, as given. The representative firm's maximization problem (assuming that $\delta = 0$) is given by (3.2), and profit maximization requires that conditions (3.3) and (3.4) are satisfied.

To derive the market equilibrium we need to find conditions for equilibrium in the goods and factor markets. Regarding equilibrium in the factor markets, the equilibrium conditions are those given by (3.3) and (3.4). Hence, equilibrium in the factor markets obtains when labor is hired to the point where the marginal product of labor equals the real wage rate and capital is rented to the point where the marginal product of capital equals the real rental rate.

Equilibrium in the goods market requires that the demand for goods equals the supply of goods or, equivalently, that investment equals saving

$$K_{t+1} - K_t = L_t s(w_t, r_{t+1}) - K_t. \tag{3.16}$$

In equation (3.16), $K_{t+1} - K_t$ is net investment, $L_t s(w_t, r_{t+1})$ is the saving of the young, and K_t is the dissaving of the old. This equation says that the capital stock increases only if the amount saved by the young, $L_t s(w_t, r_{t+1})$, exceeds the amount set aside last period by the current old, K_t, who withdraw their savings in this period.

Eliminating K_t from both sides of (3.16), we get

$$K_{t+1} = L_t s(w_t, r_{t+1}),$$

---

[6] Consider, for example, the case where utility is log linear,

$$\mathcal{U} = \log c_{1t} + \beta \log c_{2t+1},$$

in which case the Euler equation (3.15) can be written as

$$\frac{c_{2t+1}}{\beta c_{1t}} = (1 + r_{t+1}).$$

By substituting the intertemporal budget constraint into the Euler equation to eliminate c_{2t+1} we get (after solving for c_{1t})

$$c_{1t} = \frac{w_t}{1 + \beta} \quad \text{or} \quad s_t = w_t - c_{1t} = \frac{\beta w_t}{1 + \beta}.$$

Clearly, in this (log linear utility) case, saving does not depend on the interest rate, implying that the income and intertemporal substitution effects offset each other exactly.

which says that the capital stock at time $t+1$ equals the saving of the young people at time t. Dividing both sides of the above by L_t gives the following *capital accumulation equation*

$$(1+\nu)k_{t+1} = s(w_t, r_{t+1}). \tag{3.17}$$

The capital accumulation equation (3.17), together with the factor market equilibrium conditions (3.3) and (3.4), yields the following relationship between k_{t+1} and k_t

$$(1+\nu)\, k_{t+1} = s\left(f(k_t) - k_t f'(k_t),\ f'(k_{t+1}) \right). \tag{3.18}$$

We will refer to this equation as the *saving locus*. To study this equation is to study equilibria in the overlapping generations model.[7]

As Olivier Blanchard and Stanley Fischer (1989, p. 95) argue, the properties of the saving locus depend on the derivative

$$\frac{dk_{t+1}}{dk_t} = \frac{-s_w(k_t)k_t f''(k_t)}{(1+\nu) - s_r(k_{t+1})f''(k_{t+1})},$$

and the model does not, without further assumptions about utility and production, guarantee either existence or uniqueness of a steady state equilibrium with a positive capital stock.[8] One way to obtain definite results on the properties of the model is to specify explicit functional forms for the underlying utility and production functions.

---

[7] Let's see how equation (3.18) looks like with logarithmic utility, $\mathcal{U} = \log c_{1t} + \beta \log c_{2t+1}$, and a Cobb-Douglas functional form, $y = k^\alpha$, for the production function. We have

$$s_t = \frac{\beta w_t}{1+\beta}, \quad r_t = \alpha k_t^{\alpha-1}, \quad \text{and} \quad w_t = (1-\alpha)k_t^\alpha$$

so that the capital accumulation equation becomes

$$k_{t+1} = \frac{s_t}{(1+\nu)} = \frac{\beta w_t}{(1+\nu)(1+\beta)} = \frac{(1-\alpha)\beta}{(1+\nu)(1+\beta)} k_t^\alpha,$$

which is a difference equation for k_t. If we can solve this equation then we can have a complete solution, since we can read off w_t, r_t, and s_t (and hence consumption).

[8] If we are willing to assume that a unique equilibrium with positive capital stock exists, then stability requires that dk_{t+1}/dk_t is less than one in absolute value. That is, the stability condition is

$$\left| \frac{-s_w k^* f''(k^*)}{(1+\nu) - s_r f''(k^*)} \right| < 1.$$

As an example, consider the case where utility is log linear, $\mathcal{U} = \log c_{1t} + \beta \log c_{2t+1}$, and the production function is Cobb-Douglas, $y_t = k_t^\alpha$. We know (from footnote 7) that in this case the capital accumulation equation is

$$k_{t+1} = \frac{(1-\alpha)\beta}{(1+\nu)(1+\beta)} k_t^\alpha,$$

suggesting that the steady state capital stock is

$$k^* = \left[\frac{(1-\alpha)\beta}{(1+\nu)(1+\beta)} \right]^{\frac{1}{1-\alpha}}.$$

In this case, $dk_{t+1}/dk_t > 0$. Stability requires that $|dk_{t+1}/dk_t| < 1$, and we can check if this is true for given values of the technology parameter α and the preference parameter, β. Notice that the properties of the economy, once it has converged to its balanced growth path, are the same as those in the optimal growth model — the saving rate is constant, per capita output is growing at the rate ν, the capital-output ratio is constant, and so on.

To see how the economy responds to shocks, consider a fall in ρ, when the economy is initially on its balanced growth path. The fall in ρ causes the young to save a greater fraction of their labor income, thereby increasing k^*. Thus the effects of a fall in the utility rate of time preference in the Diamond model (in the case we are considering, with logarithmic utility and Cobb-Douglas technology) are similar to the effects of a fall in ρ in the optimal growth model and to the effects of a rise in the saving rate in the Solow model.

The change shifts the paths over time of output and capital per worker permanently up, but it leads only to a temporary increase in the growth rates of these variables. The reader should also notice that in the Diamond model, as in the Ramsey model, the saving rate is not constant during the adjustment process.

3.4   Conclusion

We have reviewed basic, one-sector models of neoclassical growth theory and showed that these models, unlike the static IS-LM and AD-AS models that we discussed in Chapters 1 and 2, are dynamic structures built on solid microeconomic foundations. These models are also extremely versatile. They can be extended to deal with a number of issues in growth theory such as, for example, increasing returns to scale, human capital, endogenous population growth, and technological progress — see Robert Lucas (1988), Paul Romer (1986, 1990), Barro and Sala-i-Martin (1995), and Solow (1999, 2000) for references.

Neoclassical growth theory, however, also has uses in monetary economics and macroeconomics. As Costas Azariadis (1993, p. xii) puts it, neoclassical growth theory has

> " ... evolved into a *language* in which many macroeconomists, especially of the younger generation, choose to express their work and communicate their findings."

In fact, mainstream macroeconomic analysis amounts to 'complicating' one of the models discussed in this chapter. Introducing, for example, taxes and government debt we can study the effects of fiscal policy. Introducing money, we can explore the effects of monetary policy. Excellent treatments can be found in Blanchard and Fischer (1989), Athanasios Orphanides and Solow (1990), McCallum (1990), Azariadis (1993), and David Romer (2000).

In the next chapter, we review the ongoing debates about the role of money and the money demand function in neoclassical growth theory.

Chapter 4

Monetary Growth Theory

The neoclassical growth models that we studied in Chapter 3 are models of a nonmonetary economy. In this chapter, we review monetary versions of neoclassical growth theory. This involves putting money in the models of neoclassical growth theory and studying the implications for monetary policy. We begin with James Tobin (1965) who, as Orphanides and Solow (1990, p. 224) put it,

> " ... asked the question that has mainly preoccupied the literature ever since 1965. Different long-run rates of growth of the money supply will certainly be reflected eventually in different rates of inflation; but will there be any *real* effects in the long-run? Tobin studied this ("superneutrality") question in a simple "descriptive" model with aggregate saving depending only on current income, and seigniorage distributed in such a way as to preclude any distributional effects. He found that faster money growth is associated with higher capital stock and output per person in the steady state."

We also discuss an optimizing framework, originally due to Miguel Sidrauski (1967), that has played an important role in the development of monetary theory and has been used widely to study a variety of issues in monetary economics. In the Sidrauski, infinite-horizon optimization model superneutrality prevails.

Since lump-sum transfers are equal to the real per capita value of the change in nominal balances, or

$$v_t = \frac{M_{t+1} - M_t}{P_{t+1}L_{t+1}} = \frac{\mu_t}{(1 + \pi_t)(1 + \nu_t)} m_t,$$

equation (4.2) reduces to

$$(1 + \nu_t)k_{t+1} = sf(k_t) - \left(1 - \frac{s}{1 + \nu_t}\right) \frac{\mu_t - \pi_t}{1 + \pi_t} m_t + k_t. \qquad (4.3)$$

Equation (4.3) is the Tobin model, clearly showing that anything that increases real per capita money balances will result in a lower level of per capita capital and output. The basic intuition can be stated as follows. People regard the transfer of money as income and therefore raise their total saving, but only by a fraction s of the increase in real money holdings. Thus, they are induced to consume more and hence save less for capital accumulation.

Using the Tobin model, and assuming that the population growth rate and the growth rate of nominal balances are constant, we now consider properties of steady states. Since m_t is real per capita money balances, $m_t = M_t/P_t L_t$, its evolution through time is given by

$$\frac{dm}{dt} = (\mu - \pi - \nu)m,$$

suggesting that in the steady state (where m is constant)

$$\pi = \mu - \nu. \qquad (4.4)$$

Condition (4.4) states that steady-state inflation is directly determined by the monetary growth rate, μ.

In the steady state we also have $k_{t+1} = k_t$, so that equation (4.3) reduces to[3]

$$sf(k) = \left[\left(1 - \frac{s}{1 + \nu}\right) \frac{1}{1 + \pi} m + k\right] \nu$$

$$= \left[\left(1 - \frac{s}{1 + \nu}\right) \frac{1}{1 + \pi} \frac{m}{k} + 1\right] \nu k. \qquad (4.5)$$

---

[3] In deriving (4.5), we used (4.4) and the approximation that $\pi \nu \to 0$.

Equation (4.5) is the steady-state equation in the Tobin monetary growth model. For $m = 0$, it reduces to the standard equation of the Solow non-monetary growth model, with $\delta = 0$.

It is immediately clear from (4.5) that monetary neutrality prevails in this model, since changes in the supply of nominal money balances produce proportional changes in the aggregate price level, leaving the real equilibrium unaffected. Notice that this property follows from the fact that $m = M/PL$ in (4.5), implying that proportional changes in M and P do not affect the equilibrium level of per capita capital and output.

To investigate the issue regarding the superneutrality of money, we close the model by assuming that the ratio of money holdings to capital holdings, m/k, is a function of the real rates of return yielded by the two assets. Since r is the real rate of return on capital and $-\pi/(1+\pi)$ the real rate of return on money, m/k depends negatively on r and positively on $-\pi/(1+\pi)$, or, equivalently, negatively on π. Algebraically, we have the following money demand function

$$\frac{m}{k} = \Phi(r, \pi), \tag{4.6}$$

with $\Phi_r < 0$ and $\Phi_\pi < 0$.

With profit maximization and perfect competition in factor and output markets, we know that $r = f'(k)$ and equation (4.6) becomes

$$\frac{m}{k} = \Phi\left(f'(k), \pi \right),$$

and the steady-state equation (4.5) in terms of s, π, and ν becomes

$$sf(k) = \left[\left(1 - \frac{s}{1+\nu} \right) \frac{1}{1+\pi} \Phi\left(f'(k), \pi \right) + 1 \right] \nu k. \tag{4.7}$$

Totally differentiating (4.7) with respect to μ yields

$$\frac{dk}{d\mu} = \frac{\left(\Phi_\pi - \dfrac{1}{1+\pi} \right) \vartheta \nu k}{sf'(k) - \nu \left[1 + \vartheta \Phi + \vartheta \Phi_r f''(k)k \right]} \frac{d\pi}{d\mu},$$

where $\vartheta = 1/(1+\pi) - s/(1+\nu)(1+\pi)$. Clearly, $dk/d\mu$ is positive, meaning that the Tobin model does not have the property of superneutrality, in the sense that changes in the monetary growth rate affect real variables.

Intuitively, an increase in the growth rate of money raises the steady-state rate of inflation and lowers the real rate of return on money relative to physical capital. This reduces the ratio of money holdings to capital holdings and increases the steady-state level of per capita capital. This *portfolio substitution effect* of money growth on the equilibrium capital intensity of the economy is known as the *Tobin effect*.

4.2   The Sidrauski Model

The descriptive Tobin model, like the Solow model, assumes that the saving rate is an exogenous parameter. As Carl Walsh (1998, p. 49) puts it,

> "[t]his limitation can lead to problems when we try to understand the effects of changes in the economic environment, such as changes in the rate of inflation. The effects will depend, in part, on the way in which individual agents adjust, so we need to be able to predict how they will respond. If the behavioral relationships in the model are simply specified in an ad hoc manner, we will be unable to predict how the demand function for money might shift if the underlying time-series behavior of the inflation process were to change."

Sidrauski (1967), in his paper "Rational Choice and Patterns of Growth in a Monetary Economy," studied the superneutrality of money question in the context of a monetary growth model in an explicitly optimizing framework. In particular, he incorporated money balances into the utility function of the representative economic agent of the Ramsey (1928) optimal growth model, discussed in Chapter 3.

Sidrauski (1967) assumes that the representative household's lifetime utility function is of the form

$$\mathcal{U} = \sum_{t=0}^{\infty} \beta^t u(c_t, m_t), \tag{4.8}$$

where c_t and m_t are per capita consumption and real balances at time t. The within-period utility function, $u(c_t, m_t)$, satisfies the conditions, $u_i(c_t, m_t) > 0$, $u_{ii}(c_t, m_t) < 0$, for $i = 1, 2$, where $u_i(c_t, m_t)$ denotes the partial derivatives of $u(c_t, m_t)$ with respect to the ith argument.

Assuming (for simplicity) that there is no population growth (i.e., $\nu = 0$) and that the inflation rate from period t to period $t + 1$ is $\pi_t = (P_{t+1} - P_t)/P_t$, the household's budget constraint (in per capita terms) can be written as

$$f(k_t) + v_t = c_t + i_t$$

$$= c_t + k_{t+1} - (1 - \delta)k_t + (1 + \pi_t)m_{t+1} - m_t, \qquad (4.9)$$

where m_t are real (time t) cash holdings and v_t denotes (lump-sum) real government transfers (net of taxes), received at the start of the period.[4]

The problem is solved by maximizing (4.8) subject to the constraint (4.9), taking k_0 and m_0 as given. The Lagrangian expression is

$$\mathcal{L} = \sum_{t=0}^{\infty} \beta^t u(c_t, m_t) + \sum_{t=0}^{\infty} \beta^t \lambda_t \left[f(k_t) + v_t \right.$$

$$\left. -c_t - k_{t+1} + (1 - \delta)k_t - (1 + \pi_t)m_{t+1} + m_t \right].$$

The necessary first-order conditions for optimality can be obtained by differentiating $\mathcal{L}$ with respect to c_t, m_{t+1}, and k_{t+1}. They are (for all t)

$$u_1(c_t, m_t) - \lambda_t = 0, \qquad (4.10)$$

$$\beta u_2(c_t, m_t) - \lambda_t (1 + \pi_t) + \beta \lambda_{t+1} = 0, \qquad (4.11)$$

$$-\lambda_t + \beta \lambda_{t+1} \left[f'(k_{t+1}) + 1 - \delta \right] = 0. \qquad (4.12)$$

Conditions (4.9)-(4.12) are necessary for a maximum. In addition, there are two transversality conditions,

$$\lim_{t \to \infty} m_{t+1} \beta^t \lambda_t (1 + \pi_t) = 0, \qquad (4.13)$$

$$\lim_{t \to \infty} k_{t+1} \beta^t \lambda_t = 0. \qquad (4.14)$$

---

[4]The term $(1 + \pi_t)m_{t+1} - m_t$ on the right-hand side of (4.9) gives the change in real money holdings from period t to period $t + 1$. In particular, it is

$$\frac{M_{t+1} - M_t}{P_t} = \frac{M_{t+1}}{P_t} - \frac{M_t}{P_t} = \frac{M_{t+1}}{P_{t+1}} \frac{P_{t+1}}{P_t} - m_t = (1 + \pi_t)m_{t+1} - m_t.$$

In this setting, (4.9)-(4.12) are necessary for a maximum, while (4.9)-(4.14) are jointly sufficient. In other words, if (4.13)-(4.14) are satisfied, the household's choices of c_t, m_{t+1}, and k_{t+1} will be described by (4.9)-(4.12).

We can now consider properties of steady states. Under present assumptions (with $\nu = 0$ and no technological progress), c_t, k_t, m_t, v_t, and λ_t will be constant over time. With zero growth, conditions (4.10)-(4.12) reduce to

$$\beta u_2 = (1 + \pi - \beta)u_1, \qquad (4.15)$$

$$\beta\left[f'(k) + 1 - \delta\right] = 1, \qquad (4.16)$$

with (4.15) coming from (4.10) and (4.11) and (4.16) from (4.12). As equation (4.16) shows, in the steady state the marginal product of capital, $f'(k)$, is independent of π (and μ). This means that the real rate of interest (which equals the marginal product of capital) is independent of π (and μ) and that the Fisherian link between the nominal interest rate and the inflation rate holds across steady states. Moreover, because of the one-to-one mapping from $f'(k)$ to k, the capital intensity is also independent of π (and μ). Thus, superneutrality prevails and the Tobin effect is invalidated.

The superneutrality of money, however, is not a general result. Even minor modifications of Sidrauski's optimizing framework can lead to quite different results. In what follows, we consider a variation of the Sidrauski model, due to William Brock (1974), in which superneutrality fails.

4.3   A Variation of the Sidrauski Model

The Ramsey and Sidrauski models are both based on the assumption that labor is supplied inelastically. This is an unreasonable assumption and we can drop it, by introducing the amount of work as another decision variable. In doing so, we include labor input as an argument in the utility function of the representative economic agent, as follows

$$\mathcal{U} = \sum_{t=0}^{\infty} \beta^t u(c_t, m_t, n_t),$$

where c_t and m_t are (as before) per capita consumption and real balances at time t and n_t is the amount of work during period t. The within-period utility function, $u(c_t, m_t, n_t)$, satisfies the conditions, $u_i(c_t, m_t, n_t) > 0$, $u_{ii}(c_t, m_t, n_t) < 0$, for $i = 1, 2$, and $u_3(c_t, m_t, n_t) < 0$, $u_{33}(c_t, m_t, n_t) < 0$.

When labor supply is not inelastic, the production function can also be written as $y_t = f(k_t, n_t)$, with $f_i > 0$ and $f_{ii} < 0$, for $i = 1, 2$. The household's budget constraint (in per capita terms) can then be written as

$$f(k_t, n_t) + v_t = c_t + i_t$$

$$= c_t + k_{t+1} - (1 - \delta)k_t + (1 + \pi_t)m_{t+1} - m_t.$$

The new Lagrangian expression is

$$\mathcal{L} = \sum_{t=0}^{\infty} \beta^t u(c_t, m_t, n_t) + \sum_{t=0}^{\infty} \beta^t \lambda_t \left[f(k_t, n_t) + v_t \right.$$

$$\left. -c_t - k_{t+1} + (1 - \delta)k_t - (1 + \pi_t)m_{t+1} + m_t \right],$$

and the necessary first-order conditions for optimality can be obtained by differentiating $\mathcal{L}$ with respect to c_t, m_{t+1}, k_{t+1}, and n_t. They are (for all t)

$$u_1(c_t, m_t, n_t) - \lambda_t = 0,$$

$$\beta u_2(c_{t+1}, m_{t+1}, n_{t+1}) - \lambda_t (1 + \pi_t) + \beta \lambda_{t+1} = 0,$$

$$-\lambda_t + \beta \lambda_{t+1} \left[f_1(k_t, n_t) + 1 - \delta \right] = 0,$$

$$u_3(c_t, m_t, n_t) + \lambda_t f_2(k_t, n_t) = 0,$$

and the steady-state conditions that determine c, k, m, n, v, and λ become

$$\beta u_2(c, m, n) = (1 + \pi - \beta)u_1(c, m, n), \qquad (4.17)$$

$$\beta \left[f_1(k, n) + 1 - \delta \right] = 1, \qquad (4.18)$$

$$u_3(c, m, n) = -u_1(c, m, n)f_2(k, n). \qquad (4.19)$$

Part 3:

Theoretical Approaches
to the Demand
for Money

Overview of Part 3

Chapters 5, 6, and 7 deal with conventional theoretical approaches to the demand for money. As in Laidler (1993), I discuss Fisher, Keynes, Friedman, Baumol and Tobin, McCallum, and Sargent and Wallace. Some of this theoretical literature on money demand, unlike the 'micro-foundations' approach to be discussed in Part 5 of the book, contains the result that the demand for money should be linear (or linear in the logs) and should have as arguments a small set of variables, themselves representing significant links to spending and economic activity in the other sectors of the economy.

Chapter 5

The Classics, Keynes, and Friedman

In this chapter we survey the early theoretical literature on the macroeconomic demand for money. We begin with the classical version of the quantity theory of money, which remains considerably relevant even today. Then we move on to the Keynesian liquidity preference theory and we end with Milton Friedman's modern quantity theory.

A central question in this literature, crucial to how we view money's effects on aggregate economic activity, is whether and to what extent the demand for money is affected by changes in the interest rate. If the demand for money is insensitive to interest rates, the velocity of money is constant and the quantity of money is the primary determinant of nominal aggregate spending. If, however, the demand for money is affected by changes in interest rates, then velocity is not constant and money is not the primary determinant of aggregate spending.

For discussing these theories of the demand for money, the equation of exchange is a useful point of departure.

5.1   The Equation of Exchange

We begin with the *transactions version* of the *equation of exchange*, introduced by Irving Fisher in his 1911 book, *The Purchasing Power of Money*,

$$M^s V = PT,$$

where M^s is the actual stock of money, V its transactions velocity of circulation (or more simply velocity — the average number of times per period that the stock of money changes hands to finance transactions), P is the price level, and T is the volume of transactions. The equation of exchange states that the quantity of money multiplied by the average number of times that it changes hands per period in making transactions (which equals the number of purchases) must equal the number of transactions conducted over the period multiplied by the average price at which they take place (which equals the value of sales).

In the literature one finds a second presentation of the equation of exchange, known as the *income version* of the equation of exchange,

$$M^s V = PY, \qquad\qquad (5.1)$$

where instead of the volume of transactions, T, real output, Y, appears in the equation and the income velocity (the rate of circulation of money relative to the rate of production of real income) replaces the transactions velocity. Underlying this substitution is the assumption that real income and the volume of transactions are proportionately related. In what follows, we adopt the convention of working with the income version of the equation of exchange.

5.2   The Quantity Theory of Money

Although equation (5.1) is nothing more than an identity, it can be used to develop a theory by postulating certain things about the determinants of the equation of exchange variables. In particular, assuming (as Fisher did) that real activity and money are exogenously determined, that velocity has a constant equilibrium long-run value, and that, within the monetary sector, the price level is the only endogenous variable, the equation of exchange (5.1) can be transformed into a version of the *quantity theory of money*, which can be written as

$$\overline{M^s}\,\overline{V} = P\overline{Y}, \qquad\qquad (5.2)$$

with bars over M^s, V, and Y indicating that they are determined independently of the other variables. Equation (5.2) is the quantity theory of money, which states the conditions under which nominal income is determined solely by movements in the quantity of money. Alternatively, equation (5.2) can be viewed as a theory of price level determination, suggesting that the equilibrium price level is strictly proportional to the quantity of money.

5.3 The Quantity Theory Demand for Money

The quantity theory of money becomes a theory of the demand for money once one assumes that the money market is in equilibrium, so that $M^s = M^d = M$. In that case, equation (5.2) becomes (when solved for M^d)

$$M^d = kPY \quad \text{or} \quad \frac{M^d}{P} = kY, \tag{5.3}$$

where $k = 1/V$. Equation (5.3) is the long-run demand for money function, interpreted from the viewpoint of the quantity theory of money. It says that the demand for nominal (real) money is proportional to nominal (real) income.

A convenient linearization of equation (5.3) is achieved if we write it in logarithmic form as

$$\log M - \log P = \alpha + \log Y \tag{5.4}$$

where $\alpha = \log k$. Equation (5.4) implies that for given values of real income, the demand for real money balances, $\log M - \log P$, is unaffected by exogenous changes in nominal money. In fact equation (5.4) implies that the price level elasticity of the demand for nominal money balances, $\eta(M, P)$, is[1]

$$\eta(M, P) = \frac{d \log M}{d \log P} = 1,$$

---

[1] The reader should note that the above mentioned price level homogeneity condition can easily be tested by reformulating equation (5.4) as

$$\log P = -\alpha - \beta \log Y + \gamma \log M,$$

and testing the hypothesis that $\gamma = 1$. In fact, the above equation can also be written in differenced form as

$$\Delta \log P = -\alpha - \beta \Delta \log Y + \gamma \Delta \log M,$$

where Δ is the difference operator, and be used to test the steady-state hypothesis between the inflation rate, $\Delta \log P$, and the monetary growth rate, $\Delta \log M$, by testing that $\gamma = 1$.

tive' — suggesting that people regard holding of money for one motive, at least in part, as separate from holdings of money for another motive.

In his discussions of the transactions demand for money, Keynes followed closely Fisher and the Cambridge economists and listed the transactions motive as an important (but not the only) motive underlying the demand for money. He postulated that the transactions (or business) demand for money is a stable function of the level of income. In fact, he wrote the transactions demand for money as in equation (5.3). Also, regarding the precautionary motive for holding money, Keynes suggested that the demand for precautionary money balances depends on the level of income and slightly on the interest rate, but for the most part, on the level of uncertainty about the future.

However, the most important innovation in Keynes's analysis of the demand for money is his *speculative demand* for money, or the demand for money as an asset alternative to other interest-yielding assets. The primary result of the Keynesian speculative theory is that the demand for money depends negatively on the interest rate. Keynes derived this result by analyzing only the choice between interest-yielding bonds and money as an issue of liquidity preference. In doing so, however, he raised to a position of importance variables such as interest rates, expectations, and uncertainty, which although considered by the Cambridge economists, were ultimately accorded a secondary role.

We may illustrate the Keynesian speculative theory of money demand by dividing the assets into two broad categories: money and bonds. Assume that the expected return on money is zero, as Keynes did (in his time, unlike today, this was a reasonable assumption, since money was mostly of the outside type). The expected rate of return on bonds is the sum of the current yield and the expected rate of capital gain (or loss).

If people expect interest rates to increase in the future (and therefore bond prices to decline), the expected rate of return on bonds would be less than the current yield, because the expected rate of capital gain is negative — that is, an expected capital loss. In fact, if people expect future interest rates to increase substantially, the expected rate of capital loss might outweigh the current yield, so that the expected rate of return on their bonds would be negative. In this case, they will put all of their liquid wealth into money. On the other hand, if people expect a substantial decline in interest rates (and therefore a significant increase in bond prices), the expected rate of return on bonds will exceed the current yield, because the expected rate of capital gain is positive. In this case, people will hold all bonds and no money for speculative purposes.

The implication of this is that the demand for speculative money balances depends on both the observable market (nominal) interest rate and people's expectation concerning that rate in the future. The decision with respect to holding bonds or money is described in Keynes in terms of some *normal value* that interest rates tend to. If interest rates are above this normal value, people will expect them to fall, bond prices to rise, and capital gains to be realized. As a result, people will be more likely to hold their liquid wealth as bonds rather than money, and the demand for money will be low.

If interest rates are below the normal value, people will expect them to rise, bond prices to fall, and capital losses to be realized. They will be more likely to hold money than bonds and the demand for money will be high. In fact, at some very low interest rate, everyone will expect it to rise and the demand for money in the aggregate will be perfectly elastic with respect to the interest rate — this is known as the *liquidity trap*. Overall, assuming a normal distribution on the population's expectations of the future interest rate, the aggregate demand for money will be negatively related to the level of interest rates.

We have discussed three separate demands for money — the transactions demand, the precautionary demand, and the speculative (or asset) demand for money. Combining these three demands, we get the Keynesian *liquidity preference function*, describing the total demand for money

$$\frac{M^d}{P} = \Phi(R, Y)$$

with $\Phi_1 < 0$ and $\Phi_2 > 0$, where Φ_i denotes the partial derivative of $\Phi(\cdot)$ with respect to its ith argument. That is, the demand for real money balances is negatively related to the nominal interest rate, R, and positively related to real income, Y.

One implication of the Keynesian liquidity preference theory of the demand for money, which contrasts sharply with the classical quantity theory approach, is that velocity is not constant but instead positively related to nominal interest rates. We can see this by writing down the velocity that is implied by the liquidity preference function

$$V = \frac{Y}{M/P} = \frac{Y}{\Phi(R, Y)}$$

We know that when the interest rate increases the demand for money declines and therefore velocity rises. Hence, in contrast to the quantity theorists' view of a constant velocity, the Keynesian liquidity preference

Friedman did not take the expected rate of return on money to be a constant, as did Keynes, and by assuming that the demand for money depends on the incentives for holding other assets relative to money, he argued that the demand for money is insensitive to interest rates. In particular, in Friedman's view, when interest rates rise in the economy the expected rate of return on money held as bank deposits also rises (along with the rise in the expected rates of return on other assets), so that there is no change in the incentive terms, $R_b - R_m$, $R_e - R_m$, and $\pi^e - R_m$, in the money demand function.

Hence, unlike Keynes's liquidity preference theory in which interest rates are an important determinant of the demand for money, Friedman's theory suggests that although the demand for money is sensitive to changes in the incentives for holding other assets relative to money, these incentives stay relatively constant when interest rates change, implying that the demand for money is insensitive to interest rates. Therefore, Friedman's money demand function, equation (5.6), can be approximated by

$$\frac{M^d}{P} = \Phi(Y_p),$$

which indicates that real permanent income is the only determinant of real money demand.

The second issue Friedman stressed is the stability of the money demand function. In particular, unlike Keynes (who felt that the demand for money is erratic and shifts with changed expectations of the rate of interest), Friedman suggested that the money demand function is highly stable, implying that the quantity of money demanded can be predicted accurately by the money demand function. Also, when combined with his view that the demand for money is insensitive to interest rates, this means that the velocity of money is highly predictable.

The reader should notice that the stability of the money demand function and the consequent predictability of the velocity of money derive from the relationship between current income and permanent income. In particular, according to equation (5.8), a permanent change in income changes permanent income by the same amount, whereas a temporary change in income (as, for example, in a business cycle expansion or recession) changes permanent income by a small amount.[5]

---

[5] Mathematically, suppose that $r = 10\%$ and consider a temporary change in income, such as $\Delta Y_t = 1$ with $\Delta Y_{t+j} = 0$, $j = 1, 2, \cdots$. According to equation (5.8), we have

$$\Delta Y_p = \frac{.10}{1 + .10} \Delta Y_t = .09,$$

We can see this implication of Friedman's theory, by converting the money demand function to the corresponding velocity of money function

$$V = \frac{Y}{M/P} = \frac{Y}{\Phi(Y_p)},$$

which suggests that since the relationship between current income, Y, and permanent income, Y_p, is usually quite predictable, the velocity of money is predictable (although not constant) as well. This means that a given change in the nominal money supply will produce a predictable change in aggregate spending. Therefore, Friedman's theory of the demand for money is indeed a reformulation of the quantity theory of money, because it leads to the quantity theory conclusion that money is the primary determinant of aggregate nominal spending.

Finally, Friedman's money demand formulation can also explain the procyclical movements of velocity we find in the data, by the relationship between the demand for real money balances and permanent income and by the relationship between permanent income and actual measured income. For example, in a business cycle expansion the demand for money rises less than income because the increase in permanent income is small relative to the increase in actual measured income [see equation (5.8)], and velocity rises. Similarly, in a recession, the demand for money falls less than income because the decline in permanent income is small relative to the decline in actual measured income, and velocity falls.

5.7   Conclusion

We have discussed the early theories of money demand and identified similarities and differences that exist among them. According to the classical quantity theory (developed by Fisher and the Cambridge economists), nominal income is determined primarily by the quantity of money. This proposition, however, rests on the classical economists' assumption that velocity could be treated as reasonably constant.

Keynes criticized the quantity theorists for their assumption of a constant velocity and argued that velocity is affected by behavioral economic variables, most importantly by the nominal interest rate. His conclusion that the demand for money is negatively related to the nominal interest rate is a significant departure from the classical quantity theory of

---

that is, permanent income changes by only .09. A permanent change in income, however, such as $\Delta Y_{t+j} = 1$, $j = 0, 1, 2, \cdots$, produces an equal change in permanent income, since

$$\Delta Y_p = \frac{r}{1+r} \frac{1+r}{r} = 1.$$

money demand. It is, however, less of a departure from the classical Cambridge approach, which did not rule out such a relationship.

Friedman's theory of the demand for money used a similar approach to that of Keynes and the earlier Cambridge economists, but did not deal with the motives for holding money. By using the theory of portfolio choice, Friedman argued that the demand for money depends on permanent income and the incentives for holding other assets relative to money. In contrast to Keynes, however, he concluded that the demand for money is stable and insensitive to interest rates. This implies that velocity is predictable, yielding the quantity theory conclusion that money is the primary determinant of nominal aggregate spending.

Chapter 6

Transactions Theories of Money Demand

Theories of the demand for money that emphasize money's medium-of-exchange role in the economy are called *transactions theories*. These theories emphasize that money, unlike other assets, is held to make purchases and in general show that the average amount of real money held involves a trade-off between transactions costs (that arise when people economize on their holdings of money) and interest income foregone.

Transactions theories of the demand for money take many different forms, depending on how the process of obtaining money and making transactions is modeled. To see how these theories explain the demand for money, in this chapter we develop explicitly three prominent models of this type.

6.1 The Baumol-Tobin Model

The choice of when and how often to exchange bonds for money is an important margin of choice for individuals and has been analyzed independently by William Baumol (1952) and James Tobin (1956). Both emphasize the costs and benefits of holding money, coming to similar conclusions about the variables that determine the transactions demand for money. It is argued, for example, that the benefit of holding money is convenience and that the cost of this convenience is the interest income foregone by not holding interest-yielding assets, such as bonds.

To see how maximizing economic agents trade off these benefits, we follow Baumol's (slightly simpler) approach and consider an individual agent who plans to spend Y, in real terms, gradually over the course of a year. The agent has a choice of holding his wealth in the form of (non-interest-yielding) money or in the form of interest-yielding bonds — bonds yield an interest rate of R per period, which is assumed constant over the period and reflects the opportunity cost of holding money. In addition, it is also assumed that each exchange of interest-bearing bonds for money involves a lump-sum transactions cost b in real terms — b is what Baumol calls the *brokerage fee*.

In the setting described, assuming that K is the real value of bonds turned into money each time such a transfer takes place, the total cost of making transactions is the sum of the brokerage cost, $b\,(Y/K)$, where (Y/K) is the number of withdrawals, and the foregone interest if money is held instead of bonds, which is $R(K/2)$, where $K/2$ is the average amount of real money holdings $(= M/P)$. Thus, the total cost can be written as

$$\text{Total Cost} = b\frac{Y}{K} + R\frac{K}{2} \qquad (6.1)$$

Clearly, the fewer the withdrawals, Y/K (and as a result the larger the money balances, $K/2$, held by the individual), the lower will be the brokerage cost and the higher the interest cost. In fact the number of withdrawals that minimizes the total cost of making transactions occurs when the increase in brokerage cost as the result of an additional withdrawal is just offset by the reduction in the interest cost as a result of this withdrawal.

By taking the partial derivative of equation (6.1) with respect to K, setting it equal to zero and solving for K we find the optimal value of K — the value that minimizes total cost. Thus

$$\frac{\partial(\text{Total Cost})}{\partial K} = -\frac{bY}{K^2} + \frac{R}{2} = 0$$

which yields the following *square root* relationship between K and Y, b, and R

$$K = \sqrt{\frac{2bY}{R}}\ .$$

At this value of K, average money holding in real terms is, as noted earlier

$$\frac{M}{P} = \frac{K}{2} = \frac{1}{2}\sqrt{\frac{2bY}{R}} \qquad (6.2)$$

suggesting that the demand for real (transactions) money balances is proportional to the square root of Y and inversely proportional to the square root of R. Notice that as $b \to 0$, $M/P \to 0$, meaning that without transactions costs there would be no demand for money, since in this case the individual will be synchronizing cash withdrawals with the purchase of goods and services. Hence, transactions costs have an important role in determining average money balances held, suggesting that the demand for money emerges from a trade-off between transactions costs and interest earnings.

The merit of this approach to the demand for money is that it produces testable relationships between the demand for money and its determinants. For example, taking logarithms of equation (6.2), we can express it as

$$\log \left(\frac{M}{P} \right) = \alpha + \frac{1}{2} \log Y - \frac{1}{2} \log R \qquad (6.3)$$

where $\alpha = \log (1/2) \sqrt{2b}$. In the log-linear equation (6.3), the elasticity of M/P with respect to Y is

$$\eta \left(\frac{M}{P}, Y \right) = \frac{d \log(M/P)}{d \log Y} = \frac{1}{2}$$

implying that a rise in real spending leads to a less-than-proportionate increase in the average holding of real money. Economists refer to this result as *economies of scale* in money holding, meaning that individuals with a larger scale of spending hold less money when expressed as a ratio to their expenditures.

Also the elasticity of M/P with respect to the interest rate is

$$\eta \left(\frac{M}{P}, R \right) = \frac{d \log(M/P)}{d \log R} = -\frac{1}{2}$$

and the elasticity of nominal money, M, with respect to the price level is

$$\eta(M, P) = \frac{d \log M}{d \log P} = 1.$$

Clearly, the Baumol-Tobin model represents a significant departure from the classical quantity theory of money, as it implies economies of scale in the demand for money and an interest elasticity away from zero. This conflict between the Baumol-Tobin model and the quantity theory led Karl Brunner and Allan Meltzer (1967) to reformulate the Baumol-Tobin model and show that for large values of Y or small values of b,

$$\mathcal{L} = \sum_{t=0}^{\infty} \beta^t u\left[c_t, \psi(c_t, m_t)\right] + \sum_{t=0}^{\infty} \beta^t \lambda_t \left[f(k_t) + v_t \right.$$

$$\left. - c_t - k_{t+1} + k_t - (1+\pi_t)m_{t+1} + m_t - \frac{b_{t+1}}{1+r_t} + b_t \right]$$

where $\psi(c_t, m_t)$ is substituted for ℓ_t, and λ_t is the Lagrange multiplier associated with the household's period t budget constraint. The necessary first-order conditions for optimality can be obtained by differentiating $\mathcal{L}$ with respect to c_t, m_{t+1}, k_{t+1}, and b_{t+1}. They are (for all t)

$$u_1(c_t, \ell_t) + u_2(c_t, \ell_t)\psi_1(c_t, m_t) - \lambda_t = 0 \qquad (6.5)$$

$$\beta u_2(c_{t+1}, \ell_{t+1})\psi_2(c_{t+1}, m_{t+1}) - \lambda_t(1+\pi_t) + \beta\lambda_{t+1} = 0 \qquad (6.6)$$

$$-\lambda_t + \beta\lambda_{t+1}\left[f'(k_{t+1}) + 1\right] = 0 \qquad (6.7)$$

$$-\frac{\lambda_t}{1+r_t} + \beta\lambda_{t+1} = 0 \qquad (6.8)$$

where $u_i(c_t, \ell_t)$ and $\psi_i(c_t, m_t)$ denote the partial derivatives of $u(c_t, \ell_t)$ and $\psi(c_t, m_t)$ with respect to the ith argument and $f'(k_{t+1})$ is the rate of return on capital between periods t and $t+1$. Conditions (6.4)-(6.8) are necessary for a maximum. In addition, there are three transversality conditions,

$$\lim_{t\to\infty} m_{t+1}\beta^t \lambda_t(1+\pi_t) = 0 \qquad (6.9)$$

$$\lim_{t\to\infty} k_{t+1}\beta^t \lambda_t = 0 \qquad (6.10)$$

$$\lim_{t\to\infty} b_{t+1}\beta^t \frac{\lambda_t}{1+r_t} = 0. \qquad (6.11)$$

In this setting, (6.4)-(6.8) are necessary for a maximum, while (6.4)-(6.11) are jointly sufficient. In other words, if (6.9)-(6.11) are satisfied, the household's choices of c_t, m_{t+1}, k_{t+1}, and b_{t+1} will be described by (6.4)-(6.8).

Eliminating $\beta\lambda_{t+1}$ between (6.6) and (6.8) and λ_t from the resultant equation, by using (6.5), we get the following optimality condition[3]

$$\frac{u_1(c_t, l_t) + u_2(c_t, l_t)\psi_1(c_t, m_t)}{\beta u_2(c_{t+1}, \ell_{t+1})\psi_2(c_{t+1}, m_{t+1})} = \frac{1 + r_t}{R_t} \tag{6.12}$$

The optimality condition (6.12) involves only three variables: c_t, m_t, and R_t. Assuming that it can be uniquely solved for m_t as a function of c_t and R_t we obtain an exact *equilibrium* relationship,

$$\frac{M_t}{P_t} = \Phi(c_t, R_t), \tag{6.13}$$

relating the household's optimal consumption, his demand for real balances and the nominal interest rate. Since M_t/P_t and c_t are choice variables, equation (6.13) is not a (money) demand function but, instead, an equilibrium condition among choice variables that the demand functions must satisfy. However, the practice of calling relations like (6.13) money demand functions is extremely common, and although improper, we shall use that terminology.

The foregoing theoretical model, although it is explicit and general, is lacking in one way. In particular, it does not imply, as the Baumol (1952) and Tobin (1956) models do, that c_t enters positively and R_t negatively on the right-hand side of (6.13). To complete the model, we assume that $\Phi(\cdot)$ possesses partial derivatives and that $\Phi_1 > 0$ and $\Phi_2 < 0$. It is to be noted, however, that it is not true that those signs are strictly implied for all functions satisfying the assumptions that we placed on $u(c_t, l_t)$ and $\psi(c_t, M_t/P_t)$.

6.3   Cash-in-Advance Models

Another popular device for introducing money into macroeconomic equilibrium models is the cash-in-advance constraint, proposed by Robert Clower (1967). This approach captures the role of money as a medium of exchange by requiring that a transaction can take place only if the money needed for the transaction is held in advance. Moreover, it provides an explanation as to why rational economic agents hold money

---

[3]From (6.7) and (6.8) we also get

$$1 + f'(k_{t+1}) = \frac{1 + R_t}{1 + \pi_{t+1}}$$

which is basically the Fisher equation, linking the nominal interest rate to the real interest rate and the inflation rate.

So far, however, we have assumed that the liquidity-cash-in-advance constraint pertains only to the purchases of consumption goods, c_t. We now investigate the robustness of our results regarding the superneutrality of money in cash-in-advance models, by assuming that the cash-in-advance constraint pertains to purchases of consumption as well as capital. Under this assumption, we write the cash-in-advance constraint as

$$\frac{M_t}{P_t} + v_t \geq c_t + k_{t+1} - (1 - \delta)k_t, \tag{6.22}$$

where $k_{t+1} - (1 - \delta)k_t$ is gross investment. The cash-in-advance constraint (6.22) states that the individual must be able to finance current consumption and gross investment out of money balances carried over from the previous period plus current transfers.

Now the problem of a private agent is to maximize (6.14) subject to (6.15) and (6.22). The Lagrangian associated with this problem is

$$\mathcal{L} = \sum_{t=0}^{\infty} \beta^t \left\{ u\left(c_t\right) \right.$$

$$+ \lambda_t \left[f(k_t) + v_t - c_t - k_{t+1} + (1 - \delta)k_t - \frac{M_{t+1} - M_t}{P_t} \right]$$

$$\left. + \gamma_t \left[\frac{M_t}{P_t} + v_t - c_t - k_{t+1} + (1 - \delta)k_t \right] \right\},$$

and the necessary first-order conditions are

$$u'(c_t) = \lambda_t + \gamma_t, \tag{6.23}$$

$$\beta\lambda_{t+1}\left[f'(k_{t+1}) + 1 - \delta \right] + \beta\gamma_{t+1}(1 - \delta) = \lambda_t + \gamma_t, \tag{6.24}$$

$$\beta\lambda_{t+1}\frac{1}{P_{t+1}} + \beta\gamma_{t+1}\frac{1}{P_{t+1}} = \lambda_t\frac{1}{P_t}. \tag{6.25}$$

Using (6.23)-(6.25), we again turn to steady state analysis. As before, the capital stock and consumption are constant in the steady state, implying that $\lambda+\gamma$ is constant over time. Hence, in the steady state (6.25) becomes

$$\beta(\lambda_{t+1} + \gamma_{t+1}) = \lambda_t \frac{P_{t+1}}{P_t},$$

which yields

$$\gamma = \frac{1+\pi}{\beta}\lambda - \lambda,$$

since λ and γ are each constant over time and $P_{t+1}/P_t = 1+\pi$. Substituting the last expression into (6.24) and rearranging yields the steady-state condition

$$f'(k^*) = (1+\pi)\frac{1 - (1-\delta)\beta}{\beta^2}.$$

Thus, when both consumption and gross-investment are subject to the liquidity constraint, higher inflation rates are associated with higher steady-state real rates of interest and lower capital stock and money balances.

The reason for this result is the complementarity of money and capital. In particular, as Orphanides and Solow (1990, p. 256) put it

"[i]nvestment of an additional unit of capital in period $t+1$ requires an additional unit of money holdings in period t. Higher inflation increases the cost of the additional unit of investment by increasing the cost of holding the money necessary for the investment. Thus, it reduces the (net of money holding costs) return on a unit of investment. As a result, the demand for capital is reduced and less money is held."

Finally, since consumption and the capital stock are constant in the steady-state market equilibrium, the cash-in-advance constraint is satisfied as an equality, implying the following money demand function

$$\frac{M_t}{P_t} = f(k),$$

which is similar to the quantity-theoretic money demand function.

We have presented a simple cash-in-advance model and seen that the specification of the transactions subject to the liquidity constraint is important. For other (more recent) cash-in-advance frameworks, see Lars Svennson (1985), Lucas and Nancy Stokey (1987), and Thomas Cooley and Gary Hansen (1989).

being the basis for his Nobel Prize in economics. He refers to his theory
as a theory of *liquidity preference*, following Keynes's terminology.

Tobin assumes that the individual holds a portfolio consisting of a
proportion of wealth w_1 in money and w_2 in the risky asset, say perpetual
bonds. Notice that $w_1 + w_2 = 1$. Money has a riskless rate of return
$E_1 = R_f$ (≥ 0) and therefore a variance of return that is exactly zero,
$\sigma_1^2 = 0$. The risky asset has an expected rate of return E_2 ($> R_f$) and
a variance of return σ_2^2 ($> \sigma_1^2$).

The expected return on the portfolio, E_p, is simply a weighted average
of the expected returns on each of the assets, with the weights being the
proportion of wealth invested in each asset,

$$E_p = \sum_{i=1}^{k} w_i E_i,$$

where k is the number of assets in the portfolio and E_i is the expected
return on asset i. Since $k = 2$, $E_1 = R_f$, and $w_1 = 1 - w_2$, we have

$$E_p = (1 - w_2)R_f + w_2 E_2. \tag{7.1}$$

The total variance of the portfolio, σ_p^2, is

$$\sigma_p^2 = \sum_{i=1}^{k}\sum_{j=1}^{k} w_i w_j R_{ij}\sigma_i\sigma_j,$$

where R_{ij} is the simple correlation between returns on assets i and j.
However, since $k = 2$ and $R_{11} = R_{22} = 1$ we have

$$\sigma_p^2 = w_1^2\sigma_1^2 + w_2^2\sigma_2^2 + 2w_1 w_2 R_{12}\sigma_1\sigma_2.$$

Finally, since $\sigma_1 = 0$ and the assets are independent (i.e., $R_{12} = 0$), the
last equation reduces to

$$\sigma_p^2 = w_2^2\sigma_2^2. \tag{7.2}$$

Rearranging equation (7.2) yields $w_2 = \sigma_p/\sigma_2$ which, after substituting back into equation (7.1) and rearranging terms, gives

$$E_p = R_f + \left(\frac{E_2 - R_f}{\sigma_2}\right)\sigma_p. \tag{7.3}$$

This equation shows a simple linear relationship between expected portfolio return, E_p, and portfolio risk, σ_p. Specifically, expected portfolio
return is the sum of the risk-free rate of return, R_f, and $(E_2 - R_f)/\sigma_2$

times the portfolio risk, σ_p. The slope $(E_2 - R_f)/\sigma_2$ is referred to as the *price of risk*, since it measures how σ_p and E_p can be traded off in making portfolio choices.

Equation (7.3) describes the options available to investors with respect to holding alternative portfolios. To examine, however, how investors determine what portfolios to hold, we must first examine investor preferences over expected portfolio return and portfolio risk. In doing so, we assume that the individual wishes to maximize a utility function depending on E_p and σ_p^2, as follows

$$\mathcal{U} = u(E_p, \sigma_p^2),$$

with $u_1 > 0$, $u_2 < 0$, $u_{11} < 0$, and $u_{22} < 0$. Approximating the explicit utility function by

$$\mathcal{U} = E_p - \frac{\gamma}{2}\sigma_p^2,$$

where γ is a constant representing the degree of risk aversion, and using equations (7.1) and (7.2), the individual's (unconstrained) optimization problem is to maximize

$$\mathcal{U} = (1 - w_2)R_f + w_2 E_2 - \frac{\gamma}{2}w_2^2\sigma_2^2,$$

with respect to w_2.

The first-order condition for maximization is

$$\frac{\partial \mathcal{U}}{\partial w_2} = -R_f + E_2 - \gamma w_2 \sigma_2^2 = 0,$$

which implies the optimal proportion of the holding of the risky asset, w_2^*,

$$w_2^* = \frac{E_2 - R_f}{\gamma \sigma_2^2}. \tag{7.4}$$

Equation (7.4) is Tobin's (1958) *mean-variance model* of asset demands and holds for any risky portfolio.

Consider now the effects of an increase in the interest rate, with no change in the perceived riskiness of bonds. Clearly, according to Tobin's asset demand model the optimal proportion of the holding of the risky asset will increase and money holdings will decline. That is, the increase in the interest rate reduces the demand for money. Hence, Tobin's model implies a negative interest rate elasticity of the same general form as we saw in the Keynesian and Baumol-Tobin models.

$$c_{1t} + \frac{M_t^d}{P_t} = 1,$$

$$c_{2t+1} = \frac{M_t^d}{P_{t+1}},$$

where M_t^d is the individual's demand for money at time t, which equals $1 - c_{1t}$. The first equation is the budget constraint facing the individual in the first period of life. The right-hand side represents the individual's total sources of goods (his endowment) and the left-hand side the individual's total uses of goods (consumption and the acquisition of money — $1/P_t$ is the value of one unit of money in terms of goods). The second equation is the budget constraint facing the individual in the second period of life (period $t+1$). This equation makes clear that since the individual receives no endowment when old, he can acquire second-period consumption goods only be spending the money acquired in the previous period.

By substituting the period-$(t+1)$ budget constraint into the period-t budget constraint to eliminate M_t^d we can obtain the individual's lifetime budget constraint

$$c_{1t} + \frac{P_{t+1}}{P_t} c_{2t+1} = 1,$$

which shows combinations of first- and second-period consumption that an individual can afford over his lifetime.

To solve the individual's problem we set up the Lagrangian

$$\mathcal{L} = u(c_{1t}) + \beta u(c_{2t+1}) + \lambda \left(1 - c_{1t} - \frac{P_{t+1}}{P_t} c_{2t+1} \right),$$

where λ is the Lagrange multiplier on the lifetime budget constraint. The first-order conditions are

$$u'(c_{1t}) = \lambda,$$

$$\beta u'(c_{2t+1}) = \lambda \frac{P_{t+1}}{P_t}.$$

These combine to give the Euler equation

$$\frac{u'(c_{1t})}{\beta u'(c_{2t+1})} = \frac{P_t}{P_{t+1}},$$

which states that the marginal rate of substitution between first- and second-period consumption equals the rate of return on money, P_t/P_{t+1}.

The Euler equation implies a money demand function (which is a saving function)

$$\frac{M_t^d}{P_t} = \Phi\left(\frac{P_t}{P_{t+1}}\right).$$

If we define the deflation rate, π_t, by $(1 + \pi_t) = P_t/P_{t+1}$, we can write the money demand function as

$$\frac{M_t^d}{P_t} = \Phi(1 + \pi_t).$$

Let us now describe equilibrium in the money market and find an equilibrium time path of the value of money. Since the old supply inelastically the money they have (which is H) and the young buy money according to the above equation, the money market — or equivalently, by Walras' law the goods market — will be in equilibrium when

$$(1 + \nu)^t M_t^d = H,$$

where ν is the constant population growth rate and $(1 + \nu)^t M_t^d$ is the total demand for money by all individuals in the economy at time t. Using the above two equations at time t and $t + 1$ we obtain

$$\frac{1 + \nu}{1 + \pi_t} = \frac{\Phi(1 + \pi_t)}{\Phi(1 + \pi_{t+1})}.$$

To simplify, we consider a stationary allocation, where the members of every generation have the same lifetime consumption pattern, that is, $c_{1t} = c_1$ and $c_{2t+1} = c_2$ for every period t. This definition implies that the price ratio, P_t/P_{t+1} will also be independent of time and that $\Phi(1 + \pi_t) = \Phi(1 + \pi_{t+1})$. In turn, our definition of a stationary equilibrium and the last equation imply that the rate of deflation must be equal to the constant population growth rate ($\pi = \nu$).

Since $\nu > 0, \pi = \nu$ means that the price of the consumption good is falling over time, or, equivalently, that the value of money is increasing

Part 4:
Empirical Approaches
to the Demand
for Money

Overview of Part 4

Chapter 8 deals with the empirical relevance of some of the theories presented in Part 3, taking a conventional approach to estimation and hypothesis testing. In Chapters 9, 10, and 11, we turn to a discussion of the same issues using recent advances in the field for applied econometrics, such as integration and cointegration theory. The approach here is similar to that taken by Hoffman and Rasche (1996). That is, we pay explicit attention to the econometric consequences of nonstationary data and their implications for the study of money demand.

In both Chapters 8 and 11, comparisons are made among simple-sum, Divisia, and CE monetary aggregates (of M1, M2, M3, and MZM) using the Anderson *et al.* (1997) data set. Similar comparisons will be provided in Chapter 14, as one of the objectives of this textbook is to provide empirical evidence regarding the relative merits of alternative monetary aggregation procedures.

Chapter 8

Conventional Demand for Money Functions

In our discussions of theories of macroeconomic behavior, we have talked about the demand for money function. As we saw, this function is a critical component in the formulation of monetary policy. Moreover, it has been argued over the years that a stable demand function for money is a necessary condition for money to exert a predictable influence on the economy so that control of the monetary aggregates can be a useful instrument of economic policy.

Not surprisingly, then, numerous empirical studies have been conducted in many countries to evaluate the determinants and stability of the demand for money. As Stephen Goldfeld and Daniel Sichel (1990, p. 300) put it

> "[t]he evidence that emerged, at least prior to the mid-1970s, suggested that a few variables (essentially income and interest rates, with appropriate allowance for lags) were capable of providing a plausible and stable explanation of money demand."

In this chapter we look at the factors that have shaped the evolution of the research on modeling and estimating money demand functions. In doing so, we discuss measurement issues on a variable-by-variable basis, and distinguish the long-run and short-run concepts of the demand for money by the absence of adjustment costs in the former and their presence in the latter. We conclude that conventional money demand functions are seriously misspecified, and argue for new modelling approaches.

8.1   The Basic Specification

As we have seen there are different money demand theories, emphasizing different considerations and implying different testable theoretical hypotheses. These theories, however, share common important elements. In particular, most of them suggest a relationship between the quantity of money demanded and a few important variables that represent significant links to the level of economic activity. In general, this theoretical money demand relationship can be written as

$$\frac{M_t}{P_t} = \Phi(R_t, Y_t),$$

where M_t is nominal money balances demanded, P_t is the price index used to convert nominal balances to real balances, Y_t is the *scale* variable relating to activity in the real sector of the economy, and R_t is the *opportunity cost* of holding money.

In what follows, we discuss the choice of variables as suggested by the different theories of the demand for money. For other similar, and perhaps more detailed discussions, see Edgar Feige and Douglas Pearce (1977), Judd and Scadding (1982), Laidler (1993), and Goldfeld and Sichel (1990).

8.1.1   Definition of Money

The first problem in the empirical estimation of money demand functions is the selection of an explicit measure of money. In general, transactions-based theories of the demand for money emphasize narrow definitions of money that include currency and checkable deposits. Once one moves away, however, from a transactions approach, there are problems in determining which monetary assets belong to which monetary aggregate — see, for example, Goldfeld and Sichel (1990) for a discussion of the relevant issues as they pertain to the United States.

In addition to problems of determining the monetary assets over which to aggregate, the monetary aggregates currently in use by most central banks around the world have been criticized for being based on the simple-sum method of aggregation. The essential property of this method of monetary aggregation is its assigning all monetary components a constant and equal (unitary weight). This index is M_t in

$$M_t = \sum_{i=1}^{n} x_{it}, \tag{8.1}$$

where x_{it} is one of the n monetary components of the monetary aggregate M_t. This summation index implies that all monetary components contribute equally to the money total and it views all components as dollar for dollar perfect substitutes. Such an index, there is no question, represents an index of the stock of nominal monetary wealth, but cannot, in general, represent a valid structural economic variable for the services of the quantity of money.

Over the years, there has been a steady stream of attempts at properly weighting monetary components within a simple-sum aggregate. With no theory, however, any weighting scheme is questionable. As we will see in later chapters, it was Barnett (1980) who derived the theoretical linkage between monetary theory and aggregation and index number theory. He applied economic aggregation and index number theory and constructed monetary aggregates based upon Erwin Diewert's (1976) class of superlative quantity index numbers, to be discussed in more detail later in this book. The new aggregates are Divisia quantity indexes which are elements of the superlative class. The Divisia index (in discrete time) is defined as

$$\log M_t^D - \log M_{t-1}^D = \sum_{i=1}^{n} \overline{w}_{it}(\log x_{it} - \log x_{i,t-1}). \tag{8.2}$$

According to equation (8.2) the growth rate of the aggregate is the weighted average of the growth rates of the component quantities, with the Divisia weights being defined as the expenditure shares averaged over the two periods of the change, $\overline{w}_{it} = (1/2)(w_{it} + w_{i,t-1})$ for $i = 1, ..., n$, where $w_{it} = p_{it}x_{it}/\sum_{k=1}^{n} p_{kt}x_{kt}$ is the expenditure share of asset i during period t, and p_{it} is the *user cost* of asset i, derived in Barnett (1978),

$$p_{it} = \frac{(R_t - r_{it})}{(1 + R_t)}, \tag{8.3}$$

which is just the opportunity cost of holding a dollar's worth of the ith asset. In equation (8.3), r_{it} is the market yield on the ith asset, and R_t is the yield available on a *benchmark* asset that is held only to carry wealth between multiperiods.

More recently, Rotemberg(1991) and Rotemberg, Driscoll, and Poterba (1995) proposed the currency equivalent (CE) index

$$CE_t = \sum_{i=1}^{n} \frac{R_t - r_{it}}{R_t} x_{it}. \qquad (8.4)$$

In (8.4), as long as currency yields no interest, units of currency are added together with a weight of one. Other assets are added to currency but with a weight that declines toward zero as their return increases toward R_t.

Clearly, the problem of the definition of money is an aggregation problem. We will not get into the specific aggregation issues in this discussion, but will reserve the topic for Part 5 of the book. There we will consider some important theoretical issues and approach the topic by means of a system of demand equations for the various monetary assets, estimating the degree of substitution between monetary assets and testing for weakly separable asset groupings.

8.1.2   Scale Variables

The scale variable in the money demand function is used as a measure of transactions relating to economic activity. As we saw in earlier chapters, transactions theories of money demand emphasize the level of income as the relevant scale variable whereas asset theories place more emphasis on wealth. Wealth, however, is difficult to measure. In fact, only in a handful of countries like the United Kingdom and the United States it is possible to construct long time series on financial wealth. Moreover, these measures are less inclusive than a general measure of wealth that includes the value of human as well as nonhuman capital, as suggested by Friedman's (1956) modern quantity theory discussed in Chapter 5.

To measure this more inclusive concept of wealth, as Laidler (1993, p. 99-100) put it

> " ... presents formidable difficulties of its own, and virtually all attempts to come to grips with them have started from the simple idea that wealth is the discounted present value of expected future income. So long as the rate of discount used can be regarded as constant, wealth varies in exactly the same fashion as expected income. If expected income rises by 10%, so will wealth; if it falls, so will wealth, and so on. One is interested in studying the relationship between *variations* in the level of wealth and *variations* in the demand for money and, because this is the case, it is not important whether wealth is measured directly or whether *expected*

income, or, as it is often called, *permanent income*, is used as a proxy for this variable."

One way to measure expected income is to use the expectational model that Philip Cagan (1956) developed as part of his study of hyperinflations. This model became known as the model of *adaptive expectations*. In terms of our notation, the adaptive expectations model for the unobserved expected level of income at time t, Y_t^e, can be expressed as

$$Y_t^e - Y_{t-1}^e = \theta \left(Y_t - Y_{t-1}^e \right),$$

where $0 \leq \theta \leq 1$. The adaptive expectations model states that the change in the expected level of income form period $t-1$ to period t, $Y_t^e - Y_{t-1}^e$, is proportional to the forecast error — the discrepancy between the current actual and last period's anticipated level of income, $Y_t - Y_{t-1}^e$ — with the factor of proportionality being θ. Clearly, the adaptive expectations model expresses the ability of economic agents to learn from their past mistakes, and this is why it is also known as the *error learning* hypothesis. In particular, if expectations are realized, then there will be no revision in expectations. If, however, income turns out to be surprisingly high, then there will be an upward revision in expectations, and if it turns out to be surprisingly low, then there will be a downward revision in expectations.

A simple rearrangement of the adaptive expectations model yields

$$Y_t^e = \theta Y_t + (1 - \theta) Y_{t-1}^e$$

This formulation states that the expected level of income at time t is a weighted average of the current actual level of income and last period's expected value of income, with the weights being the adjustment parameters θ and $1 - \theta$. Finally, through continuous back-substitution, the second presentation of the adaptive expectations model yields

$$Y_t^e = \theta Y_t + \theta (1 - \theta) Y_{t-1} + \theta (1 - \theta)^2 Y_{t-2} + \cdots$$

$$= \theta \sum_{i=1}^{\infty} (1 - \theta)^{i-1} Y_{t-i+1},$$

according to which the unobserved expected level of income at time t is a weighted average of the current actual level of income and already known income levels of the past, Y_{t-1}, Y_{t-2}, and so on. The weighting scheme, θ, $\theta (1 - \theta)$, $\theta (1 - \theta)^2$, and so on, represents a memory expressing the influence of past income levels on the formation of expectations.

If, for example, θ is close to zero, then the weights decline slowly and the economic agent is said to have a 'long memory,' in the sense that information from the distant past significantly influences the formation of expectations. If θ is close to one, then the weights decline quickly and the agent is said to have a 'short memory,' in the sense that only information from the recent past influences the formation of expectations.

The adaptive expectations model, however, has been faulted on the grounds that it doesn't assume enough rationality on the part of economic agents. In particular, according to the third presentation of the adaptive expectations hypothesis, economic agents use only current and past values of the variable in question when formulating expectations for the future. An alternative hypothesis for economic analysis of expectational behavior is John Muth's (1961) *rational expectations* hypothesis. According to the rational expectations notion, economic agents use all of the available and economically usable information, including relevant economic theory, in the formation of expectations for the future.

As it happens, the concept of rational expectations has been embraced by the economics profession and the theory has been enhanced by important contributions by Lucas (1972, 1973), Sargent and Wallace (1975), and Barro (1976). Of course, in order to implement the notion of rational expectations empirically, it is necessary to quantify the concepts of 'available information' and 'relevant economic theory.' Such quantification, although potentially fruitful, is very difficult, since it also requires an explicit treatment of a large number of other issues, such as, for example, structural shifts in the income growth process.[1]

As an empirical matter, the level of current income is most often used to represent the scale variable in the money demand function. As Laidler (1993, p. 98-99) put it

> "[t]he measurement of this variable presents little problem because, although gross national product series, net national product series and gross domestic product series have been used to measure it, these variables move rather closely together over time and no important difference in results is obtained by using one or the other."

The level of income, however, is less inclusive than a more comprehensive measure of transactions. For example, gross national product (GNP) excludes transactions in financial assets, sales of intermediate goods, transfers, and purchases of existing goods, all of which are likely

---

[1] For empirical work along these lines, see Barro (1977, 1978).

to affect the demand for money. For this reason, in recent years research has focused on the construction of scale variables based on more general measures of transactions. It is too early, however, to tell if these new data will yield significant improvements in the explanation of aggregate money demand.

Recent research has also focused on the disaggregation of GNP into several scale variables, reflecting the notion that not all transactions are equally money intensive. For example, Gregory Mankiw and Lawrence Summers (1986) argue that consumption is a more empirically successful scale variable in estimated money demand functions than GNP. It has also been argued that the disaggregation of GNP into components that reflect the nature of international transactions is likely to be important for open economies. However, there is no firm evidence that disaggregation of GNP improves the performance of money demand functions.

8.1.3 Opportunity Costs

For a given definition of money, the opportunity cost of holding money is the difference between the rate of return on assets alternative to money and the own rate on money. Regarding the rate of return on alternative assets, those researchers that adopt a transactions approach and use a narrow definition of money typically use one or more short-term interest rates, such as the Treasury bill rate, the commercial paper rate, or the saving deposit rate. On the other hand, those that adopt an asset approach and use broader definitions of money typically use longer-term rates of interest.

As to the own rate on money, most researchers treat it as zero, implicitly assuming that the explicit rate of return on most forms of money (i.e., currency, demand deposits, etc.) is zero. This is not correct, however, because even when the explicit return is zero, money earns an *implicit rate* of return, in the form of gifts, services, or reduced transactions fees, when deposit holders maintain a minimum level of deposits. The measurement, however, of this implicit rate of return is a difficult matter and it is perhaps for this reason that this issue has generally been ignored — see Benjamin Klein (1974) and Richard Startz (1979) for exceptions.

Of course, there are other variables that may play a role in the money demand function. For a discussion with further references see Goldfeld and Sichel (1990), Laidler (1993), Subramanian Sriram (1999).

8.2   The Long-Run Function

In general, the starting point in the empirical estimation of money demand functions is the long-run, log linear function of the form

$$\log\left(\frac{M_t^*}{P_t}\right) = \alpha + \beta_1 \log Y_t + \beta_2 R_t + \varepsilon_t, \qquad (8.5)$$

where M^* denotes the *desired* stock of nominal money, P is the price index used to convert nominal balances to real balances, Y is the scale variable, and R is the opportunity cost variable.

As an example of estimated long-run money demand functions, in Table 8.1 we report estimation results based on quarterly observations for the United States over the 1960:1 to 1999:4 period. In doing so, we use real GNP as the scale variable, the 90-day T-bill rate as the opportunity cost variable, and make comparisons between simple-sum, Divisia, and currency equivalent monetary aggregates (of M1, M2, M3, and MZM). The monetary aggregates were obtained from the St. Louis MSI database, maintained by the Federal Reserve Bank of St. Louis as a part of the Bank's Federal Reserve Economic Database (FRED). The three different monetary aggregation procedures will be discussed in detail in Chapters 12-14.

The numbers in parentheses, under the ordinary least squares (OLS) coefficients are t-statistics. Other notation is: R^2 is the unadjusted squared multiple correlation coefficient and DW is the conventional Durbin-Watson statistic. Q is the Ljung-Box (1978) Q-statistic for testing residual serial correlation, asymptotically distributed as a $\chi^2(36)$ on the null of no autocorrelation; RESET is (an F-version of) Ramsey's (1969) test of functional form (using the square of the fitted values), and has an asymptotic F distribution on the null of no misspecification; J-B is the Jarque-Bera (1980) test for normality of the regression residuals, distributed as a $\chi^2(2)$ under the null hypothesis of normality; ARCH is Robert Engle's (1982) Autoregressive Conditional Heteroskedasticity (ARCH) test, distributed as a $\chi^2(1)$ on the null of no ARCH; CHOW is (an F-version of) Gregory Chow's (1960) test for parameter constancy over the 1960:1 – 1979:3 and 1979:4 – 1999:4 sample periods, and has an asymptotic F distribution on the null of parameter constancy.

Table 8.1. Long-Run Money Demand Functions

Aggregate	Coefficients			R^2	DW	Q	RESET	J-B	ARCH	CHOW
	Constant	log Y	R							
Sum M1	1.37 (27.5)	.51 (38.5)	−.03 (15.6)	.91	.17	.000	.000	.807	.000	.000
Divisia M1	−1.55 (33.8)	.55 (45.2)	−.03 (15.9)	.93	.17	.000	.000	.988	.000	.000
CE M1	.69 (10.4)	.62 (35.3)	−.04 (14.9)	.89	.19	.000	.000	.067	.000	.000
Sum M2	1.13 (29.2)	.84 (81.3)	.00 (1.5)	.98	.05	.000	.000	.102	.000	.000
Divisia M2	−.17 (3.9)	.49 (47.2)	.01 (3.8)	.93	.04	.000	.000	.204	.000	.000
CE M2	−.57 (5.0)	1.14 (38.1)	−.00 (0.6)	.91	.27	.000	.009	.000	.000	.000
Sum M3	.39 (7.9)	1.06 (81.2)	.01 (5.8)	.98	.07	.000	.000	.677	.000	.000
Divisia M3	−.38 (8.3)	.58 (47.2)	.01 (4.8)	.94	.05	.000	.000	.049	.000	.000
CE M3	−1.03 (8.2)	1.29 (38.7)	−.01 (1.6)	.91	.25	.000	.001	.001	.000	.000
Sum MZM	1.67 (31.5)	.69 (48.9)	−.04 (21.7)	.94	.32	.000	.002	.086	.000	.000
Divisia MZM	−.01 (0.2)	.39 (30.5)	−.03 (19.3)	.87	.26	.000	.024	.039	.000	.000
CE MZM	.26 (2.7)	.90 (34.9)	−.04 (10.8)	.89	.33	.000	.000	.327	.000	.000

NOTES: Sample period, quarterly observations, 1960:1 - 1999:4. The numbers in parentheses (next to the OLS coefficients) are t-values. Q is the Ljung-Box (1978) Q-statistic for testing serial correlation (asymptotically) distributed as a $\chi^2(36)$ on the null of no autocorrelation. The RESET statistic is the outcome of (an F-version of) Ramsey's (1969) test of functional form (using the square of the fitted values), and has an asymptotic F distribution on the null of no misspecification. J-B is the Jarque-Bera's (1980) test statistic distributed as a $\chi^2(2)$ under the null hypothesis of normality. ARCH is Engle's (1982) Autoregressive Conditional Heteroskedasticity (ARCH) χ^2 test statistic, distributed as a $\chi^2(1)$ on the null of no ARCH. The CHOW statistic is the outcome of (an F-version of) Chow's (1960) test for parameter constancy over the 1960:1 - 1979:3 and 1979:4 - 1999:4 sample periods, and has an asymptotic F distribution on the null of parameter constancy.

The estimates seem reasonable by conventional standards. The coefficient on real income is statistically significant, has the correct sign (i.e., $\beta_1 > 0$), and is of reasonable magnitude. The coefficient on the opportunity cost variable is also as the theory implies (i.e., $\beta_2 < 0$), although it is not always statistically significant. The test statistics, however, give indication of model misspecification. In particular the Q-statistic indicates significant residual serial correlation and this is consistent with the DW statistic. The Chow test statistic reveals parameter non-constancy of the regression model and the RESET statistic indicates model misspecification.

8.3   Money Demand Dynamics

Many of the early studies tended to ignore dynamic aspects of the money demand specification. However, the standard practice of using quarterly, instead of annual, observations and hence the need to take account of sluggish adjustment by money holders to fluctuations in the determinants of money demand, prompted a number of researchers to address this issue, most frequently by assuming that agents behave as posited by the *partial adjustment* model. This model posits the existence of a desired level of real money balances M^*/P — reflecting what real money demand would be if there were no adjustment costs — and further assumes that the actual level of money balances adjusts in each period only part of the way toward its desired level.

If the adjustment of actual to desired money holdings is in real terms, the adjustment mechanism is

$$\log\left(\frac{M_t}{P_t}\right) - \log\left(\frac{M_{t-1}}{P_{t-1}}\right) = \lambda\left[\log\left(\frac{M_t^*}{P_t}\right) - \log\left(\frac{M_{t-1}}{P_{t-1}}\right)\right] \qquad (8.6)$$

where M_t/P_t denotes the actual value of real money balances and λ is a measure of the speed of adjustment, with $0 \leq \lambda \leq 1$; $\lambda = 1$ corresponds to full immediate adjustment while smaller values represent slower, more sluggish, adjustment. Implementation of the real partial adjustment model is achieved by assuming that $\log\left(M_t^*/P_t\right)$ is given by an equation of the form (8.5) and by substituting equation (8.5) into equation (8.6) to obtain the short-run demand for money function with real [e.g., Chow (1966) and Goldfeld (1973)] partial adjustment

$$\log\left(\frac{M_t}{P_t}\right) = \lambda\alpha + \lambda\beta_1\log Y_t$$

$$+ \lambda\beta_2\log R_t + (1 - \lambda)\log\left(\frac{M_{t-1}}{P_{t-1}}\right) + \varepsilon_t \qquad (8.7)$$

where ε_t is a random error term.

The real partial adjustment model of equation (8.6), however, is not without its shortcomings. One aspect of this can be seen by rewriting (8.6) as follows

$$\log M_t - \log M_{t-1} = \lambda\left[\log\left(\frac{M_t^*}{P_t}\right) - \log\left(\frac{M_{t-1}}{P_{t-1}}\right)\right] + \Delta\log P_t$$

As this equation shows, since the coefficient of $\Delta\log P_t$ is unity, the real partial adjustment specification presumes an immediate adjustment to changes in the price level. As this assumption is unlikely to hold, more recent research has used the so-called nominal adjustment model given by

$$\log M_t - \log M_{t-1} = \lambda\left[\log M_t^* - \log M_{t-1}\right] \qquad (8.8)$$

Implementation of the nominal adjustment model (8.8) is achieved by assuming again that $\log(M_t^*/P_t)$ is given by an equation of the form (8.5) and substituting equation (8.5) into equation (8.8) to obtain the short-run demand for money function with nominal [e.g., Goldfeld (1976)] partial adjustment

$$\log\left(\frac{M_t}{P_t}\right) = \lambda\alpha + \lambda\beta_1\log Y_t$$

$$+ \lambda\beta_2\log R_t + (1 - \lambda)\log\left(\frac{M_{t-1}}{P_t}\right) + v_t \qquad (8.9)$$

where v_t is a stochastic disturbance term. A number of empirical tests suggest that the nominal model is to be preferred.

A final attack on the real and nominal partial adjustment models involves a more general reconsideration of the adjustment process. In particular, if we assume that the monetary authorities exogenously fix the nominal money supply, then the desired nominal stock of money must adjust to the given stock, presumably by adjustments in the price

level. A particularly simple version of this idea would replace equation
(8.8) with an adjustment equation in prices as in

$$\log P_t - \log P_{t-1} = \lambda \left[\log P_t^* - \log P_{t-1} \right] \tag{8.10}$$

Implementation of (8.10) is achieved by assuming that $\log(M_t^*/P_t)$ is
given by an equation of the form (8.5) and by substituting equation (8.5)
into equation (8.5) to obtain the short-run demand for money function
with price [e.g., Robert Gordon (1984)] adjustment

$$\log \left(\frac{M_t}{P_t} \right) = \lambda\alpha + \lambda\beta_1 \log Y_t$$

$$+ \lambda\beta_2 \log R_t + (1 - \lambda) \log \left(\frac{M_t}{P_{t-1}} \right) + \zeta_t \tag{8.11}$$

where ζ_t is a stochastic disturbance term.

Equations (8.7), (8.9), and (8.11) differ in the lagged money term.
In equation (8.7), which is the real adjustment specification, the lagged
dependent variable is M_{t-1}/P_{t-1}, whereas in equation (8.9), which is
the nominal adjustment specification, the lagged dependent variable is
M_{t-1}/P_t, and in equation (8.11), which is the price adjustment specification, the lagged dependent variable is M_t/P_{t-1}.

Because specifications (8.7), (8.9), and (8.11) are not nested hypotheses, each should be evaluated for its stability and its consistency with
the theory, the latter meaning that the coefficients should be correctly
signed, statistically significant, and the adjustment coefficient should
obey its restriction. Ordinary least squares estimates of the real, nominal, and price adjustment equations appear in Table 8.2. Durbin's h-
statistic (instead of the DW statistic) is reported with the real ljust-
ment equations.

In general, all the coefficient estimates are correctly signed (although
they are not always statistically significant). Overall, the results suggest that the currency equivalent monetary aggregates perform better
than the corresponding simple-sum and Divisia aggregates and that the
nominal model is to be preferred. However, the evidence also clearly
indicates that this change does not repair the money demand function,
since the test statistics indicate model misspecification with almost all
money measures (irrespective of the method of aggregation) and for all
partial adjustment specifications.

Table 8.2. Estimates of the Three Basic Adjustment Equations for Sum, Divisia, and CE M1 Monetary Aggregates

Aggregate & Type of Adjustment	Coefficients						R^2	DW	Tail Areas of Tests				
	Constant	$\log Y$	R	$\log\left(\frac{M_{t-1}}{P_{t-1}}\right)$	$\log\left(\frac{M_{t-1}}{P_t}\right)$	$\log\left(\frac{M_t}{P_{t-1}}\right)$			Q	RESET	$J\text{-}B$	ARCH	CHOW
Sum M1:													
Real	.09 (4.4)	.04 (5.0)	−.00 (6.0)	.93 (68.5)			.99	.73	.000	.023	.108	.000	.000
Nominal	.12 (6.0)	.04 (5.2)	−.00 (3.4)		.92 (71.4)		.99	.73	.000	.000	.047	.000	.000
Price	−.02 (2.6)	.00 (0.4)	−.00 (6.9)			1.01 (162.4)	.99	.44	.000	.013	.000	.000	.000
Divisia M1:													
Real	−.10 (4.6)	.04 (5.0)	−.00 (5.9)	.93 (70.0)			.99	.75	.000	.015	.199	.000	.000
Nominal	−.10 (4.9)	.04 (5.6)	−.00 (3.2)		.92 (73.5)		.99	.75	.000	.000	.072	.000	.000
Price	−.00 (0.3)	−.00 (0.1)	−.00 (6.6)			1.01 (148.6)	.99	.44	.000	.007	.000	.000	.000
CE M1:													
Real	.05 (2.2)	.06 (4.1)	−.00 (4.5)	.92 (44.1)			.99	1.52	.008	.209	.001	.305	.004
Nominal	.06 (2.8)	.05 (3.7)	−.00 (2.8)		.92 (43.9)		.99	1.51	.001	.711	.000	.162	.013
Price	−.01 (2.4)	.01 (2.6)	−.00 (8.8)			.99 (214.8)	.99	.45	.000	.000	.000	.000	.000

Table 8.2 (continued). Estimates of the Three Basic Adjustment Equations for Sum, Divisia, and CE M2 Monetary Aggregates

Aggregate & Type of Adjustment	Constant	log Y	R	$\log\left(\frac{M_{t-1}}{P_{t-1}}\right)$	$\log\left(\frac{M_{t-1}}{P_t}\right)$	$\log\left(\frac{M_t}{P_{t-1}}\right)$	R^2	DW	Q	RESET	J-B	ARCH	CHOW
Sum M2:													
Real	.04 (2.3)	.00 (0.3)	−.00 (3.8)	.99 (62.9)			.99	.67	.000	.491	.000	.020	.000
Nominal	.03 (1.9)	−.02 (1.7)	.00 (2.3)		1.01 (69.6)		.99	.69	.000	.000	.000	.056	.000
Price	.01 (1.5)	.03 (4.1)	−.00 (11.3)			.97 (128.3)	.99	.45	.000	.000	.000	.000	.000
Divisia M2:													
Real	.02 (3.4)	.00 (0.1)	−.00 (5.2)	.99 (78.6)			.99	.56	.000	.195	.148	.000	.000
Nominal	.05 (7.7)	−.03 (5.1)	.00 (0.2)		1.05 (86.1)		.99	.52	.000	.002	.980	.000	.000
Price	−.02 (7.3)	.03 (10.5)	−.00 (10.6)			.95 (173.4)	.99	.62	.000	.003	.000	.000	.000
CE M2:													
Real	−.08 (1.3)	.16 (3.4)	−.00 (0.6)	.86 (22.1)			.98	1.77	.651	.204	.000	.017	.046
Nominal	−.06 (1.0)	.15 (3.2)	.00 (0.1)		.87 (21.8)		.98	1.76	.700	.107	.000	.014	.034
Price	−.02 (5.6)	.02 (5.2)	−.00 (12.5)			.99 (384.0)	.99	.47	.000	.000	.000	.000	.000

Table 8.2 (continued). Estimates of the Three Basic Adjustment Equations for Sum, Divisia, and CE M3 Monetary Aggregates

Aggregate & Type of		Coefficients								Tail Areas of Tests					
Adjustment	Constant	$\log Y$	R	$\log\left(\frac{M_{t-1}}{P_{t-1}}\right)$	$\log\left(\frac{M_{t-1}}{P_t}\right)$	$\log\left(\frac{M_t}{P_{t-1}}\right)$	R^2	DW	Q	RESET	$J\text{-}B$	ARCH	CHOW		
Sum M3:															
Real	.04 (4.0)	.00 (0.3)	−.00 (1.9)	.99 (77.3)			.99	.45	.000	.456	.014	.000	.000		
Nominal	.05 (6.0)	−.01 (0.5)	.00 (3.4)		1.00 (82.9)		.99	.41	.000	.003	.276	.000	.000		
Price	−.01 (2.8)	.01 (2.0)	−.00 (9.9)			.99 (159.1)	.99	.43	.000	.000	.000	.000	.000		
Divisia M3:															
Real	.02 (2.5)	.00 (0.1)	−.00 (4.6)	.99 (76.7)			.99	.44	.000	.939	.050	.000	.000		
Nominal	.06 (6.9)	−.03 (4.2)	−.00 (0.2)		1.04 (83.9)		.99	.41	.000	.026	.378	.000	.000		
Price	−.03 (8.4)	.03 (9.2)	−.00 (9.5)			.96 (176.2)	.99	.56	.000	.000	.002	.000	.000		
CE M3:															
Real	−.13 (1.7)	.17 (3.2)	−.00 (0.9)	.87 (22.8)			.98	1.70	.427	.162	.000	.056	.004		
Nominal	−.11 (1.5)	.16 (3.0)	−.00 (0.2)		.88 (22.6)		.98	1.69	.446	.084	.000	.048	.004		
Price	−.02 (5.5)	.01 (4.5)	−.00 (12.5)			.99 (421.8)	.99	.45	.000	.000	.000	.000	.000		

levels) except with the price adjustment specification when Sum M1 and Divisia M1 are used. Furthermore, the first-difference specifications appear to have eliminated some of the autocorrelation problems in comparison with the log-levels specifications, suggesting that the econometric estimates obtained with differenced data might be more reliable. However, the first-difference specifications are not consistent with the theory, since the coefficients are not always "correctly" signed neither are they always statistically significant.

Regarding the levels versus first-difference formulations, many researchers, under the assumption that the (log) levels of the variables are nonstationary, carried out the empirical analysis in terms of first differences of the variables. This practice, however, of first differencing to induce stationarity has recently been questioned by Engle and Clive Granger in their 1987 article "Co-Integration and Error Correction: Representation, Estimation and Testing". They argue that the traditional approach of first differencing to induce stationarity disregards potentially important equilibrium relationships among the levels of the series to which the hypotheses of economic theory are usually taken to apply.

Hence, a strategy that is consistent with recent developments in the theory of nonstationary regressors should be applied to analyze the money demand variables.

8.5   Conclusion

We have looked at the factors that have shaped the evolution of the research on the demand for money function and discussed some specific results on the demand for money in the United States. We have determined that, irrespective of how money is measured, conventional money demand functions are seriously misspecified and that recent developments in the theory of nonstationary regressors should be used to analyze aggregate money demand. These developments are the subject matter of the next two chapters.

Table 8.3. Estimates of the Three Basic Adjustment Equations With First-Differenced Data for Sum, Divisia, and CE M1 Monetary Aggregates

Aggregate & Type of Adjustment	Coefficients								Tail Areas of Tests				
	Constant	$\Delta \log Y$	ΔR	$\Delta \log\left(\frac{M_{t-1}}{P_{t-1}}\right)$	$\Delta \log\left(\frac{M_{t-1}}{P_t}\right)$	$\Delta \log\left(\frac{M_t}{P_{t-1}}\right)$	R^2	DW	Q	RESET	J-B	ARCH	CHOW
Sum M1:													
Real	.00 (0.0)	.14 (1.6)	−.00 (2.9)	.67 (11.0)			.47	2.36	.003	.001	.000	.000	.661
Nominal	.00 (0.1)	.12 (1.5)	−.00 (2.6)		.69 (11.7)		.50	2.40	.000	.007	.000	.000	.894
Price	.00 (0.2)	.02 (0.8)	−.00 (2.0)			.96 (48.6)	.94	2.54	.000	.840	.211	.002	.001
Divisia M1:													
Real	.00 (0.2)	.14 (1.9)	−.00 (2.6)	.65 (10.7)			.46	2.35	.011	.063	.000	.000	.607
Nominal	.00 (0.2)	.13 (1.6)	−.00 (2.3)		.69 (11.7)		.50	2.40	.000	.157	.000	.000	.901
Price	.00 (0.0)	.02 (0.9)	−.00 (2.0)			.95 (42.9)	.93	2.54	.000	.761	.220	.003	.000
CE M1:													
Real	.00 (1.1)	.08 (0.4)	−.00 (1.2)	.27 (0.1)			.09	2.00	.241	.060	.011	.121	.072
Nominal	.00 (1.1)	.08 (0.4)	−.00 (1.1)		.26 (3.4)		.08	1.99	.224	.048	.008	.132	.053
Price	.00 (0.0)	.01 (0.5)	−.00 (2.1)			.97 (98.5)	.98	2.59	.000	.537	.215	.002	.084

Table 8.3 (continued). Estimates of the Three Basic Adjustment Equations With First-Differenced Data for Sum, Divisia, and CE MZM Monetary Aggregates

Aggregate & Type of Adjustment	Coefficients						Tail Areas of Tests						
	Constant	$\Delta \log Y$	ΔR	$\Delta \log \left(\dfrac{M_{t-1}}{P_{t-1}} \right)$	$\Delta \log \left(\dfrac{M_{t-1}}{P_t} \right)$	$\Delta \log \left(\dfrac{M_t}{P_{t-1}} \right)$	R^2	DW	Q	RESET	J-B	ARCH	CHOW
Sum MZM:													
Real	.00 (1.0)	.12 (0.7)	–.01 (3.6)	.55 (7.9)			.35	2.19	.216	.044	.000	.164	.365
Nominal	.00 (1.0)	.09 (0.5)	–.01 (3.5)		.58 (8.4)		.37	2.23	.269	.018	.000	.113	.312
Price	–.00 (0.2)	.01 (0.4)	–.00 (1.8)			1.00 (85.7)	.98	2.57	.000	.213	.112	.001	.129
Divisia MZM:													
Real	.00 (0.6)	.09 (0.7)	–.01 (4.0)	.63 (9.6)			.44	2.26	.030	.365	.000	.004	.636
Nominal	.00 (0.7)	.05 (0.4)	–.01 (3.9)		.67 (10.3)		.47	2.30	.065	.212	.000	.002	.551
Price	–.00 (0.3)	.02 (0.5)	–.00 (1.9)			.99 (72.2)	.97	2.57	.000	.261	.124	.001	.110
CE MZM:													
Real	.01 (0.8)	.27 (0.5)	–.00 (0.4)	.01 (0.2)			.00	1.98	.780	.920	.000	.000	.164
Nominal	.01 (0.8)	.27 (0.5)	–.00 (0.4)		.01 (0.1)		.00	1.97	.778	.797	.000	.000	.164
Price	–.00 (0.2)	.01 (0.4)	–.00 (1.8)			.99 (252.2)	.99	2.62	.000	.737	.094	.001	.201

NOTES: Sample period, quarterly observations, 1960:1 - 1999:4. The numbers in parentheses (next to the OLS coefficients) are t-values. Q is the Ljung-Box (1978) Q-statistic for testing serial correlation (asymptotically) distributed as a $\chi^2(36)$ on the null of no autocorrelation. The RESET statistic is the outcome of (an F-version of) Ramsey's (1969) test of functional form (using the square of the fitted values), and has an asymptotic F distribution on the null of no misspecification. J-B is the Jarque-Bera's (1980) test statistic distributed as a $\chi^2(2)$ under the null hypothesis of normality. ARCH is Engle's (1982) Autoregressive Conditional Heteroskedasticity (ARCH) χ^2 test statistic, distributed as a $\chi^2(1)$ on the null of no ARCH. The CHOW statistic is the outcome of (an F-version of) Chow's (1960) test for parameter constancy over the 1960:1 - 1979:3 and 1979:4 - 1999:4 sample periods, and has an asymptotic F distribution on the null of parameter constancy.

Chapter 9

Modeling Trends in the Variables of the Money Demand Function

As discussed in the previous chapter the issue of whether economic time series are nonstationary or not is important for both estimation and hypothesis testing, both of which rely on asymptotic distribution theory. Moreover, the nature of nonstationarity has important implications for the appropriate transformation to attain a stationary series as well as for the estimation of long-run relationships between nonstationary variables.

In this chapter we explore recent exciting developments in the field of applied econometrics to distinguish between two different types of nonstationary time series — those with a deterministic trend and those with a stochastic trend. We also use tools from dynamical systems theory to distinguish between stochastic and deterministic behavior in the money demand variables. As we shall see, such a distinction is an important part of the analysis of data on the demand for money.

9.1   Deterministic and Stochastic Trends

The money demand variables (and most economic and financial time series in general) are nonstationary and the basic statistical issue is the appropriate representation of the nature of nonstationarity. Nonstationary time series are frequently assumed to be *trend-stationary* (TS) and are detrended in empirical investigations by regressing the series on time or a function of time. However, Charles Nelson and Charles Plosser (1982) show that most economic time series are better characterized as *difference-stationary* (DS) processes rather than TS processes. As a result, differencing rather than detrending is preferable to achieve stationarity.

The issue of whether economic time series are TS or DS has also important implications for the nature and existence of business cycles. For example, according to Nelson and Plosser (1982), trend stationarity in aggregate output would be evidence for traditional (monetary or Keynesian) business cycle models — according to which output fluctuations from a variety of macroeconomic disturbances are temporary deviations from trend. On the other hand, difference stationarity in output would be providing support for the *real business cycle* (RBC) theory of economic fluctuations — according to which most disturbances to output are permanent.

To distinguish between TS and DS processes, let us start with the time series model most commonly used to describe trend stationarity

$$y_t = \mu t + \sum_{j=0}^{\infty} a_j \epsilon_{t-j}, \tag{9.1}$$

where μt describes the trend and ϵ_t is a random disturbance. If a_j approaches zero as $j \to \infty$, $\sum_{j=0}^{\infty} a_j \epsilon_{t-j}$ is a stationary stochastic process. In this case, fluctuations in y_t are temporary and y_t is called trend stationary. As a result, a one-unit shock to y, say in period 1 (i.e., $\epsilon_1 = 1$) with no further shocks (i.e., $\epsilon_t = 0$, for $t > 1$), increases the growth rate of y above its historical average for a few periods, but does not change the long-range forecast of the level of y.

The simplest time series model most commonly used to describe difference stationarity is the 'random walk with drift' which is a first-order autoregressive process with unit coefficient (also known as a *unit root* process)

$$y_t = \mu + y_{t-1} + \epsilon_t, \tag{9.2}$$

where ϵ_t is white noise with zero mean and variance σ_ϵ, and where μ is the (fixed) mean of the first differences, often called the 'drift.' When $\mu = 0$, equation (9.2) reduces to a 'pure random walk' (i.e., random walk with no drift), $y_t = y_{t-1} + \epsilon_t$.

The conditional mean of y_t is

$$E(y_t | y_0) = y_0 + \mu t,$$

which increases or decreases without limit as t increases. It is for this reason that a random walk with drift model is also known as a model of *stochastic trend*, because the trend is driven by stochastic shocks. Also, the 'conditional variance' of y_t is

$$
\begin{aligned}
\text{var}\,(y_t\,|y_0) &= E\,[y_t - E\,(y_t\,|y_0)]^2 \\
&= E\,[\epsilon_t + \epsilon_{t-1} + ... + \epsilon_1]^2 \\
&= t\sigma_\epsilon^2,
\end{aligned}
$$

with $\lim_{t \to \infty} t\sigma_\epsilon^2 = \infty$. Hence, the conditional variance of a random walk increases without limit, rather than converging to some finite unconditional variance. In fact, the unconditional mean and variance of a random walk do not exist. Hence, the random walk is also nonstationary.

Fluctuations in a random walk are permanent in the following sense. Accumulating changes in y from some initial value y_0 at time 0, we get from (9.2)

$$
y_t = y_0 + \mu t + \sum_{j=1}^{t} \epsilon_j, \tag{9.3}
$$

which has the same form as equation (9.1), but is fundamentally different from (9.1). In particular, the intercept in (9.3) is not a fixed parameter but rather depends on the initial value y_0. Also, equation (9.3) implies that a one-unit shock to y, say in period 1 (i.e., $\epsilon_1 = 1$) with no further shocks (i.e., $\epsilon_t = 0$, for $t > 1$), will forever increase y by one unit. Hence fluctuations in a random walk are permanent. Nelson and Plosser (1982) refer to processes like (9.2) as DS processes. Such processes are also known as *integrated* with an 'order of integration' of one, denoted $I(1)$, meaning that they need to be differenced once to yield a stationary series.[1]

We have distinguished between two different types of nonstationary time series — those with a deterministic trend and those with a stochastic trend. We have also argued that time series with a deterministic trend can be transformed into stationary series by removing the deterministic trend and those with a stochastic trend by first-differencing. Obviously, subtracting a deterministic trend from a DS process or first-differencing a TS process will result in serious misspecification errors in applied work. Thus, the issue is how to distinguish between time series with and without a unit root.

---

[1] A stationary series is said to be integrated of order zero, $I(0)$.

9.2   Testing for Unit Roots

The literature on unit root testing is vast — see Francis Diebold and Mark Nerlove (1990), John Campbell and Pierre Perron (1991), and James Stock (1994) for selective surveys, and Walter Enders (1995, Chapter 4) for a textbook treatment. In what follows, we shall only briefly illustrate some of the issues that have arisen in the broader search for unit roots in economic and financial time series

9.2.1   Dickey-Fuller (DF) Tests

The point of tests for unit roots is to distinguish between TS and DS processes. In the simplest case one starts with a zero-mean AR(1) process

$$y_t = \phi_1 y_{t-1} + e_t, \tag{9.4}$$

where the shock e_t is white noise. By subtracting y_{t-1} from both sides of (9.4) we obtain

$$\Delta y_t = \alpha_1 y_{t-1} + e_t, \tag{9.5}$$

where $\alpha_1 = (\phi_1 - 1)$. Notice that testing the hypothesis $\phi_1 = 1$ is equivalent to testing the hypothesis $\alpha_1 = 0$. With this in mind, in what follows we shall consider regression equations of the form (9.5).

Hence, we can test for the presence of a unit root by estimating [by ordinary least squares (OLS)] the coefficients in (9.5) and using the standard t-test, labeled $\hat{\tau}$, to test the null $H_0 : \alpha_1 = 0$. When the null is true, equation (9.5) reduces to

$$\Delta y_t = e_t,$$

so that y_t is a pure random walk and thus nonstationary.

In the context of (9.5) we test the null hypothesis of a pure random walk against the alternative hypothesis of a zero-mean, covariance-stationary AR(1) process. However, given that economic time series rarely have zero mean, we should allow for a nonzero mean, α_0, under the alternative hypothesis. In this case, we can estimate the regression equation

$$\Delta y_t = \alpha_0 + \alpha_1 y_{t-1} + e_t, \tag{9.6}$$

and use the standard t-test, now labeled $\hat{\tau}_\mu$ (since a nonzero mean is allowed), to test the null $H_0 : \alpha_1 = 0$. Under the null hypothesis of a unit root, equation (9.6) reduces to

$$\Delta y_t = \alpha_0 + e_t,$$

so that y_t is a random walk with drift and thus nonstationary.

Finally, we can also allow for a deterministic trend under the alternative hypothesis, by estimating the regression equation

$$\Delta y_t = \alpha_0 + \alpha_1 y_{t-1} + \alpha_2 t + e_t, \tag{9.7}$$

and using the standard t-test, in this case labeled $\hat{\tau}_\tau$ (since a linear trend is allowed), we can test the null hypothesis $H_0 : \alpha_1 = 0$.

A key result is that, under the null hypothesis $H_0 : \alpha_1 = 0$, in each of (9.5), (9.6), and (9.7) the y_t sequence is generated by a nonstationary process and the t-statistic for testing $\alpha_1 = 0$, $\hat{\tau}$, $\hat{\tau}_\mu$, and $\hat{\tau}_\tau$, respectively, does not have the usual t-distribution. This problem has been solved by David Dickey and Wayne Fuller (1979, 1981) who devised special distributions, now called the 'Dickey-Fuller distributions' — see Fuller (1976) for the Dickey-Fuller tables.

9.2.2   Augmented Dickey-Fuller (ADF) Tests

The Dickey-Fuller test can also be generalized to allow for higher-order autoregressive dynamics, in case that an AR(1) process is inadequate to render e_t white noise. Consider, for example, the zero-mean AR(p) process

$$y_t = \sum_{j=1}^{p} \alpha_j y_{t-j} + e_t, \tag{9.8}$$

which can be written as[2]

$$\Delta y_t = \alpha y_{t-1} + \sum_{j=1}^{k} c_j \Delta y_{t-j} + e_t, \tag{9.9}$$

---

[2] To obtain (9.9), first subtract y_{t-1} from both sides of (9.8) to obtain

$$\Delta y_t = -(1 - \alpha_1) y_{t-1} + \sum_{j=2}^{p} \alpha_j y_{t-j} + e_t.$$

Then add and subtract $\alpha_p y_{t-p+1}$ to obtain

$$\Delta y_t = -(1 - \alpha_1) y_{t-1} + \alpha_2 y_{t-2} + \dots + (\alpha_{p-1} + \alpha_p) y_{t-p+1} - \alpha_p \Delta y_{t-p+1} + e_t.$$

Next, add and subtract $(\alpha_{p-1} + \alpha_p) y_{t-p+2}$. Continuing in this fashion, we obtain (9.9), with α and c_j ($j = 1, ..., p-1$) defined as in (9.10).

In general, existing empirical evidence indicates that the unit root hypothesis could be rejected if allowance is made for the possibility of a one-time break in the intercept or in the slope (or both) of the trend function, irrespective of whether the break point is estimated or fixed. Hence, whether the unit root model is rejected or not depends on how big shocks are treated. If big shocks are treated like any other shock, then ADF unit root testing procedures are appropriate and the unit root null hypothesis cannot (in general) be rejected. If, however, they are treated differently, then Perron-type procedures are appropriate and the null hypothesis of a unit root will most likely be rejected.

9.3   Testing for Stationarity

It is important to note that in the tests that we have discussed so far the unit root is the null hypothesis to be tested and that the way in which classical hypothesis testing is carried out ensures that the null hypothesis is accepted unless there is strong evidence against it. In fact, Denis Kwiatkowski, Peter Phillips, Peter Schmidt, and Yoncheol Shin (1992) argue that such unit root tests fail to reject a unit root because they have low power against relevant alternatives (meaning that they do nor reject the hypothesis $\alpha = 1$, but they do not reject the hypothesis $\alpha = 0.95$ either).

Kwiatkowski *et al.* (1992) propose tests (known as the KPSS tests) of the null hypothesis of stationarity against the alternative of a unit root. They argue that such tests should complement unit root tests and that by testing both the unit root hypothesis and the stationarity hypothesis, one can distinguish series that appear to be stationary, series that appear to be integrated, and series that are not very informative about whether or not they are stationary or have a unit root.

In particular, the null hypothesis of *level stationarity* in y_t is tested by calculating the test statistic

$$\widehat{\eta}_\mu = \frac{1}{T^2} \sum_{t=1}^{T} \frac{S_t^2}{\widehat{\sigma}_k^2},$$

where $S_t = \sum_{i=1}^{t} e_i$, $t = 1, 2, ..., T$, e_t is the residuals from the regression of y_t on an intercept, and $\widehat{\sigma}_k$ is a consistent estimate of the long-run variance of y_t calculated, using the Whitney Newey and Kenneth West (1987) method, as

$$\widehat{\sigma}_k = \frac{1}{T} \sum_{t=1}^{T} e_t^2 + \frac{2}{T} \sum_{s=1}^{T} b(s,k) \sum_{t=s+1}^{T} e_t e_{t-s},$$

where T is the number of observations, $b(s,k) = 1 + s/(1+k)$ is a weighing function and k is the lag truncation parameter.

The null hypothesis of *trend stationarity* in y_t can also be tested by defining e_t as the residuals from the regression of y_t on an intercept and time trend (instead of as above) and calculating the $\widehat{\eta}_\tau$ test statistic as above.

9.4   Testing for Nonlinearity and Chaos

Most of the empirical tests that we discussed so far are designed to detect *linear* structure in the data. However, as John Campbell, Andrew Lo, and Craig MacKinlay (1997, pp. 467) argue

" ... many aspects of economic behavior may not be linear. Experimental evidence and casual introspection suggest that investors' attitudes towards risk and expected return are nonlinear. The terms of many financial contracts such as options and other derivative securities are nonlinear. And the strategic interactions among market participants, the process by which information is incorporated into security prices, and the dynamics of economy-wide fluctuations are all inherently nonlinear."

It is for such reasons that interest in deterministic nonlinear chaotic processes has in the recent past experienced a tremendous rate of development. Besides its obvious intellectual appeal, chaos is interesting because of its ability to generate output that mimics the output of stochastic systems, thereby offering an alternative explanation for the behavior of economic variables. Clearly then, an important research inquiry is to test for chaos in the money demand variables. In other words, we are interested in whether it is possible for the money demand variables to appear to be random but not to be really random.

Sensitive dependence on initial conditions is the most relevant property of chaos to economics and finance and its characterization in terms of Lyapunov exponents is the most satisfactory from a computable (i.e. possible to estimate) perspective. Lyapunov exponents measure average exponential divergence or convergence between trajectories that differ only in having an 'infinitesimally small' difference in their initial conditions and remain well-defined for noisy systems. A bounded system with

model. In particular, one can prefilter the stationary series by the following autoregression

$$z_t = b_0 + \sum_{j=1}^{q} b_j z_{t-j} + \varepsilon_t, \quad \varepsilon_t | I_{t-1} \sim N(0, w_0),$$

using for each series the number of lags, q, for which the Ljung-Box (1978) $Q(36)$ statistic, for example, is not significant at the 5% level.

Finally, since the interest is in deterministic nonlinear dependence, one should remove any stochastic nonlinear dependence by fitting a GARCH model with the same AR structure as the one determined above, using the $Q(36)$ statistic. In particular, one can estimate the following GARCH (1,1) model

$$z_t = b_0 + \sum_{j=1}^{q} b_j z_{t-j} + \varepsilon_t, \quad \varepsilon_t | I_{t-1} \sim N(0, \sigma_t^2),$$

$$\sigma_t^2 = w_0 + \alpha_1 \varepsilon_{t-1}^2 + \beta_1 \sigma_{t-1}^2,$$

where $N(0, \sigma_t^2)$ represents the normal distribution with mean zero and variance σ_t^2. Lyapunov exponent estimates can then be calculated for the standardized GARCH (1,1) residuals, $\hat{\varepsilon}_t / \hat{\sigma}_t$.[7]

In general, it has been proven difficult to produce reliable evidence regarding the existence of chaotic processes in the money demand variables, or in macroeconomic and financial variables in general — see, for example, Barnett and Ping Chen (1988), Serletis (1995), Barnett and Serletis (2000b), Serletis and Andreadis (2000) and Serletis and Mototsugu Shintani (2001). In fact, as Barnett and Serletis (2000b, p. 721) conclude

> "[e]xisting tests cannot tell whether the source of detected chaos comes from within the structure of the economy, or from chaotic external shocks, as from the weather. Thus, we do not have the slightest idea of whether or not asset prices exhibit chaotic nonlinear dynamics produced from the nonlinear structure of the economy (and hence we are not justified in excluding the possibility).

---

[7] See Serletis (1995) or Serletis and Ioannis Andreadis (2000) for more details regarding these issues.

Until the difficult problems of testing for chaos 'within the structure of the economic system' are solved, the best that we can do is to test for chaos in economic time series data, without being able to isolate its source. But even that objective has proven to be difficult. While there have been many published tests for chaotic nonlinear dynamics, little agreement exists among economists about the correct conclusions."

9.5   Conclusion

We have argued that the first step in estimating money demand functions is to test for stochastic trends (unit roots) in the autoregressive representation of each individual time series. Moreover, since the power of unit root tests against alternative hypotheses near the null hypothesis is low, we should use alternative testing procedures (such as, for example, the KPSS level and trend stationarity tests) to deal with anomalies that arise when the data are not very informative about whether or not there is a unit root.

In a univariate time series modeling context, unit root and stationarity tests are useful in regard to the decision of whether to specify models [such as, for example, moving-average (MA) models, autoregressive (AR) models, and autoregressive moving-average (ARMA) models] in levels or first differences. If the series are stationary (i.e., there is no unit root), then it is desirable to work in levels, and if the series are integrated (i.e., there is a unit root), then differencing is appropriate.

At one time, the conventional wisdom was to generalize this idea and difference all integrated variables used in a multivariate context. Recently, however, Engle and Granger (1987) argue that the appropriate way to treat integrated variables is not so straightforward in a regression analysis. It is possible, for example, that the integrated variables cointegrate — in the sense that a linear relationship among the variables is stationary. Differencing such an already stationary relationship entails a misspecification error, which we should avoid. It is to these issues that the next chapter is devoted.

empirical issues in modeling and estimating aggregate money demand functions.

10.1   Cointegration and Common Trends

Cointegration is a relatively new statistical concept, introduced into the economics literature by Engle and Granger (1987). It is designed to deal explicitly with the analysis of the relationship between integrated series. In particular, it allows individual time series to be integrated, but requires a linear combination of the series to be stationary. Therefore, the basic idea behind cointegration is to search for a linear combination of individually integrated time series that is itself stationary.

Consider the null hypothesis that there is no cointegration between two integrated series, y_t and x_t, or equivalently, there are no shared stochastic trends (i.e., there are two distinct stochastic trends) between these series, in the terminology of Stock and Mark Watson (1988). The alternative hypothesis is that there is cointegration (or equivalently, y_t and x_t share a stochastic trend). Following Engle and Granger (1987), one can estimate the so-called *cointegrating regression* (selecting arbitrarily a normalization)

$$y_t = a + bx_t + \varepsilon_t. \tag{10.1}$$

A test of the null hypothesis of no cointegration (against the alternative of cointegration) is based on testing for a unit root in the ordinary least squares (OLS) regression residuals $\widehat{\varepsilon}_t$.

10.2   Error Correction Models

If a cointegrating relationship is identified, for example $\widehat{\varepsilon}_t$ is integrated of order zero, then according to the Engle and Granger (1987) representation theorem there must exist an error correction representation relating current and lagged first differences of y_t and x_t, and at least one lagged value of $\widehat{\varepsilon}_t$. In particular, in the present context the error correction model can be written as

$$\Delta y_t = \alpha_1 + \alpha_y \widehat{\varepsilon}_{t-1} + \sum_{j=1}^{r} \alpha_{11}(j)\Delta y_{t-j} + \sum_{j=1}^{s} \alpha_{12}(j)\Delta x_{t-j} + \varepsilon_{yt}, \tag{10.2}$$

$$\Delta x_t = \alpha_2 + \alpha_x \widehat{\varepsilon}_{t-1} + \sum_{j=1}^{r} \alpha_{21}(j)\Delta y_{t-j} + \sum_{j=1}^{s} \alpha_{22}(j)\Delta x_{t-j} + \varepsilon_{xt}, \tag{10.3}$$

where $\alpha_1, \alpha_2, \alpha_y, \alpha_x, \alpha_{11}(j), \alpha_{12}(j), \alpha_{21}(j)$, and $\alpha_{22}(j)$ are all parameters, ε_{yt} and ε_{xt} are white noise disturbances, and $\widehat{\varepsilon}_{t-1}$ estimates the deviation from long-run equilibrium in period $t-1$.

The purpose of the error correction model is to focus on the short-run dynamics while making them consistent with the long-run equilibrium. In particular, the error correction model shows how y_t and x_t change in response to stochastic shocks, represented by ε_{yt} and ε_{xt}, and to the previous period's deviation from long-run equilibrium, represented by $\widehat{\varepsilon}_{t-1}$. If, for example, $\widehat{\varepsilon}_{t-1}$ is positive (so that $y_t - a - bx_t > 0$), x_t would rise and y_t would fall until long-run equilibrium is attained, when $y_t = a + bx_t$.

Notice that α_y and α_x can be interpreted as *speed of adjustment* parameters. For example, the larger is α_y, the greater the response of y_t to the previous period's deviation from long-run equilibrium. On the other hand, very small values of α_y imply that y_t is relatively unresponsive to last period's equilibrium error. In fact, for y_t to be unaffected by x_t, α_y and all the $\alpha_{12}(j)$ coefficients in (10.2) must be equal to zero. This is the empirical definition of Granger causality in cointegrated systems. In other words, the absence of Granger causality for cointegrated variables requires the additional condition that the speed of adjustment coefficient be equal to zero.

In fact, in the context of two integrated variables, y_t and x_t, that cointegrate, the causal relationship between y_t and x_t can be determined by first fitting equation (10.2) by ordinary least squares and obtaining the unrestricted sum of squared residuals, SSR_u. Then by running another regression equation under the null hypothesis that α_y and all the coefficients of the lagged values of Δx_t are zero, the restricted sum of squared residuals, SSR_r, is obtained. The statistic

$$\frac{(SSR_r - SSR_u)/(s+1)}{SSR_u/(T-r-s-2)},$$

has an asymptotic F-distribution with numerator degrees of freedom $(s+1)$ and denominator degrees of freedom $(T-r-s-2)$. T is the number of observations, r represents the number of lags of Δy_t in equation (10.2), s represents the number of lags for Δx_t, and 2 is subtracted in order to account for the constant term and the error correction term in equation (10.2).

If the null hypothesis cannot be rejected, than the conclusion is that the data do not show causality. If the null hypothesis is rejected, then the conclusion is that the data do show causality. The roles of y_t and

(1996). In what follows, we consider two of the most frequently used cointegration testing approaches — the Engle and Granger (1987) approach and the Soren Johansen (1988) approach.

10.4.1   The Engle-Granger Approach

The Engle and Granger (1987) approach is to select arbitrarily a normalization and regress one variable against the others to obtain the ordinary least squares (OLS) regression residuals. In the context of the money demand function, this involves estimating the long-run equilibrium relationship (10.4) to obtain the residual sequence $\widehat{\varepsilon}_t$. A test of the null hypothesis of no cointegration (against the alternative of cointegration) could then be based on testing for a unit root in $\widehat{\varepsilon}_t$ using a Dickey-Fuller test.

In particular, we could estimate the following autoregression of the residuals [without an intercept and trend term, since the $\widehat{\varepsilon}_t$ sequence is a residual from a regression],

$$\Delta\widehat{\varepsilon}_t = \alpha_1\widehat{\varepsilon}_{t-1} + \xi_t, \tag{10.5}$$

and test the null hypothesis that $\alpha_1 = 0$, using critical values that reflect the fact that the $\widehat{\varepsilon}_t$ sequence is generated from a regression equation.[3] If we cannot reject the null hypothesis $\alpha_1 = 0$, we can conclude that the $\widehat{\varepsilon}_t$ sequence contains a unit root, suggesting that the money demand variables are not cointegrated. If, however, we can reject the null hypothesis $\alpha_1 = 0$, we can conclude that the residual series is stationary and that the money demand variables are cointegrated.

If the residual sequence $\widehat{\xi}_t$ of (10.5) does not appear to be white noise, we could perform an augmented Dickey-Fuller test on the sequence $\widehat{\varepsilon}_t$. That is, instead of using (10.5), we could estimate the following autoregression

$$\Delta\widehat{\varepsilon}_t = \alpha_1\widehat{\varepsilon}_{t-1} + \sum_{j=1}^{k} c_j\Delta\widehat{\varepsilon}_{t-j} + \xi_t, \tag{10.6}$$

and test the null hypothesis $\alpha_1 = 0$, using simulated critical values which correctly take into account the number of variables in the cointegrating regression — see Engle and Yoo (1987) for the appropriate tables.

The Engle-Granger procedure has several important defects. One defect is that it is a 'two-stage' estimator. In the first stage we generate

---

[3] The problem here is that we cannot use the ordinary Dickey-Fuller tables. This is so because $\widehat{\varepsilon}_t$ is not the actual error, but an estimate of the error.

the residual sequence $\widehat{\varepsilon}_t$, by estimating the long-run equilibrium relationship (10.4). In the second stage we use the generated sequence $\widehat{\varepsilon}_t$ to test the null hypothesis of a unit root in the context of a regression equation of the form (10.5) or (10.6), depending on whether or not the $\widehat{\xi}_t$ sequence exhibits serial correlation. This is an undesirable feature of the procedure, since any errors introduced in the first stage are carried into the second stage.

Another defect of the Engle-Granger procedure is that (with limited amounts of data typically available in economics) the test for cointegration depends on the arbitrary normalization implicit in the selection of the 'dependent' variable in the regression equation. In the context, for example, of the nonstationary stochastic process $\mathbf{X}_t = [\log(M/P)_t \; \log Y_t \; \log R_t]'$, the long-run equilibrium regression can be estimated using either $\log(M/P)_t$, $\log Y_t$, or $\log R_t$ as the dependent variable. The problem is that it is possible to find that the variables are cointegrated using one variable as the dependent variable, but are not cointegrated using another variable. This possible ambiguity is a weakness of the test.

Moreover, in tests using three or more variables, the Engle-Granger procedure does not distinguish between the existence of one or more cointegrating vectors. As a consequence, the Engle-Granger approach is well suited for the bivariate case which can have at most one cointegrating vector. All these problems can be avoided by using Johansen's (1988) maximum likelihood (ML) extension of the Engle and Granger (1987) cointegration approach. This approach is sufficiently flexible to account for long-run properties as well as short-run dynamics, in the context of multivariate vector autoregressive models.

10.4.2 The Johansen ML Approach

The Johansen procedure is a multivariate generalization of the ADF test. Following Johansen and Katarina Juselius (1992), let us consider the following p-dimensional vector autoregressive (VAR) model of order k

$$\mathbf{X}_t = \sum_{i=1}^{k} \mathbf{A}_i \mathbf{X}_{t-i} + u_t, \tag{10.7}$$

where $\mathbf{X}_t$ is a $p \times 1$ vector and u_t is an independently and identically distributed p-dimensional vector of innovations with zero mean and variance matrix Σ_u. In the case of the stochastic process $\mathbf{X}_t = [\log(M/P)_t \; \log Y_t \; \log R_t]'$ and $p = 3$.

The maximum likelihood estimation and likelihood ratio test of this model has been investigated by Johansen (1988), and can be described as follows. First, letting $\Delta = 1 - L$, where L is the lag operator, Johansen and Juselius (1992) suggest writing equation (10.7) as

$$\Delta \mathbf{X}_t = \sum_{i=1}^{k-1} \Gamma_i \Delta \mathbf{X}_{t-i} + \Pi \mathbf{X}_{t-k} + u_t, \tag{10.8}$$

where

$$\Gamma_i = -\left(\mathbf{I} - \sum_{j=1}^{i} \mathbf{A}_j\right) \quad \text{and} \quad \Pi = -\left(\mathbf{I} - \sum_{i=1}^{k} \mathbf{A}_i\right), \tag{10.9}$$

with the $p \times p$ 'total impact' matrix Π containing information about the long-run relationships between the variables in $\mathbf{X}_t$.[4]

In the context of (10.8), the number of distinct cointegrating vectors that exist between the p elements of $\mathbf{X}_t$ will be given by the rank of Π, denoted as r. The rank of a (square) matrix is the number of linearly independent rows (columns) in the matrix and is given by the number of its 'eigenvalues' that are significantly different from zero.

To recall some linear algebra, note that for an $n \times n$ square matrix $\mathbf{A}$, a real number λ is an eigenvalue (or 'characteristic root') of $\mathbf{A}$ if the system of linear equations

$$\mathbf{A}\mathbf{z} = \lambda \mathbf{z},$$

(where $\mathbf{z}$ is an $n \times 1$ vector) has nonzero solutions $\mathbf{z}$ (called 'eigenvectors' or 'characteristic vectors'). The condition $\mathbf{A}\mathbf{z} = \lambda \mathbf{z}$ can be written as

$$(\mathbf{A} - \lambda \mathbf{I})\mathbf{z} = 0,$$

where $\mathbf{I}$ is the $n \times n$ identity matrix. Hence, λ is an eigenvalue of $\mathbf{A}$ if and only if $\mathbf{A} - \lambda \mathbf{I}$ is not invertible, which in turn means that the determinant $|\mathbf{A} - \lambda \mathbf{I}| = 0$. Thus, we can find the eigenvalues of $\mathbf{A}$ by finding the values of λ that satisfy the 'characteristic equation'

$$|\mathbf{A} - \lambda \mathbf{I}| = 0.$$

---

[4] Equation (10.8) can be obtained as follows. Subtract $\mathbf{X}_{t-1}$ from both sides of (10.7) to get

$$\Delta \mathbf{X}_t = (\mathbf{A}_1 - \mathbf{I})\mathbf{X}_{t-1} + \sum_{i=2}^{k} \mathbf{A}_i \mathbf{X}_{t-i} + u_t.$$

Now, add and subtract $(\mathbf{A}_1 - \mathbf{I})\mathbf{X}_{t-2}$ to obtain

$$\Delta \mathbf{X}_t = (\mathbf{A}_1 - \mathbf{I})\Delta \mathbf{X}_{t-1} + (\mathbf{A}_2 + \mathbf{A}_1 - \mathbf{I})\mathbf{X}_{t-2} + \sum_{i=3}^{k} \mathbf{A}_i \mathbf{X}_{t-i} + u_t.$$

Next add and subtract $(\mathbf{A}_2 + \mathbf{A}_1 - \mathbf{I})\mathbf{X}_{t-3}$. Continuing in this fashion, we obtain (10.8).

In the context of (10.8), if Π consists of all zeros, its characteristic equation has solutions $\lambda_1 = \lambda_2 = ... = \lambda_p = 0$, and rank($\Pi$) = 0. In this case, (10.8) is the usual VAR model in first differences and there are p unit roots and no cointegration — that is, all elements of $\mathbf{X}_t$ have unit roots and so do all linear combinations of these elements.

If all rows of Π are linearly independent, Π has full rank so that rank(Π) = p, and the vector process is stationary — that is, all elements of $\mathbf{X}_t$ (as well as any linear combination of these elements) will be stationary. In the more interesting case when $0 <$ rank(Π) = $r < p$, there are r cointegrating relations among the elements of $\mathbf{X}_t$ and $p - r$ common stochastic trends.

Johansen proposes two tests for the number of distinct cointegrating vectors — the *trace* and *maximum eigenvalue* tests. In the trace test, the null hypothesis that there are at most r cointegrating vectors is tested (against a general alternative) by calculating the test statistic

$$\lambda_{\text{trace}}(r) = -T \sum_{i=r+1}^{p} \log(1 - \widehat{\lambda}_i),$$

where $\widehat{\lambda}_i$ ($i = 1, ..., p$) are the estimated eigenvalues, obtained from the estimated Π matrix. If the variables do not cointegrate, rank(Π) = 0, and the characteristic equation of Π has solutions $\lambda_1 = \lambda_2 = ... = \lambda_p = 0$. In this case, each $\log(1 - \widehat{\lambda}_i)$ will equal zero (since $\log 1 = 0$), and λ_{trace} equals zero. However, the farther the estimated eigenvalues are from zero, the more negative is each of the expressions $\log(1 - \widehat{\lambda}_i)$, and the larger the λ_{trace} statistic.

In the maximum eigenvalue test, the null hypothesis of r cointegrating vectors is tested against the alternative of $r + 1$ cointegrating vectors by calculating the test statistic

$$\lambda_{\max}(r, r + 1) = -T \log(1 - \widehat{\lambda}_{r+1}).$$

Again, if the estimated eigenvalue, $\widehat{\lambda}_{r+1}$, is close to zero, $\lambda_{\max}$ will be small, and the null hypothesis that the number of cointegrating vectors is r will not be rejected.

The cointegration and error-correction frameworks have proved to be successful tools in the identification and estimation of aggregate money demand functions. This type of approach to the demand for money captures the long-run equilibrium relationship between money and its determinants as well as the short-run variation and dynamics. It does so by allowing economic theory to specify the long-term equilibrium while the underlying data-generating process determines the short-term dynamics. It is in this sense that this approach represents a significant improvement over the partial adjustment specifications that we discussed in Chapter 8, which severely restrict the lag structure by relying solely on ad hoc economic theory without examining the actual data.

There is a growing literature on the application of cointegration and error-correction models to the examination of aggregate money demand functions. The earlier applications tended to be based on the Engle and Granger (1987) cointegration approach. Further research, however, suggests that we undertake the identification and estimation of aggregate money demand functions in a multivariate framework, using procedures developed by Johansen (1988) and Johansen and Juselius (1992). For an excellent textbook treatment see Hoffman and Rasche (1996) and for further references regarding the existing empirical literature on the demand for money in different countries (including developing countries) see Sriram (1999).

10.5   A Bounds Testing Approach

Although the demand for money has been investigated in a large number of recent studies taking a cointegration and error-correction approach, this approach requires the researcher to take a stance on a common order of integration for the individual variables in the money demand function. As a result, most of the literature ignores a recent important contribution to this topic by Serena Ng and Perron (1997) who show that we should be very wary of estimation and inference in 'nearly unbalanced,' 'nearly cointegrated' systems.

In this section we discuss a new econometric technique developed by Hashem Pesaran, Yongcheol Shin, and Richard Smith (1999). Their autoregressive distributed lag (ARDL), bounds test approach to testing for the existence of a single long-run relationship among a set of variables is particularly relevant as it does not require that we take a stand on the time series properties of the data. Therefore one is able to test for the existence of a long-run relationship without having to assume that the money demand variables are I(0), I(1), or even integrated of the same order.

Let us consider the existence of a single long-run relationship between the logarithm of real money balances, $(m - p)_t$, which here we will also denote by s_t, and $\mathbf{x}_t$, where $\mathbf{x}_t$ is the vector time series $[\log Y_t \ \log R_t]$. In describing the Pesaran et al. (1999) methodology, we begin with an unrestricted vector autoregression

$$\mathbf{Z}_t = \boldsymbol{\mu} + \boldsymbol{\delta} t + \sum_{j=1}^{p} \boldsymbol{\phi}_j \mathbf{Z}_{t-j} + \boldsymbol{\varepsilon}_t \qquad (10.10)$$

where $\mathbf{Z}_t = [s_t\ \mathbf{x}_t]'$, $\boldsymbol{\mu}$ is a vector of constant terms, $\boldsymbol{\mu} = [\mu_s\ \boldsymbol{\mu}_\mathbf{x}]'$, t is a linear time trend, $\boldsymbol{\delta} = [\delta_s\ \boldsymbol{\delta}_\mathbf{x}]'$ and $\boldsymbol{\phi}_j$ is a matrix of VAR parameters for lag j. As noted earlier, the money demand variables can be either I(0) or I(1). In this case, equation (10.10) describes a trivariate VAR.

The vector of error terms $\boldsymbol{\varepsilon}_t = [\varepsilon_{s,t}\ \varepsilon_{\mathbf{x},t}]' \sim IN(0,\Omega)$ where Ω is positive definite and given by

$$\Omega = \begin{bmatrix} \omega_{ss} & \omega_{s\mathbf{x}} \\ \omega_{s\mathbf{x}} & \omega_{\mathbf{x}\mathbf{x}} \end{bmatrix}.$$

Given this, $\varepsilon_{s,t}$ can be expressed in terms of $\varepsilon_{\mathbf{x},t}$ as

$$\varepsilon_{s,t} = \omega \varepsilon_{\mathbf{x},t} + u_t \qquad (10.11)$$

where $\omega = \omega_{s\mathbf{x}}/\omega_{\mathbf{x}\mathbf{x}}$ and $u_t \sim IN(0,\omega_{ss})$.

Manipulation of equation (10.10) allows us to write it as a vector error correction model, as follows

$$\Delta \mathbf{Z}_t = \boldsymbol{\mu} + \boldsymbol{\delta} t + \boldsymbol{\lambda} \mathbf{Z}_{t-1} + \sum_{j=1}^{p-1} \boldsymbol{\gamma}_j \Delta \mathbf{Z}_{t-j} + \boldsymbol{\varepsilon}_t \qquad (10.12)$$

where $\Delta = 1 - L$, and

$$\boldsymbol{\gamma}_j = \begin{bmatrix} \gamma_{ss,j} & \gamma_{s\mathbf{x},j} \\ \gamma_{s\mathbf{x},j} & \gamma_{\mathbf{x}\mathbf{x},j} \end{bmatrix} = - \sum_{k=j+1}^{p} \boldsymbol{\phi}_k.$$

Here $\boldsymbol{\lambda}$ is the long-run multiplier matrix and is given by

$$\boldsymbol{\lambda} = \begin{bmatrix} \lambda_{ss} & \lambda_{s\mathbf{x}} \\ \lambda_{\mathbf{x}s} & \lambda_{\mathbf{x}\mathbf{x}} \end{bmatrix} = - \left(\mathbf{I} - \sum_{j=1}^{p} \boldsymbol{\phi}_j \right)$$

where $\mathbf{I}$ is an identity matrix. The diagonal elements of this matrix are left unrestricted. This allows for the possibility that each of the series can be either I(0) or I(1) — for example, $\lambda_{ss} = 0$ implies that the real balances series is I(1) and $\lambda_{ss} < 0$ implies that it is I(0).

This procedure allows for the testing for the existence of a maximum of one long-run relationship that includes both $(m-p)_t$ and $\mathbf{x}_t$. This implies that only one of $\lambda_{\mathbf{x}s}$ and $\lambda_{s\mathbf{x}}$ can be non-zero. As our interest is on the long-run effect of real output and the nominal interest rate on real money balances, one can impose the restriction $\lambda_{xs} = 0$. This implies that real balances have no long-run impact on real output and the nominal interest rate or that the real output and nominal interest rate series are *long-run forcing* for real money balances, in the terminology of Pesaran *et al.* (1999). Note that this does not preclude real money balances being Granger causal for the real output and nominal interest rate series in the short-run. These effects are captured through the short-run response coefficients described by the matrices ϕ_1 to ϕ_p.

Under the assumption $\lambda_{xs} = 0$, and using (10.11), the equation for real money balances from (10.12) can be written as

$$\Delta(m - p)_t = \alpha_0 + \alpha_1 t + \varphi s_{t-1} + \psi \mathbf{x}_{t-1}$$

$$(10.13)$$

$$+ \sum_{j=1}^{p-1} \beta_{s,j} \Delta(m - p)_{t-j} + \sum_{j=1}^{q-1} \beta_{\mathbf{x},j} \Delta \mathbf{x}_{t-j} + \omega \Delta \mathbf{x}_t + u_t$$

where $\alpha_0 = \mu_s - \boldsymbol{\omega}' \boldsymbol{\mu}_{\mathbf{x}}$, $\alpha_1 = \delta_s + \boldsymbol{\omega}' \boldsymbol{\delta}_{\mathbf{x}}$, $\varphi = \lambda_{ss}$, $\psi = \lambda_{sx} - \boldsymbol{\omega}' \lambda_{\mathbf{xx}}$, $\beta_{s,j} = \gamma_{ss,j} - \boldsymbol{\omega}' \gamma_{\mathbf{xs},j}$ and $\beta_{\mathbf{x},j} = \gamma_{sx,j} - \boldsymbol{\omega}' \gamma_{\mathbf{xx},j}$. This can also be interpreted as an autoregressive distributed lag [ARDL(p, q)] model. One can estimate equation (10.13) by ordinary least squares and test the absence of a long-run relationship between s_t and $\mathbf{x}_t$, by calculating the F statistic for the null hypothesis of $\varphi = \psi = 0$. Under the alternative of interest, $\varphi \neq 0$ and $\psi \neq 0$, there is a stable long-run relationship between $(m - p)_t$ and $\mathbf{x}_t$, which is described by

$$(m - p)_t = \theta_0 + \theta_1 t + \boldsymbol{\theta}_2 \mathbf{x}_t + v_t$$

where $\theta_0 = -\alpha_0/\varphi$, $\theta_1 = -\alpha_1/\varphi$, $\boldsymbol{\theta}_2 = \boldsymbol{\delta}/\varphi$ and v_t is a mean zero stationary process.

The distribution of the test statistic under the null depends on the order of integration of $(m - p)_t$ and $\mathbf{x}_t$. In the trivariate case where all variables are I(0), and the regression includes an unrestricted intercept and trend, the appropriate 95% asymptotic critical value is 4.87. When all variables are I(1) this critical value is 5.85. For cases in which one series is I(0) and the other is I(1), the 95% asymptotic critical value falls in-between these two bounds — see Pesaran *et al.* (1999, Table C1.v).[5]

---

[5] See Patrick Coe and Serletis (2001) for an application of the Pesaran *et al.* (1999) methodology in the context of purchasing power parity tests.

10.6   Conclusion

We have argued that cointegration provides a correct method of estimating and testing hypotheses in models characterized by long-run relations between nonstationary time series data. It avoids the spurious regression problem and indicates whether it is possible to model the integrated data in an error correction model. In particular, if the variables are integrated and cointegrate, then there is an error-correction representation that enables the estimation of long-run equilibrium relationships without simultaneously having to take a strong position on how to model short-run dynamics. If, however, the variables are integrated and do not cointegrate, then the only valid relationship that can exist between them is in terms of their first differences.

More detailed discussion of the issues raised in this chapter is best carried on in the context of a specific investigation. Such an investigation forms the subject matter of the next chapter. In particular, we examine the evidence for an equilibrium aggregate money demand function in the United States, using quarterly data and making comparisons among simple-sum, Divisia, and currency equivalent methods of monetary aggregation. We also discuss the implications of such an equilibrium relationship for the sources of shocks in the U.S. economy.

Chapter 11

Balanced Growth, the Demand for Money, and Monetary Aggregation

In this chapter, building on a previous empirical study by King, Plosser, Stock, and Watson (1991), we apply the Johansen (1988) maximum likelihood approach for estimating long-run steady-state relations in multivariate vector autoregressive models, to test the implications of neoclassical stochastic growth theory and traditional money demand theory. As we argued in Chapter 10, the Johansen approach is superior to the Engle and Granger (1987) methodology, because it fully captures the underlying time series properties of the data, provides estimates of all the cointegrating relations among a given set of variables, offers a set of test statistics for the number of cointegrating vectors, and allows direct hypothesis tests on the elements of the cointegrating vectors.

Our objective is to apply the Johansen methodology to U.S. quarterly observations over the 1960:1 to 1999:4 period, and also determine whether the evidence supports certain theoretical claims in the real business cycle literature as well as in the traditional money demand literature. In doing so, we make comparisons among simple-sum, Divisia, and currency equivalent monetary aggregates (of M1, M2, M3, and MZM), to deal with the possible anomalies that arise because of different definitions of money. The monetary aggregates were obtained from the

St. Louis MSI database, maintained by the Federal Reserve Bank of St. Louis as a part of the Bank's Federal Reserve Economic Database (FRED). The monetary data and the different monetary aggregation procedures will be discussed in great detail in Chapters 12-14.

11.1   Theoretical Background

Following King *et al.* (1991), let's consider the following simple real business cycle model. The single final good, Y_t, is produced via a constant-returns-to-scale Cobb-Douglas production function,

$$Y_t = \lambda_t K_t^{1-\theta} L_t^{\theta}, \qquad (11.1)$$

where K_t is the predetermined capital stock, chosen in period $t-1$, and L_t is labor input in period t. Total factor productivity, λ_t, follows a logarithmic random walk

$$\log(\lambda_t) = \mu_\lambda + \log(\lambda_{t-1}) + \xi_t, \qquad (11.2)$$

where μ_λ represents the average productivity growth rate and ξ_t is an independent and identically distributed process with mean zero and variance σ^2. In equation (11.2), $\mu_\lambda + \log(\lambda_{t-1})$ represents the deterministic part of the productivity evolution and ξ_t represents the stochastic innovations (or shocks).

Under the assumption that the intertemporal elasticity of substitution in consumption is constant and independent of the level of consumption, the basic neoclassical growth model with deterministic trends implies that the two great ratios — the log output-consumption ratio and the log output-investment ratio — are constant along the steady-state growth path, since the deterministic model's steady-state common growth rate is μ_λ/θ. With stochastic trends, however, there is a common stochastic trend $\log(\lambda_t)/\theta$ with a growth rate of $(\mu_\lambda + \xi_t)/\theta$, implying that the great ratios, $c_t - y_t$ and $i_t - y_t$ become stationary stochastic processes — see King, Plosser, and Sergio Rebelo (1988) for more details.

As we argued in Chapter 10, these theoretical results can be formulated as testable hypotheses in a cointegration framework. Let $\mathbf{X}_t$ be the multivariate stochastic process consisting of the logarithms of real per capita consumption, investment, and output, $\mathbf{X}_t = [c_t, i_t, y_t]$. Each component of $\mathbf{X}_t$ is integrated of order one [or I(1) in the terminology of Engle and Granger (1987)] — because of the random walk nature of productivity. The balanced growth implication of the neoclassical growth model with stochastic trends is that the differences $c_t - y_t$ and $i_t - y_t$ will be I(0) variables. That is, there should be two cointegrating vectors, $[1, 0, -1]$ and $[0, 1, -1]$.

If $\mathbf{X}_t$ is augmented to include real per capita money balances, $(m-p)_t$ and the nominal interest rate, R_t, that is if $\mathbf{X}_t = [c_t, i_t, (m-p)_t, y_t, R_t]$, and if $(m-p)_t$ and R_t are each integrated of order one, then according to the theory we would expect to find three cointegrating vectors — the two great ratios, $[1, 0, 0, -1, 0]$ and $[0, 1, 0, -1, 0]$, and the money demand relation, $[0, 0, 1, \beta_y, \beta_R]$. In fact, according to the theory we expect $\beta_y = -1$ and β_R to be small and positive. These coefficients in the cointegrating vector imply a one-to-one positive relation between real money balances and real output and a small but negative relation between real balances and the nominal rate of interest.

11.2   Univariate Tests for Unit Roots

As we argued earlier meaningful cointegration tests can only be conducted if both nominal and real variables are integrated of order one and of the same order of integration. Hence, the first step before conducting Johansen maximum likelihood cointegration tests is to test for stochastic trends (unit roots) in the autoregressive representation of each individual time series. In doing so, in what follows we use four alternative testing procedures to deal with anomalies that arise when the data are not very informative about whether or not there is a unit root.

In the first three columns of panel A of Table 11.1, we report p-values for the augmented Weighted Symmetric (WS) unit root test [see Pantula *et al.* (1994)], the augmented Dickey-Fuller (ADF) test [see Dickey and Fuller (1981)], and the nonparametric, $Z(t_{\hat{\alpha}})$, test of Phillips (1987) and Phillips and Perron (1988). These p-values (calculated using TSP 4.5) are based on the response surface estimates given by MacKinnon (1994). As discussed in Pantula *et al.* (1994), the WS test dominates the ADF test in terms of power. Also, the $Z(t_{\hat{\alpha}})$ test is robust to a wide variety of serial correlation and time-dependent heteroskedasticity. For the WS and ADF tests, the optimal lag length was taken to be the order selected by the Akaike information criterion (AIC) plus 2 — see Pantula *et al.* (1992) for details regarding the advantages of this rule for choosing the number of augmenting lags. The $Z(t_{\hat{\alpha}})$ test is done with the same Dickey-Fuller regression variables, using no augmenting lags. Based on the p-values for the WS, ADF, and $Z(t_{\hat{\alpha}})$ test statistics reported in panel A of Table 11.1, the null hypothesis of a unit root in levels cannot in general be rejected for each of the variables, except for the CE M2 and CE M3 monetary aggregates.

Table 11.1. Unit Root Test Results

| Variable | A. Log Levels | | | | | B. First Differences of Log Levels | | | | | Decision |
| | p-values | | | KPSS | | p-values | | | KPSS | | |
	WS	ADF	$Z(t_{\hat{a}})$	$\hat{n}_\mu$	$\hat{n}_\tau$	WS	ADF	$Z(t_{\hat{a}})$	$\hat{n}_\mu$	$\hat{n}_\tau$	
Sum M1	.819	.772	.721	.771*	.337*	.003	.010	.000	.110	.085	I(1)
Sum M2	.998	.227	.524	1.948*	.276*	.004	.013	.000	.220	.063	I(1)
Sum M3	.970	.192	.838	1.988*	.345*	.011	.031	.003	.222	.076	I(1)
Sum MZM	.894	.907	.817	1.117*	.352*	.008	.020	.000	.150	.071	I(1)
Divisia M1	.894	.821	.735	1.027*	.350*	.001	.004	.000	.122	.080	I(1)
Divisia M2	.829	.196	.546	1.151*	.317*	.008	.006	.000	.197	.073	I(1)
Divisia M3	.612	.097	.719	1.471*	.320*	.007	.023	.005	.178	.084	I(1)
Divisia MZM	.880	.927	.796	.314	.317*	.006	.016	.000	.147	.081	I(1)
CE M1	.657	.705	.870	.964*	.366*	.000	.000	.000	.119	.066	I(1)
CE M2	.011	.034	.030	1.855*	.129	.000	.000	.000	.028	.029	I(0)
CE M3	.004	.013	.026	1.895*	.127	.000	.000	.000	.027	.027	I(0)
CE MZM	.450	.526	.362	1.435*	.284*	.000	.000	.000	.125	.039	I(1)
C	.450	.067	.294	2.085*	.108	.000	.000	.000	.050	.050	I(1)
I	.124	.041	.315	1.974*	.128	.000	.000	.000	.067	.056	I(1)
Y	.766	.239	.374	2.055*	.317*	.000	.000	.000	.055	.043	I(1)
R	.494	.518	.447	.429	.340*	.000	.001	.000	.071	.038	I(1)

Notes: Numbers in the WS, ADF, and $Z(t_{\hat{a}})$ columns are tail areas of unit root tests. An asterisk (next to a t-statistic) indicates significance at the 5 percent level. The 5 percent critical values for the KPSS $\hat{n}_\mu$ and $\hat{n}_\tau$ test statistics [given in Kwiatkowski *et al.* (1992)] are .463 and .146, respectively.

Given that unit root tests have low power against relevant (trend stationary) alternatives, we also follow Kwiatkowski *et al.* (1992) and test for level and trend stationarity to distinguish between series that appear to be stationary, series that appear to be integrated, and series that are not very informative about whether or not they are stationary or have a unit root. KPSS tests for level and trend stationarity are presented in columns 4 and 5 of panel A of Table 11.1. As can be seen, the t-statistic $\widehat{\eta}_{\mu}$ that tests the null hypothesis of level stationarity is large relative to the 5% critical value of .463 given in Kwiatkowski *et al.* (1992). Also, the t-statistic $\widehat{\eta}_{\tau}$ that tests the null hypothesis of trend stationarity exceeds the 5% critical value of .146 [also given in Kwiatkowski *et al.* (1992)], except for the CE M2 and CE M3 monetary aggregates and the consumption and investment series. Hence, combining the results of our tests of the stationarity hypothesis with the results of our tests of the unit root hypothesis, we conclude that all the series have at least one unit root, except for the CE M2 and CE M3 money measures that appear to be stationary.

To test the null hypothesis of a second unit root, in panel B of Table 11.1 we test the null hypothesis of a unit root (using the WS, ADF, and $Z(t_{\widehat{\alpha}})$ tests) as well as the null hypotheses of level and trend stationarity in the first (logged) differences of the series. Clearly, all the series appear to be stationary in first differences, since the null hypothesis of a unit root is rejected and the null hypotheses of level and trend stationarity cannot be rejected. The decision of the order of integration of the series is documented in the last column of Table 11.1.

11.3 Testing the c, i, y System

In this section, we apply the Johansen and Juselius (1992) maximum likelihood cointegration tests to test the balanced growth hypothesis in a three-variable model containing the real variables, c, i, and y on a per capita basis. According to the theory, we expect two cointegrating relationships among these three I(1) variables, given by the (log) differences of consumption and output and of investment and output. These are known as the 'great ratios.'

Table 11.2 reports the results of the cointegration tests on a quarterly VAR of length 6 ($k = 6$). Two test statistics are used to test for the number of cointegrating vectors: the maximum eigenvalue ($\lambda_{\max}$) and trace (λ_{trace}) test statistics. As we argued in Chapter 10, in the trace test the null hypothesis that there are at most r cointegrating vectors (where $r = 0$, 1, 2) is tested against a general alternative whereas in the maximum eigenvalue test the alternative is explicit. That is, the

Table 11.4.   Multivariate Hypothesis Testing in the $m - p, y, R$ System

| Monetary | | *p*-values | |
aggregates	Specification	$H_0 : \beta_t = 0$	$H_0 : \beta_y = -1$
Sum M1	VAR $= 6$, $r = 1$	.914	.000
Sum M2	VAR $= 6$, $r = 0$	—	—
Sum M3	VAR $= 6$, $r = 0$	—	—
Sum MZM	VAR $= 6$, $r = 1$	.003	.000
Divisia M1	VAR $= 6$, $r = 1$	.726	.000
Divisia M2	VAR $= 6$, $r = 0$	—	—
Divisia M3	VAR $= 6$, $r = 0$	—	—
Divisia MZM	VAR $= 6$, $r = 0$	—	—
CE M1	VAR $= 6$, $r = 0$	—	—
CE MZM	VAR $= 6$, $r = 0$	—	—

Notes: Sample period, quarterly data: 1960:1–1999:4. r is the
cointegration rank. Low *p*-values imply strong evidence against
the null hypothesis.

cointegrating vector cannot be rejected at the 5% level with Sum M1
and Divisia M1, but is rejected with Sum MZM.

Hence, we next impose the over-identifying restriction that $\beta_t = 0$ in
the Sum M1 and Divisia M1 systems (but not in the Sum MZM) system
and test whether the empirically determined cointegrating relation in
each of the Sum M1, Sum MZM, and Divisia M1 systems is compatible
with traditional money demand theory. In particular, we test the null
hypothesis that the output elasticity of money demand is equal to 1
(that is, $\beta_y = -1$). Clearly, the *p*-values in the last column of Table
11.4 indicate that the null hypothesis is rejected, independently of how
money is measured.

11.5   Testing the c, i, $m - p$, y, R System

We now turn to the multivariate stochastic process, $\mathbf{X}_t = [c_t, i_t,$
$(m - p)_t, y_t, R_t]$ and report results in Table 11.5, in the same fashion
as those for the trivariate system $m - p$, y, R in Table 11.3. According
to the λ_{trace} test statistic, we cannot reject the null of $r = 1$ in the Sum
M2, Sum M3, and Sum MZM systems and we cannot reject the null of
no cointegration in each of the other systems. Of course, these results

do not explain why the hypothesis of cointegration is rejected with most monetary aggregates, but they do lead one to suspect that there may be a common explanation such as, for example, differences in the time-series properties of the different monetary aggregates.

The next step is to identify the cointegrating vector in each of the Sum M2, Sum M3, and Sum MZM systems, for which we found one cointegrating relation. Clearly, the evidence in support of one cointe- grating relationship does not provide any direction as to which one of the three vectors expected by economic theory is picked up by the Jo- hansen procedure. It is more likely that the one cointegrating vector is the long-run money demand function, since in the trivariate c, i, y system we did not find evidence of cointegration.

To identify the cointegrating vector, in Table 11.6 we test the overi- dentifying restrictions that identify the consumption-output ratio, the investment-output ratio, and the money demand function, $\beta_2 = \beta_3 = \beta_5 = \beta_6 = 0$, $\beta_1 = \beta_3 = \beta_5 = \beta_6 = 0$, and $\beta_1 = \beta_2 = \beta_6 = 0$, respec- tively. Clearly, the restrictions that identify the consumption-output ratio and the investment-output ratio are rejected, suggesting that the empirically determined cointegrating relation is not compatible with the balanced growth theory. However, the overidentifying restrictions that identify the money demand function, $\beta_1 = \beta_2 = \beta_6 = 0$, cannot be rejected with the Sum M2 and Sum M3 monetary aggregates, but are rejected with the Sum MZM aggregate.

Hence, for the case of the Sum M2 and Sum M3 systems, we have been able to identify the cointegrating vector with the long-run money demand function. In the case, however, of the Sum MZM system, we cannot identify the cointegrating vector, since we have rejected all three sets of overidentifying restrictions. This means that for the Sum MZM system the one cointegrating vector that the Johansen test detects is not the money demand or any of the two great ratios that the theory predicts.

Finally, in the last column of Table 11.6 we test the restriction that $\beta_4 = -1$ for each of the Sum M2 and Sum M3 systems. This hypothesis is rejected in the Sum M2 system, but not in the Sum M3 system. In fact, with Sum M3 the estimate of the long-run income elasticity is .957 (with a standard error of .041) and that of the long-run interest elasticity is .019 (with a standard error of .005). Hence, we conclude that a money-demand cointegrating relation is consistent only with the observed behavior of the Sum M3 monetary aggregate.

Figure 11.1. Persistence Profile of the Effect of a System-Wide Shock to the Cointegrating Vector

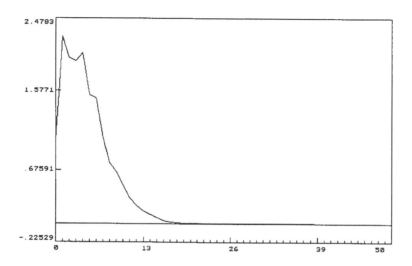

Next, we examine the effect of system-wide shocks on the Sum M3 money demand relation, by plotting the persistence profile in Figure 11.1. This profile clearly shows an overshooting of the cointegrating vector in the short-run and a strong tendency of the long-run relation to converge to its equilibrium. To see the effect of variable-specific shocks on the cointegrating vector, in Figure 11.2 we show orthogonalized impulse responses of the cointegrating vector to shocks to real per capita income (panel A) and real per capita money balances (panel B). As can be seen, the effect of the shocks on the cointegrating relation dies out, although the cointegrating vector is slow to return to its equilibrium following such shocks — it deviates from its equilibrium for periods longer than 15 quarters. Finally, in Figure 11.3 we consider the dynamic effects of shocks to real per capita income (panel A) and real per capita money balances (panel B) on real per capita income and real per capita money balances. Clearly, these shocks have permanent effects. This is an expected result, since as we have already determined that each of these series has a stochastic trend.

Figure 11.2. Orthogonalized Impulse Responses of the Cointegrating Vector to One Standard Error Shock

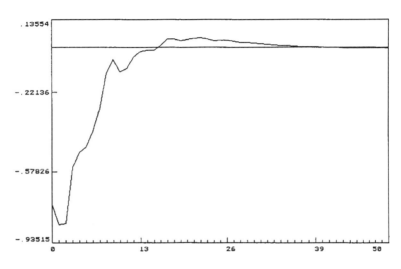

a. Shock in the Equation for Y

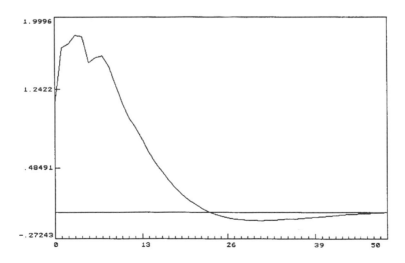

b. Shock in the Equation for Sum M3

Part 5:

Microfoundations

and Monetary

Aggregation

Overview of Part 5

Chapters 12 and 13 provide the microeconomic foundations to the problem of monetary aggregation. Most of the material here is by now well established in the monetary literature. In fact, the manifest advantages of the microfoundations approach have been laid out carefully by Barnett, Douglas Fisher, and Serletis (1992) and Barnett and Serletis (2000).

Chapter 14 investigates the cyclical behavior of the monetary variables, using the methodology suggested by Kydland and Prescott (1990). In doing so, comparisons are made among simple-sum, Divisia, and CE monetary aggregates (of M1, M2, M3, and MZM) using the Anderson *et al.* (1997) data set that we discussed in Chapters 8 and 11.

all monetary components are assigned a constant and equal (unitary) weight. This index is M in

$$M = \sum_{i=1}^{n} x_i$$

where x_i is one of the n monetary components of the monetary aggregate M. This summation index views all components as dollar-for-dollar perfect substitutes. There is no question that such an index represents an index of the stock of nominal monetary wealth, but it is a special case, at best, of the appropriate type of index for monetary services, as we will see.

Friedman and Anna Schwartz (1970, p. 151–152) dismissed simple-sum monetary aggregates when discussing the potential generalization of the simple-sum aggregates to index numbers

"[t]his (summation) procedure is a very special case of the more general approach. In brief, the general approach consists of re-garding each asset as a joint product having different degrees of *moneyness*, and defining the quantity of money as the weighted sum of the aggregate value of all assets, the weights for individual assets varying from zero to unity with a weight of unity assigned to that asset or assets regarded as having the largest quantity of "moneyness" per dollar of aggregate value. The procedure we have followed implies that all weights are either zero or unity. The more general approach has been suggested frequently but experimented with only occasionally. We conjecture that this approach deserves and will get much more attention than it has so far received."

Over the years, there has been a steady stream of attempts at prop-erly weighting the monetary components within a simple-sum aggregate. Without theory, however, any weighting scheme is questionable. Karup-pan Chetty (1969) appears to have been the first to recognize the direct relevancy of microeconomic aggregation theory to monetary aggregation, since he was the first to produce a structure for monetary aggregation embedded within a constrained optimization problem.

More recently, Barnett (1980) in a challenging paper, "Economic Mon-etary Aggregates: An Application of Index Number and Aggregation Theory," voiced objections to simple-sum aggregation procedures and argued instead for applying aggregation theory and statistical index number theory to monetary aggregation. As Barnett, Edward Offen-bacher , and Paul Spindt (1984, p. 1051) put it

"[b]y equally weighting components, aggregation by summation can badly distort an aggregate. For example, if one wished to obtain an aggregate of transportation vehicles, one would never aggregate by summation over the physical units of, say, subway trains and roller skates. Instead one could construct a quantity index (such as the Department of Commerce's indexes) using weights based on the *values* of the different modes of transportation."

Barnett has argued that a more satisfactory approach to monetary aggregation must involve consideration of the utility function underlying the demand for monetary assets. For example, the appropriate form of aggregation (simple-sum as opposed to other possibilities) will be determined by the relationship that monetary assets bear to one another and their contribution to total 'moneyness.' It turns out that simple-sum aggregation is justified, when viewed in this framework, only if the component assets are perfect substitutes.

The case for using microeconomic aggregation theory in monetary economics is now very strong. The theory has two branches, one leading to the construction of index numbers and methods derived from economic theory and one leading to the construction of money-demand functions in the context of a system of equations modeling the wealth holder's allocation of funds between money and nonmoney assets. The two branches are supported by the same structure in that the supporting theory in both cases is that of the constrained maximization of the aggregate consumer's dynamic utility function.

In what follows, we briefly spell out the microtheoretical framework to the aggregation of money, leaving the related discussion of the demand systems approach to modeling the demand for money (and monetary assets) for later chapters.

12.2 The User Cost of Money

The meaning of the *price* of money is not obvious in monetary theory. Usually this price has been viewed as varying inversely to the general price level. In this sense, the price of money is its purchasing power in terms of real goods and services. The price of money has also been viewed as an opportunity cost — the cost of not holding interest-yielding assets. In fact, as we will see later in this book, the usual assumption is that the demand for money depends negatively on the incentives for holding other assets relative to money.

In the recent literature, however, money is treated as a durable good having an infinite life and it is assumed that money retains at least some value beyond the holding period. Under such an assumption, it would be wrong to attribute a price of unity — the full purchase price — to a unit

that the demand for monetary services is independent of relative prices outside the monetary group.[1]

Whether or not the utility function (12.2) is weakly separable in monetary services is, of course, an empirical question. Ideally, instead of treating (12.3) as a maintained (untested) hypothesis, as we do here, one could test whether the utility function (12.2) is appropriately separable in monetary services — an assumption implicit in the traditional money-nonmoney dichotomization. This issue remains relatively unexplored.

If one is willing to continue focusing on the details of the demand for services of monetary assets, ignoring other types of goods, the following classical consumer problem can be utilized

$$\max_{x} f(x) \quad \text{subject to} \quad p'x = m \tag{12.4}$$

in which m is the expenditure on the services of monetary assets (determined in the first stage of the two level optimization problem) and p is as defined above, a vector of monetary asset user costs.

12.4   Aggregation Theory

In the discussion to this point, we have shown the steps that are normally taken to reduce a very general consumer choice problem to an asset-choice problem. At this point, we are prepared to proceed to results in the aggregation-theoretic literature, in which we are looking for monetary aggregates that are consistent with the optimizing behavior of rational economic agents. We begin with the monetary services utility function, $f(x)$, assuming that the utility function (12.2) is weakly separable in monetary services.

Using a specific and differentiable form for $f(x)$, and solving decision (12.4), we can derive the demand-function system. Using these derived solution functions and specific monetary data, we then could estimate the parameters and replace the unknown parameters of $f(x)$ by their estimates. The resulting estimated function is called an *economic* (or *functional*) monetary index, and its calculated value at any point in time is an economic monetary-quantity index number.

---

[1] Note that the separability structure is asymmetric. That is, c is not separable from x and ℓ in $u(\cdot)$ unless there exists a function $g(c)$ such that

$$u = u(c, \ell, x) = u\left(g(c), \ell, f(x)\right).$$

For an extensive discussion of separability, see Charles Blackorby, Daniel Primont, and Robert Russell (1978).

The problem is that the use of a specific function necessarily implies a set of implicit assumptions about the underlying preference structure of the economic agent. For example, the use of a weighted linear aggregator function

$$f(x) = \sum_{i=1}^{n} a_i x_i$$

implies perfect substitutability among the assets and hence should logically lead to specialization in consumption of the least expensive asset.[2] If this is inaccurate, obviously, we commit a specification error by using this functional form.

The use of a Cobb-Douglas functional form

$$f(x) = \prod_{i=1}^{n} x_i^{a_i}$$

imposes an elasticity of substitution equal to unity ($\sigma = 1$) between every pair of assets and its use implies that each asset always accounts for a constant share of the expenditure.[3] Again, if this proposition is at odds with the facts, as it is likely to be, the use of the Cobb-Douglas seems inappropriate.

As a last example, a constant elasticity of substitution (CES) functional form

$$f(x) = \sum_{i=1}^{n} (a_i x_i^r)^{1/r}$$

---

[2] The more restrictive unit-weighted ($a_i = 1$, $i = 1, ..., n$) aggregator function implies dollar for dollar perfect substitutability. This was the simple-sum aggregation procedure.

[3] In general, the elasticity of substitution between assets i and j is defined as

$$\sigma_{ij} = \frac{d \log(x_j/x_i)}{d \log (f_i(x)/f_j(x))}.$$

To calculate the elasticity of substitution for the simple, two-asset (i.e., $n = 2$) Cobb-Douglas utility function, we note that the numerator of the above expression is

$$d \log(x_2/x_1) = d \log x_2 - d \log x_1,$$

and that the denominator is

$$d \log (f_1(x)/f_2(x)) = d \log \left(\frac{\alpha_1}{\alpha_2} \frac{x_2}{x_1} \right) = d \log x_2 - d \log x_1.$$

Hence, $\sigma = 1$.

where $0 < a_i < 1$, $-\infty < r < 1$, relaxes the unitary elasticity of substitution restriction imposed by the Cobb-Douglas, but imposes the restriction that the elasticity of substitution between any pair of assets is always constant, $\sigma = 1/(1-r)$. Again this seems contrary to fact.

The list of specific functional forms is, of course, boundless, but the defining property of the more popular of these entities is that they imply limitations on the behavior of the consumer that may be incorrect in practice. While the issue of their usefulness is ultimately an empirical question — and we shall treat the issue that way in this book — we feel that most members of this class of functions should be rejected, partly in view of the restrictive nature of their implicit assumptions, and partly because of the existence of attractive alternatives.

Among the alternatives is a member of the class of quadratic utility functions. With a member of the quadratic class, we would be using a *flexible functional form* to approximate the unknown monetary-services aggregator function, $f(x)$. Flexible functional forms such as the translog, introduced by Laurits Christensen, Dale Jorgenson , and Lawrence Lau in their 1975 article, "Transcendental Logarithmic Utility Functions,"

$$f(x) = \alpha_0 + \sum_{i=1}^{n}\alpha_i \log x_i + \frac{1}{2}\sum_{i=1}^{n}\sum_{j=1}^{n}\beta_{ij} \log x_i \log x_j \qquad (12.5)$$

can locally approximate to the second order any unknown functional form for the monetary services aggregator function, and even higher quality approximations are available. We will consider the details of such functional forms later in this book.

If one is to do away with the simple-sum method of aggregating money and replace it with a nonlinear aggregator function as suggested, one will be able to deal with less than perfect substitutability and, for that matter, with variations over time in the elasticities of substitution among the components of the monetary aggregates. There is a problem, however, and this is that the functions must be estimated over specific data sets (and re-estimated periodically) with the attendant result that the index becomes dependent upon the specification.

This dependence is particularly troublesome to government agencies that have to justify their procedures to persons untrained in econometrics. This is a reasonable concern — and it is exacerbated by the fact that there are many possible nonlinear models from which to choose. Under these circumstances, government agencies around the world have always viewed aggregation theory as being solely a research tool, and have instead used index number formulas from statistical index number theory, to which we now turn.

12.5   Index Number Theory

Statistical index-number theory provides a class of quantity and price indexes that can be computed from price and quantity data alone, thus eliminating the need to estimate an underlying structure. In fact since the appearance of Fisher's (1922) early classic book on statistical index number theory, nearly all federal government economic data series have been based upon aggregation formulas from that literature. Well known examples are the Consumer Price Index, which is a Laspeyres price index, the Implicit Price Deflator, which is a Paasche price index, and real GNP, which is a Laspeyres quantity index.[4] The simple-sum index, often used for monetary quantities, is a member of the broad class, but the simple-sum is a special case, since it contains no prices.

Statistical indexes are mainly characterized by their statistical properties. These properties were examined in great detail by Fisher (1922) and serve as tests in assessing the quality of a particular statistical index. They have been named, after Fisher, as *Fisher's system of tests.* Wolfrang Eichhorn (1976, 1978) provides a detailed analysis as well as a comprehensive bibliography of Fisher's *test* (or *axiomatic*) approach to index numbers.

While Fisher found the simple-sum index to be the worst known index number formula, the index that he found to be the best, in the sense of possessing the largest number of appropriate statistical properties, has now become known as the *Fisher ideal* index. Another index found to possess a very large number of such properties is the (Törnqvist) discrete time approximation to the continuous Divisia index. That index commonly is called the Törnqvist index or just the Divisia index (in discrete time). We shall use the latter naming convention.

Let x_{it} be the quantity of the ith asset during period t, and let p_{it} be the rental price (i.e., user cost) for that asset during period t. Then, the Fisher ideal index, M_t^F, during period t, is the geometric average of the

---

[4]The Laspeyres quantity index is

$$M_t^L = \sum_{i=1}^{n} w_{i,t-1} \left(\frac{x_{it}}{x_{i,t-1}} \right),$$

where $w_{it} = p_{it} x_{it} / \sum_{k=1}^{n} p_{kt} x_{kt}$ is the ith asset's share in expenditure on all assets. The Paasche quantity index is

$$M_t^P = 1 \left/ \sum_{i=1}^{n} w_{it} \left(\frac{x_{i,t-1}}{x_{it}} \right) \right. .$$

Laspeyres and Paasche indexes

$$M_t^F = M_{t-1}^F \left[\sum_{i=1}^n w_{i,t-1} \left(\frac{x_{it}}{x_{i,t-1}} \right) \times 1 \left/ \sum_{i=1}^n w_{it} \left(\frac{x_{i,t-1}}{x_{it}} \right) \right. \right]^{1/2},$$

where

$$w_{it} = p_{it} x_{it} \left/ \sum_{k=1}^n p_{kt} x_{kt} \right.$$

is the ith asset's share in expenditure on the total portfolio's service flow.

On the other hand, the discrete time (Törnqvist) Divisia index, M_t^D, during period t, is

$$M_t^D = M_{t-1}^D \prod_{i=1}^n \left(\frac{x_{it}}{x_{i,t-1}} \right)^{(1/2)(w_{it}+w_{i,t-1})}.$$

It is informative to take the logarithm of each side of the above equation, so that

$$\log M_t^D - \log M_{t-1}^D = \sum_{i=1}^n \overline{w}_{it} (\log x_{it} - \log x_{i,t-1}), \qquad (12.6)$$

where $\overline{w}_{it} = (1/2)(w_{it} + w_{i,t-1})$. In this form, it is easy to see that for the Divisia index the growth rate (log change) of the aggregate is the share-weighted average of the growth rates of the component quantities.

The primary advantage of the Fisher ideal index over the Divisia index is that the Fisher ideal index satisfies Fisher's *factor reversal test* — which requires that the product of the price and quantity indexes for an aggregated asset (or good) should equal actual expenditures on the component assets (or goods) — while the Divisia index fails that test. However, the magnitude of the error is very small (third order in the changes), and the Divisia index has the very large advantage of possessing the easily interpreted functional form, given as equation (12.6).

12.6   Diewert's Link

Until relatively recently, the fields of aggregation theory and statistical index number theory developed independently. However, Diewert in his 1976 paper, "Exact and Superlative Index Numbers," provided the link between aggregation theory and statistical index number theory by attaching economic properties to statistical indexes. These properties are defined in terms of the statistical indexes' ability to approximate a particular functional form for the unknown aggregator function, $f(x)$ in our case.

For example, for a number of well known statistical indexes Diewert shows that they are equivalent to the use of a particular functional form. Such statistical indexes are called *exact*. Exactness, however is not sufficient for acceptability of a particular statistical index when the functional form for the aggregator function is not known. In this case it seems desirable to choose a statistical index which is exact for a flexible functional form. Diewert termed such statistical indexes *superlative*. Diewert also showed that the Divisia index is exact for the linearly homogeneous translog and is, therefore, superlative.

Following Diewert (1976) we will demonstrate how an exact index for the homogeneous translog functional form can be derived and that the index is the Divisia index. Consider the homogeneous (of degree one) translog functional form given by equation (12.5), with the following (homogeneity) restrictions imposed

$$\sum_{i=1}^{n} \alpha_i = 1 \quad \text{and} \quad \sum_{j=1}^{n} \beta_{ij} = 0, \quad \text{for all } j$$

and define a quantity index between periods 0 and r, $Q(p^0, x^0, p^r, x^r)$, $r = 1, ..., T$, as a function of the n prices in periods 0 and r. To ensure that the statistical index approximates the functional form for the aggregator function, it is required that the following relation is satisfied

$$\frac{f(x^r)}{f(x^0)} = Q(p^0, x^0, p^r, x^r), \quad \text{for } r = 1, ..., T \tag{12.7}$$

whenever $x^r > 0$ is the solution to the following aggregator maximization problem

$$\max_{x} \{f(x) : p^r x \le p^r x^r, \quad x \ge 0\}, \quad \text{for } r = 0, ..., T$$

For a base period normalization $f(x^0) = 1$, equation (12.7) implies that the quantity index at time t equals the aggregator function evaluated at that point. If equation (12.7) is satisfied the quantity index $Q(p^0, x^0, p^r, x^r)$ is said to be exact for the aggregator function $f(x)$.

Next, we make use of the quadratic approximation lemma of Henri Theil (1967, p. 222-223)

$$f(z^1) - f(z^0) = \frac{1}{2} \left[\nabla f(z^1) + \nabla f(z^0)\right](z^1 - z^0) \tag{12.8}$$

Chapter 13

The New Monetary Aggregates

We have argued in Chapter 12 that the simple-sum method of aggregation makes strong *a priori* assumptions about substitution effects and the result is a set of monetary aggregates that do not accurately measure the actual quantities of the monetary products that optimizing economic agents select (in the aggregate). We also surveyed the microeconomic theory of monetary aggregation, as it has evolved during the past twenty years, using a model of the optimizing behavior of representative economic agents.

Our objective in this chapter is to develop a better understanding of the Divisia monetary aggregates, by presenting the source and the underlying microeconomic theory of the Divisia index. In addition, we provide an empirical assessment of the relative merits of the Divisia versus the simple sum method of monetary aggregation as well as other, recently proposed, aggregation procedures. Our objective is to be able to settle on a satisfactory method of 'measuring' money.

13.1   The Neoclassical Monetary Problem

In the discussion to this point, we have shown that in the second stage of the two-stage maximization problem, with weak separability between monetary assets and consumer goods and leisure, the consumer faces the

Next define $P(\boldsymbol{p})$ to be the dual price index satisfying Fisher's factor reversal test[1]

$$P(\boldsymbol{p})f(\boldsymbol{x}) = \sum_{i=1}^{n} p_i x_i \quad (= m).$$

It can be shown [see Barnett, Fisher, and Serletis (1992, footnote 22)] that $\lambda = 1/P(\boldsymbol{p})$ in which case equation(13.3) reduces to

$$df(\boldsymbol{x}) = \sum_{i=1}^{n} \left(\frac{1}{P(\boldsymbol{p})}\right) p_i \, dx_i. \tag{13.4}$$

Manipulating equation (13.4) algebraically, to convert to growth rate (log change) form, we find that

$$d \log f(\boldsymbol{x}) = \sum_{i=1}^{n} \overline{w}_i d \log x_i \tag{13.5}$$

where, as in the previous chapter, $w_i = p_i x_i / \sum_{k=1}^{n} p_k x_k$ is the ith asset's value share in total expenditure on monetary services. The result is that the log change in the utility level (and therefore in the level of the aggregate) is the weighted average of the log changes of the component levels, with expenditure shares being the weights. Equation (13.5) is the Divisia index in growth rate form, as defined in chapter 8.

This exercise demonstrates the solid microeconomic foundations of the Divisia index. It is indeed, the logical choice for an index from a theoretical point of view, being the transformed first-order conditions for constrained optimization.

13.3   Divisia Second Moments

Henri Theil in his 1967 book, *Economics and Information Theory*, observed that there is an interesting stochastic interpretation of the Divisia index. In particular, he observed that the Divisia weights are nonnegative and sum to 1 in every period. Given this, we can treat the growth rates of the components as drawn randomly from a population such that the right-hand side of equation (13.5) becomes an expectation. Under this interpretation, the left-hand side of equation (13.5) is the mean of the growth rates of the components, $d \log M^D$. What this then suggests

---

[1] Recall that Fisher's factor reversal test requires that the product of the price and quantity indexes for an aggregated asset (or good) should equal actual expenditure on the component assets (or goods).

is that the Divisia quantity index is a first moment and, by appealing to Theil's sampling analogy, we can define the Divisia second moments. In particular, the Divisia quantity variance (the second moment) is

$$K_t = \sum_{i=1}^{n} \overline{w}_{it}(d\log x_{it} - d\log M_t^D)^2.$$

Also, since the Divisia price index (mean or first moment) is

$$d\log P_t = \sum_{i=1}^{n} \overline{w}_{it} d\log p_{it},$$

the corresponding Divisia price variance is

$$J_t = \sum_{i=1}^{n} \overline{w}_{it}(d\log p_{it} - d\log P_t)^2,$$

and the Divisia price-quantity covariance is

$$\Gamma_t = \sum_{i=1}^{n} \overline{w}_{it}(d\log x_{it} - d\log M_t^D)(d\log p_{it} - d\log P_t).$$

Similarly, we can define the Divisia share mean as

$$d\log W_t = \sum_{i=1}^{n} \overline{w}_{it} d\log w_{it},$$

and the Divisia share variance as

$$\Psi_t = \sum_{i=1}^{n} \overline{w}_{it}(d\log w_{it} - d\log W_t)^2.$$

Note that Theil (1967) has shown that the Divisia second moments are related by the equality

$$K_t = \Psi_t - J_t - 2\Gamma_t.$$

Recently, Barnett and Serletis (1990) applied Theil's stochastic index number theory and tested for aggregation error in the Divisia monetary aggregates. Aggregation errors can be produced when the conditions for exact aggregation are violated. As we have seen, exact aggregation (over monetary assets) requires the existence of a weakly separable and linearly homogeneous aggregator function and removes dependency of market behavior upon distributional effects.

This means that the Divisia second moments would contain no information about the economy, if one already had conditioned upon the information contained in the Divisia mean. Barnett and Serletis (1990), by implicitly assuming that the appropriate distributional variable is the Divisia quantity variance, explored its macroeconomic effects by explicitly introducing it along with the Divisia quantity mean in various tests. They found no evidence of major aggregation error in the Divisia monetary aggregates.

13.4   Measurement Matters

At this stage, it is perhaps worth asking whether 'measurement' matters. To highlight the importance of measurement, let's recall the three-year 'monetarist experiment' of November 1979 to August 1982. During that time the Federal Reserve Board embarked on an experiment in monetarist policy designed to control the money supply and permit interest rates to be determined in the money markets, free of control.

The Fed's views on monetary policy, however, were based on the simple sum monetary aggregates (in particular simple sum M2) and monetary policy during the three-year period was considerably tighter than the Fed thought and led to the recession of 1982. The following quotation, from Barnett (1997, p. 1174-1175), explains what happened:

"As I reported in Barnett (1984), the growth rate of simple sum M2 during the period of the 'monetarist experiment' averaged 9.3%, while the growth rate of Divisia M2 during the period averaged 4.5%. Similarly, the growth rate of simple sum M3 during the period averaged 10%, while the growth rate of Divisia M3 during the period averaged 4.8%. This period followed double digit growth rates of all simple sum and Divisia monetary aggregates. In short, believers in simple sum monetary aggregation, who had been the advocates of the 'monetarist experiment,' were put in the embarrassing position of witnessing an outcome (the subsequent recession) that was inconsistent with the intent of the prescribed policy and with the behavior of the simple sum aggregates during the period. This unwelcome and unexpected outcome rendered vulnerable those economists who advocated a policy based upon the assumption of a stable simple sum demand for money function.

Friedman's very visible forecast error on 26 September 1983 followed closely on the heels of the end of the monetarist experiment in August 1982 and the recession that it produced. The road buckled and collapsed below the monetarists and those who believed in stable simple sum demand for money functions. Those two associated groups have never recovered. But the recession that followed the monetarist experiment was no surprise to anyone who had followed the Divisia monetary aggregates, since those aggregates indicated that a severe deflationary shock had occurred. To those who were using data based upon valid index number and aggregation theory, rather than the obsolete simple sum monetary aggregates, the road remained smooth — no bumps, no breaks. Nothing unexpected had happened."

The above quotation shows that simple sum and Divisia monetary aggregates tell very different stories. Monetary policy, as indicated by the Divisia monetary aggregates, was tighter than indicated by the simple sum aggregates. That resulted in the severe 1982 recession, despite the fact that the Fed's intention, as indicated by the simple sum monetary aggregates, was to produce a gradual disinflation rather than a severe disinflationary shock. Hence, measurement matters and the failure to use superior aggregates can have big practical consequences.

13.5 The MQ and CE Indexes

While we are on the topic of monetary indexes, we will briefly consider two recent additions to the list of alternative index numbers, with a potential application to monetary aggregation. These are Paul Spindt's (1985) 'monetary quantities' (MQ) index (which is no longer in use in the monetary literature), and the 'currency equivalent' (CE) index more recently introduced by Rotemberg (1991) and Rotemberg , Driscoll, and Poterba (1995).

In the particular form computed by Spindt (1985), MQ is measured as a Fisher ideal index, but with the user costs replaced by monetary-asset turnover rates. That is

$$\mathrm{MQ}_t = \mathrm{MQ}_{t\text{-}1} \left[\sum_{i=1}^{n} w_{i,t-1} \left(\frac{x_{it}}{x_{i,t-1}} \right) \times 1 \middle/ \sum_{i=1}^{n} w_{it} \left(\frac{x_{i,t-1}}{x_{it}} \right) \right]^{1/2},$$

where

$$w_{it} = v_{it} x_{it} \middle/ \sum_{k=1}^{n} v_{kt} x_{kt} ,$$

with v_i being the turnover rate of monetary asset i. The problem with this procedure is that the MQ index, unlike the Divisia index, is inconsistent both with existing aggregation theory and index number theory.

The relevant foundations (both index-number theoretic and aggregation theoretic) for the Fisher-ideal index require the use of prices and quantities and not turnover rates and quantities. If nothing else, MQ can be said to be no less arbitrary than the official simple-sum aggregates.

A more recent addition to the list of alternative index numbers is the Rotemberg, Driscoll, and Poterba (1995) currency equivalent (CE) index

$$\text{CE} = \sum_{i=1}^{n} \frac{R_t - r_{it}}{R_t} x_{it}. \tag{13.6}$$

This index is basically the simple sum index with the addition of a simple weighting mechanism. In (13.6), as long as currency gives no interest, units of currency are added together with a weight of one. Other assets are added to currency, but with a weight that declines toward zero as their return increases toward R_t and the assets come to behave more like the benchmark asset (a means to transfer wealth) and less like money.

The difference between Divisia and CE methods of monetary aggregation is that the former measures the flow of monetary services whereas the latter, like simple summation aggregation, measures the stock of monetary assets. There is also a considerably less attractive interpretation of the CE index as a flow index. See Barnett, Melvin Hinich, and Piyu Yue (2000) regarding the flow interpretation, which requires stronger assumptions than those needed to derive the Divisia flow index.

13.6   Empirical Comparisons

In order to provide a quantitative assessment of the simple sum, Divisia, and currency equivalent monetary aggregation procedures, we employ (seasonally-adjusted) quarterly data, from 1960:1 to 1999:4, on United States simple sum, Divisia, and CE indexes. The data were obtained from the St. Louis MSI database, maintained by the Federal Reserve Bank of St. Louis as part of the Federal Reserve Economic Database (FRED) — see Anderson, Jones , and Nesmith (1997) for details regarding the construction of the Divisia and currency equivalent aggregates and related data.

Figures 13.1 to 13.4 provide graphical representations of the four major measures of money (M1, M2, M3, and MZM) under the simple sum, Divisia, and currency equivalent aggregation procedures. As the graphs indicate, the numbers differ considerably across the three monetary aggregation procedures. Even more interesting are the graphs of the GNP velocities for these same aggregates appearing in Figures 13.5 to 13.8. Not only are the fluctuations of the velocity series different at different levels of aggregation, but also across aggregation methods.

Finally, in Table 13.1 we provide summary statistics based upon the first and second order sample moments of the quarterly data on annual monetary growth rates.[2] Inspection of the summary statistics suggests that the average growth rate of the Divisia aggregates is, in general, less than that of the simple sum aggregates. In addition, the Divisia aggregates indicate less volatile monetary growth, during our sample period, than is indicated by the official simple sum aggregates.

However, the currency equivalent money measures tell a very different story. In particular, the average growth rate of the CE aggregates is always higher than that of the corresponding simple sum and Divisia aggregates. Also, observe that monetary policy, as measured by the CE aggregates, is much more volatile than is suggested by either the simple sum or Divisia aggregates. These differences reflect the essentially complicated monetary aggregation issues — something we mentioned when we discussed the 'monetarist experiment' of November 1979 to August 1982 and to be kept in mind throughout this book.

13.7 Conclusion

We have surveyed a growing literature on the importance of the use of microeconomic aggregation theory in monetary aggregation. The issue is of practical importance, because effective conduct of monetary policy presupposes an appropriate monetary aggregate. It is also of academic interest for the insight it provides into the nature of 'moneyness'. We have argued that the simple sum aggregates are just accounting identities, not economic aggregates. The Divisia aggregates are economic aggregates, and hence are useful indicators (or intermediate targets) for ultimate policy goals.

We have also demonstrated, on United States monthly data, some quantitative differences among simple sum, Divisia, and CE money measures, raising a number of warnings about ignoring the important monetary aggregation issues in the conduct of monetary policy. To further highlight the influence of money measurement on statistical inference, as in Michael Belongia (1996), in the following chapter we investigate the cyclical behavior of the monetary variables in the United States, using the methodology suggested by Finn Kydland and Edward Prescott (1990).

---

[2]The annual growth rates are simple percent quarterly changes at an annual rate — that is, $400 \times (x_t/x_{t-1} - 1)$.

Figure 13.1.   Logged M1 Monetary Aggregates

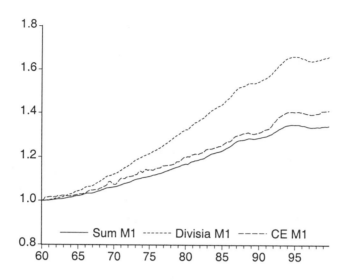

Figure 13.2.   Logged M2 Monetary Aggregates

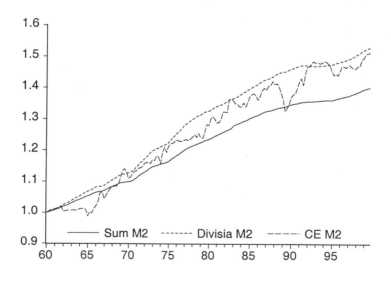

Figure 13.3.   Logged M3 Monetary Aggregates

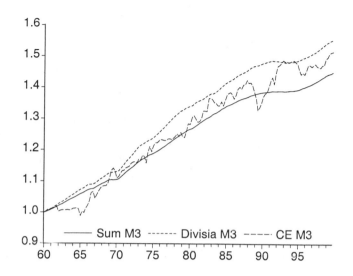

Figure 13.4.   Logged MZM Monetary Aggregates

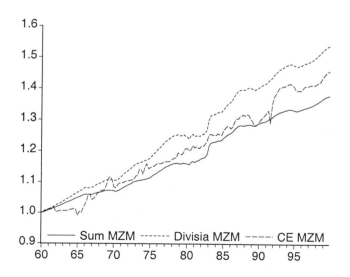

Figure 13.5.   Logged M1 Velocity Aggregates

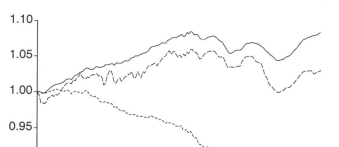

Figure 13.6.   Logged M2 Velocity Aggregates

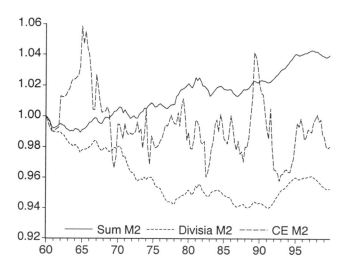

Figure 13.7.   Logged M3 Velocity Aggregates

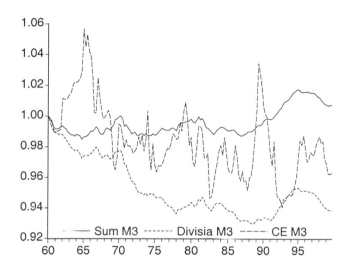

Figure 13.8.   Logged MZM Velocity Aggregates

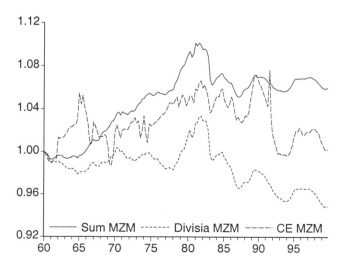

14.1   The Hodrick and Prescott Filter

For a description of the stylized facts, we follow the current practice of detrending the data with the Hodrick-Prescott (HP) filter — see Hodrick and Prescott (1980). For the logarithm of a time series X_t, for $t = 1, 2, \ldots, T$, this procedure defines the (smoothed) *trend* or growth component, denoted τ_t, for $t = 1, 2, \ldots, T$, as the solution to the following minimization problem

$$\min_{\{\tau_t\}_{t=1}^T} \sum_{t=1}^T (X_t - \tau_t)^2$$

subject to

$$\sum_{t=2}^{T-1} [(\tau_{t+1} - \tau_t) - (\tau_t - \tau_{t-1})]^2 \leq \Lambda.$$

That is, the smoothed trend component, $\{\tau_t\}_{t=1}^T$, is obtained by minimizing the sum of squared differences from the data subject to the constraint that the sum of the squared differences be less than an appropriate bound Λ.

The above minimization problem is equivalent to the following unconstrained (minimization) problem

$$\min_{\{\tau_t\}_{t=1}^T} \sum_{t=1}^T (X_t - \tau_t)^2 + \lambda \sum_{t=2}^{T-1} [(\tau_{t+1} - \tau_t) - (\tau_t - \tau_{t-1})]^2$$

for an appropriate value of λ — the Lagrange multiplier. The smaller is λ, the smoother the trend path and when $\lambda = 0$, the linear trend results. In our computations we set $\lambda = 1,600$, as it has been suggested by Kydland and Prescott (1990) for quarterly data. Notice that $X_t - \tau_t$ is the filtered series.

As noted by Kydland and Prescott (1990), the HP filter has several attractive features. In particular, it occupies an intermediate position between the linear filter (which permits most low frequency components to pass through) and the first difference filter (which permits the least). Moreover, the HP trend is a linear transformation of the original series and is a smooth curve — like one that one would draw through a plot of the original series. An illustration of the HP filter, using quarterly real GNP data for the United States, is depicted in Figures 14.1 and 14.2. Figure 14.1 plots the logs of actual and trend real GNP during 1960:1-1999:4 and Figure 14.2 the corresponding percentage deviations from trend of real GNP.

Figure 14.1.   Actual and Trend Logs of U.S. Real GNP

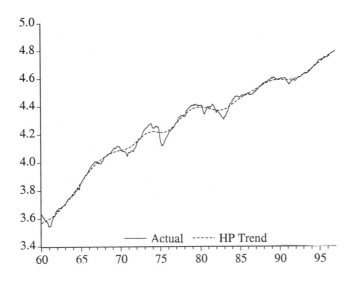

Figure 14.2.   Deviations from Trend of U.S. Real GNP

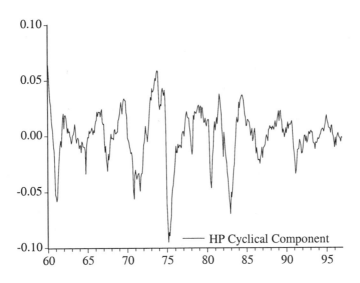

14.2   The Cyclical Behavior of Money

We describe the empirical regularities of the monetary variables, by investigating whether deviations from their HP trends are correlated —

and at what leads and lags — with the cycle. In particular, we measure the degree of comovement of a monetary aggregate with the cycle by the magnitude of the correlation coefficient $\rho(j)$, $j \in \{0, \pm 1, \pm 2, \dots\}$. All the variables are in logarithms (with the exception of the rate variables) and the statistics discussed pertain to variables that have been processed via the Hodrick and Prescott filter — that is, to stationary HP cyclical deviations.

The contemporaneous correlation coefficient — $\rho(0)$ — gives information on the degree of contemporaneous comovement between the monetary series and the cycle. In particular, if $\rho(0)$ is positive, zero, or negative, we say that the series is *procyclical, acyclical,* or *countercyclical,* respectively. In fact, for data samples of this size, it has been suggested [see, for example, Ricardo Fiorito and Tryphon Kollintzas (1994)] that for $0.5 \leq |\rho(0)| < 1$, $0.2 \leq |\rho(0)| < 0.5$, and $0 \leq |\rho(0)| < 0.2$, we say that the series is strongly contemporaneously correlated, weakly contemporaneously correlated, and contemporaneously uncorrelated with the cycle, respectively. Also, $\rho(j)$ $j \in \{\pm 1, \pm 2, \dots\}$ — the cross correlation coefficient — gives information on the phase shift of the monetary series relative to the cycle. If $|\rho(j)|$ is maximum for a positive, zero, or negative j, we say that the series is *leading* the cycle by j periods, is *synchronous,* or is *lagging* the cycle by j periods, respectively.

In Table 14.1 we report contemporaneous correlations as well as cross correlations (at lags and leads of $1, 2, 3, 6, 9,$ and 12 quarters, given the high frequency nature of the data and the traditional view that there are 'long and variable lags' in the relationship between real and monetary variables) between the cyclical components of money and the cyclical component of real GNP. We see that simple-sum and Divisia money is, in general, procyclical (with the broad monetary aggregates being more so than the narrow ones) and leads the cycle.[1] The CE aggregates are generally countercyclical, with CE M2 and CE M3 being strikingly more countercyclical than CE MZM and CE M1.

To investigate the robustness of these results to changes in the cyclical indicator, we report in Table 14.2 correlations (in the same fashion as in Table 14.1) using the unemployment rate as an indicator of the cycle. The seasonally adjusted unemployment rate includes all workers (including resident armed forces). Of course, since the cyclical compo-

---

[1] Recall that a variable leads the cycle if its cross-correlations with future real GNP are larger (in absolute value) than the contemporaneous correlation. Similarly, a variable is lagging the cycle if its cross-correlations with lagged real GNP are larger (in absolute value) than the contemporaneous correlation.

Table 14.1. Hodrick-Prescott Cyclical Correlations of Money Measures With Real GNP

Series	$\rho(M_t, Y_{t+j})$, $j = -12, -9, -6, -3, -2, -1, 0, 1, 2, 3, 6, 9, 12$												
	$j=-12$	$j=-9$	$j=-6$	$j=-3$	$j=-2$	$j=-1$	$j=0$	$j=1$	$j=2$	$j=3$	$j=6$	$j=9$	$j=12$
Sum M1	−.13	−.08	−.11	−.04	.03	.10	.18	.21	.21	.18	.08	−.02	−.09
Divisia M1	−.11	−.09	−.12	−.05	.01	.07	.14	.16	.15	.12	.06	−.00	−.07
CE M1	−.05	−.00	−.05	−.01	.00	−.03	−.05	−.05	−.07	−.06	−.00	−.01	−.07
Sum M2	−.08	−.29	−.36	−.11	.02	.19	.37	.49	.53	.51	.27	−.06	−.26
Divisia M2	−.09	−.22	−.19	.09	.21	.33	.46	.52	.53	.47	.20	−.15	−.32
CE M2	.19	.18	.10	−.09	−.16	−.21	−.25	−.27	−.27	−.23	−.03	.01	.05
Sum M3	−.13	−.12	−.03	.22	.30	.37	.43	.42	.38	.29	.01	−.26	−.40
Divisia M3	−.19	−.19	−.04	.28	.38	.46	.53	.54	.50	.40	.05	−.29	−.42
CE M3	−.22	.17	.03	−.19	−.27	−.32	−.34	−.31	−.26	−.18	.08	.10	.09
Sum MZM	−.21	−.32	−.46	−.33	−.21	−.04	.18	.36	.47	.52	.44	.22	−.01
Divisia MZM	−.25	−.30	−.39	−.24	−.11	.05	.26	.43	.53	.55	.42	.16	−.08
CE MZM	.03	.06	−.01	−.04	−.02	−.02	−.01	−.01	−.05	−.06	−.03	−.00	−.03

NOTE: Sample period, quarterly data: 1960:1 – 1999:4

Table 14.2. Hodrick-Prescott Cyclical Correlations of Money Measures With the Unemployment Rate

$\rho(M_t, u_{t+j})$, $j = -12, -9, -6, -3, -2, -1, 0, 1, 2, 3, 6, 9, 12$

Series	$j=-12$	$j=-9$	$j=-6$	$j=-3$	$j=-2$	$j=-1$	$j=0$	$j=1$	$j=2$	$j=3$	$j=6$	$j=9$	$j=12$
Sum M1	.19	.22	.22	.13	.05	-.05	-.17	-.27	-.32	-.33	-.25	-.08	.05
Divisia M1	.17	.23	.23	.15	.07	-.02	-.13	-.21	-.25	-.26	-.21	-.09	.01
CE M1	.02	.08	.14	.11	.08	.07	.05	.01	-.02	-.06	-.10	-.08	.00
Sum M2	-.09	.21	.38	.29	.19	.04	-.16	-.33	-.45	-.49	-.34	-.01	.22
Divisia M2	-.05	.16	.19	.02	-.07	-.18	-.31	-.41	-.45	-.45	-.24	.10	.30
CE M2	-.17	-.09	-.03	.12	.18	.25	.27	.27	.25	.19	-.01	-.09	-.12
Sum M3	.03	.10	.06	-.11	-.18	-.24	-.31	-.34	-.33	-.28	-.03	.22	.38
Divisia M3	.06	.16	.05	-.20	-.28	-.35	-.42	-.45	-.44	-.39	-.08	.26	.41
CE M3	-.21	-.11	.02	.22	.30	.37	.38	.35	.28	.19	-.11	-.18	-.18
Sum MZM	.13	.33	.52	.50	.39	.23	-.01	-.23	-.41	-.53	-.54	-.31	.09
Divisia MZM	.19	.35	.47	.41	.29	.12	-.11	-.33	-.49	-.59	-.55	-.26	-.02
CE MZM	.02	.06	.09	.13	.13	.11	.05	.00	-.03	-.06	-.06	-.07	-.06

NOTE: Sample period, quarterly data: 1960:1 - 1999:4

nent of real GNP and the unemployment rate are negatively correlated, a negative correlation in Table 14.2 indicates procyclical variation and a positive correlation indicates countercyclical variation. Clearly, the results in Table 14.2 strongly confirm those in Table 14.1 except that the simple-sum and Divisia aggregates appear to be less procyclical and the CE aggregates more countercyclical than when real GNP is used as the cyclical indicator.

We interpret these results as being generally consistent with the cyclical money behavior in the U.S. reported by Kydland and Prescott (1990) and Belongia (1996). Unlike Belongia (1996), and in line with Serletis and Krause (1996), however, we find no significant differences across narrow simple-sum and Divisia monetary aggregates. We find strong contemporaneous correlations between broad simple-sum and Divisia money and each of the cyclical indicators. These results illustrate some significant differences across simple-sum, Divisia, and currency equivalent monetary aggregates and appear to support a monetary effect of simple-sum and Divisia money on real GNP.

14.3   Prices, Interest Rates, and Velocity

While we are investigating nominal stylized facts, we also describe the statistical properties of the cyclical components of the price level (measured by the GNP deflator) and two short-term nominal interest rates (to deal with anomalies that arise because of different ways of measuring financial market price information) — the Treasury bill rate and the federal funds rate. The Treasury bill rate is the interest rate on short-term unsecured borrowing by the U.S. government whereas the fed funds rate is the interest rate on fed funds. Again, with the exception of the rate variables, all the other variables are in logarithms. Table 14.3 reports HP cyclical correlations of prices and short-term nominal interest rates with each of real GNP (panel A) and the unemployment rate (panel B).

Irrespective of the cyclical indicator, we see that the price level is strongly countercyclical (with the countercyclicality being more pronounced when real GNP is used as the measure of the cycle), whereas both the Treasury bill rate and the fed funds rate are strongly procyclical and lag the cycle. These results provide strong confirmation for the countercyclical price behavior in the U.S. reported by Kydland and Prescott (1990), Thomas Cooley and Lee Ohanian (1991), David Backus and Patrick Kehoe (1992), Todd Smith (1992), and Bankim Chadha and Eswar Prasad (1994). They clearly support the Kydland and Prescott (1990) claim that the perceived fact of procyclical prices is but a myth.

Table 14.4. Hodrick-Prescott Cyclical Correlations of Velocity of Money Measures With Real GNP

| | $\rho(V_t, Y_{t+j})$, $j = -12, -9, -6, -3, -2, -1, 0, 1, 2, 3, 6, 9, 12$ | | | | | | | | | | | | |
Series	$j = -12$	$j = -9$	$j = -6$	$j = -3$	$j = -2$	$j = -1$	$j = 0$	$j = 1$	$j = 2$	$j = 3$	$j = 6$	$j = 9$	$j = 12$
Sum M1	.02	.03	.10	.20	.23	.24	.22	.08	-.05	-.14	-.25	-.16	-.04
Divisia M1	.03	.04	.11	.17	.17	.17	.14	.03	-.05	-.10	-.18	-.10	-.01
CE M1	-.12	-.05	.03	.10	.14	.22	.30	.23	.18	.09	-.09	-.08	-.00
Sum M2	-.10	.17	.30	.36	.39	.38	.34	.06	-.18	-.36	-.50	-.23	-.01
Divisia M2	-.04	.19	.23	.17	.16	.14	.09	-.14	-.32	-.44	-.44	-.10	.13
CE M2	-.21	-.20	-.12	-.10	.20	.28	.35	.34	.32	.25	.00	-.04	-.07
Sum M3	-.04	.06	.05	.11	.17	.24	.28	.09	-.09	-.23	-.32	-.07	.14
Divisia M3	.07	.17	.09	-.03	-.03	-.03	-.03	-.20	-.33	-.41	-.30	.06	.26
CE M3	-.24	-.19	-.05	.20	.30	.38	.42	.37	.30	.20	-.10	-.12	-.10
Sum MZM	.13	.28	.44	.43	.37	.26	.11	-.15	-.34	-.47	-.54	-.33	-.08
Divisia MZM	.20	.29	.40	.32	.24	.12	-.06	-.29	-.45	-.55	-.52	-.24	.02
CE MZM	-.06	-.09	-.02	.06	.08	.11	.13	.11	.11	.09	-.01	-.04	-.01

NOTE: Sample period, quarterly data: 1960:1 - 1999:4.

Table 14.5.   Hodrick-Prescott Cyclical Correlations of Velocity of Money Measures With the Unemployment Rate

Series	$\rho(V_t, u_{t+j})$, $j = -12, -9, -6, -3, -2, -1, 0, 1, 2, 3, 6, 9, 12$												
	$j=-12$	$j=-9$	$j=-6$	$j=-3$	$j=-2$	$j=-1$	$j=0$	$j=1$	$j=2$	$j=3$	$j=6$	$j=9$	$j=12$
Sum M1	−.07	−.13	−.19	−.24	−.25	−.24	−.19	−.07	.06	.19	.37	.25	.08
Divisia M1	−.08	−.16	−.21	−.23	−.21	−.19	−.12	−.02	.08	.18	.30	.19	.06
CE M1	.06	−.00	−.11	−.16	−.19	−.24	−.27	−.21	−.13	−.03	.16	.17	.07
Sum M2	.23	−.06	−.31	−.43	−.47	−.50	−.43	−.24	−.01	.21	.51	.31	.03
Divisia M2	.17	−.09	−.22	−.22	−.23	−.24	−.18	−.03	.14	.30	.45	.16	−.11
CE M2	.18	.12	.06	−.11	−.20	−.30	−.34	−.33	−.30	−.22	.03	.11	.14
Sum M3	.13	.01	−.08	−.13	−.20	−.29	−.32	−.23	−.09	.07	.29	.13	−.12
Divisia M3	.05	−.10	−.10	−.00	−.02	−.05	−.04	.06	.18	.28	.31	−.01	−.25
CE M3	.22	.13	.01	−.21	−.31	−.41	−.44	−.41	−.33	−.22	.12	.20	.19
Sum MZM	−.06	−.27	−.49	−.55	−.50	−.41	−.23	−.00	.23	.42	.60	.41	.17
Divisia MZM	−.14	−.31	−.46	−.46	−.39	−.27	−.07	.16	.37	.54	.62	.35	.08
CE MZM	.01	−.02	−.06	−.14	−.16	−.18	−.15	−.10	−.05	.01	.09	.11	.09

NOTE: Sample period, quarterly data: 1960:1 - 1999:4.

Chapter 15

The Nonparametric Approach to the Demand for Monetary Assets

In Chapter 12 we showed the steps that are normally taken to reduce a very general consumer choice problem to a monetary asset choice problem. At this point, we are prepared to proceed and develop the microeconomic- and aggregation-theoretic literature on the demand for money and monetary assets. This is achieved by conducting the analysis within a microtheoretical framework, making use of a number of theoretical advances in a set of related theories — revealed preference, index numbers, duality, separability, and demand systems.

The standard approach to applied demand analysis is *parametric*, in the sense that it postulates parametric forms for the utility function and fits the derived demand functions to observed data. The estimated demand functions can then be tested for consistency with the utility-maximizing hypothesis underlying the model, used to estimate price and substitution elasticities, or used to forecast behavior for other price configurations. As Hal Varian (1982, p. 945) puts it, this approach "will be satisfactory only when the postulated parametric forms are good approximations to the 'true' demand functions."

THEOREM 15.2 *The following conditions are equivalent: (1) there exists a nonsatiated homothetic utility function that rationalizes the data; (2) the data satisfies HARP: for all distinct choices of indexes $(i, j, \cdots, m)$ we have*

$$\left(p^i x^j\right)\left(p^j x^k\right) \cdots \left(p^m x^i\right) \geq 1;$$

(3) there exist numbers $U^i > 0$, $i = 1, \cdots, T$ such that

$$U^i \leq U^j p^j x^i,$$

for $i, j = 1, ..., T$; (4) there exists a concave, monotonic, continuous, nonsatiated, homothetic utility function that rationalizes the data.

15.4   Direct Separability

The notion of separability is of considerable importance, because it provides a means of justifying the use of monetary aggregates. It also resolves the statistical problem caused by the lack of degrees of freedom, since it rationalizes the estimation of a smaller set of demand equations when one takes a parametric approach to demand analysis (as we shall do in the rest of this book). In the context of preference structures there are different separability concepts, giving rise to both different grouping patterns and different behavioral implications.[1] Here we deal with the utility relation expressed in the direct form.

Let $I = (1, 2, \cdots, n)$ be a set of integers that identify the variables over which preferences are defined and consider the partition of I into two subsets

$$I = \{I^c, I^r\}$$

such that $I^c \cup I^r = I$, $I^c \cap I^r = \emptyset$, $I^c \neq \emptyset$, and $I^r \neq \emptyset$. Corresponding to the binary partition I, denote vectors in Ω^n in ways that reflect the partition. In particular, express Ω^n as a Cartesian product of the subspaces

$$\Omega^n = \Omega^{(c)} \times \Omega^{(r)}$$

with the dimensions of $\Omega^{(c)}$ and $\Omega^{(r)}$ given by the cardinalities of I^c and I^r, respectively. An asset vector, $x \in \Omega^n$, can be written as $x = (x^c, x^r)$ and if the ith asset is in the rth category, then x_i is a component of

---

[1] For a good exposition of alternative forms of separability and their behavioral implications, see S. Pudney (1981).

the vector $\boldsymbol{x}^r \in \Omega^{(r)}$. Consider the following definition, adapted from Blackorby, Primont, and Russell (1978).[2]

DEFINITION 15.5 *I^r is weakly separable in $f(\boldsymbol{x})$ if and only if there exist functions*

$$f^r : \Omega^{(r)} \to \mathbb{R}$$

and

$$\overline{f} : \Omega^{(r)} \times \mathcal{R}(f^r) \to \mathbb{R},$$

where $\mathcal{R}(f^r)$ is the range of f^r, such that

$$f(\boldsymbol{x}) = \overline{f}(\boldsymbol{x}^c, f^r(\boldsymbol{x}^r)),$$

where $\overline{f}$ is strictly inreasing in $f^r(\boldsymbol{x}^r)$.

According to this theorem, $f(\boldsymbol{x})$ is called the *parent function*, $\overline{f}(\boldsymbol{x}^c, f^r(\boldsymbol{x}^r))$ the *macro function*, and $f^r(\boldsymbol{x}^r)$ the *aggregator function*. The requirement of weak separability is that the marginal rate of substitution between any two assets in a separable component group be invariant with respect to any asset outside the group. Algebraically, assets i and j are separable from asset k, if and only if

$$\frac{\partial}{\partial x_k}\left(\frac{f_i(\boldsymbol{x})}{f_j(\boldsymbol{x})}\right) = 0, \quad \forall \boldsymbol{x} \in \Omega^n,$$

where $f_i(\boldsymbol{x})$ is the marginal utility of asset i and $f_j(\boldsymbol{x})$ the marginal utility of asset j. Equivalently, assets i and j are separable from asset k if and only if

$$\frac{f_{ik}(\boldsymbol{x})}{f_i(\boldsymbol{x})} = \frac{f_{jk}(\boldsymbol{x})}{f_j(\boldsymbol{x})},$$

which is the explicit differential statement of the previous equation and $f_{ik}(\boldsymbol{x})$ and $f_{jk}(\boldsymbol{x})$ are the cross partial derivatives. Note that a sufficient condition for weak separability is perfect substitutability. Under perfect substitutability, the ratio of marginal utilities is constant and hence invariant to any asset change.

If the utility function $f(\boldsymbol{x})$ is weakly separable in $\boldsymbol{x}^r$, its value does not depend on the elements of $\boldsymbol{x}^r$ individually, but rather on the quantity

---

[2] Blackorby, Primont, and Russell (1978) should be consulted as a definite source concerning separability, duality, and functional structure.

index $f^r(x^r)$. As we discussed in Chapter 12, weak separability implies a sequential expenditure allocation, where in the first stage the consumer divides expenditures on x^c and x^r, and then decides the optimal allocation of expenditure among the elements of x^r independently of the choices of the elements of x^c. In other words, when the function $f(x)$ is weakly separable in x^r, the econometrician can estimate a separable demand system in the assets of x^r, disregarding the assets in x^c.

Varian (1982, 1983) provides two tests of weak separability. The first test, which is the weaker of the two, is a test of the necessary conditions for weak separability. It checks if the subdata in group r satisfy GARP. In particular, since each observation in group r must solve the problem

$$\max_{x^r} f^r(x^r) \quad \text{subject to} \quad p^r x^r \geq p^r x,$$

it is necessary for separability that Afriat numbers exist for the data in x^r. Otherwise the aggregator function $f^r(x^r)$ does not exist. The second, stronger test checks necessary and sufficient conditions for weak separability. It does so, by checking if the Afriat numbers for the aggregator function $f^r(x^r)$ are consistent with those for the parent function $f(x)$. The following theorem from Varian (1983) states the relationship precisely.

THEOREM 15.3 *The following conditions are equivalent: (1) there exists a weakly separable concave, monotonic, continuous, nonsatiated utility function that rationalizes the data; (2) there exist numbers $U^i, W^i, \lambda^i > 0, \mu^i > 0, i = 1, \cdots, T$ that satisfy:*

$$U^i \leq U^j + \lambda^j p^j (x^i - x^j) + \frac{\lambda^j}{\mu^j} (W^i - W^j),$$

$$W^i \leq W^j + \mu^j q^j (z^i - z^j),$$

for $i, j = 1, ..., T$; (3)   the data $(q^j z^j)$ and $(p^i, 1/\mu^i; x^i, W^i)$ satisfy GARP for some choices of (W^i, μ^i) that satisfy the Afriat inequalities.

Note that part 2 of the theorem provides the means for testing the necessary and sufficient conditions for direct weak separability — clearly one must construct two sets of interrelated Afriat numbers.

15.5   Indirect Separability

The utility function $f(x)$ introduced above is *direct* — it has the actual quantities of liquid assets used, $x_i, i = 1, ..., n$, as arguments. Alternatively, preferences may be represented by the indirect utility function, which indicates the indifference curve attainable at prices p and total expenditure m. In particular, the utility maximization problem

$$\max_{x} f(x) \quad \text{subject to} \quad p'x = m,$$

can be reformulated equivalently as

$$\max_{x} f(x) \quad \text{subject to} \quad \sum_{i=1}^{n} v_i x_i = 1. \tag{15.1}$$

where $v_i = p_i/m$, $i = 1, ..., n$ denotes 'expenditure-normalized' user costs. In this reformulated version, the maximization problem has two sets of n variables: monetary asset services, with values $x = (x_1, ..., x_n)$, and normalized monetary asset user costs, with values $v = (v_1, ..., v_n)$.

As we shall see in the next chapter, the solution to (15.1) is the system of demand functions

$$x_i = x_i(v_1, ..., v_n), \quad i = 1, ..., n. \tag{15.2}$$

Substituting solution (15.2) into the objective function yields the maximum attainable utility given normalized monetary asset user costs

$$V(v) = V\left(x_1(v), ..., x_n(v) \right),$$

where $V(v)$ is quasi convex, continuous, and decreasing. The function $V(v)$ reflects the fact that utility depends indirectly on prices and income rather than on quantities. For this reason, $V(v)$ is called the *indirect utility function*.

The important thing is that the direct utility function and the indirect utility function are equivalent representations of the underlying preference ordering. However, a structural property of the direct utility function does not imply the same property of the indirect utility function. The point to be stressed here is that the behavioral implications of direct separability are different from those of indirect separability. Let's consider the following definition of indirect weak separability.

DEFINITION 15.6 *I^r is weakly separable in $V(v)$ from I^c if and only if there exist continuous functions*

$$V^r : \Omega_+^{(r)} \to \mathbb{R}$$

and

$$\overline{V} : \Omega_+^{(c)} \times \mathcal{R}(V^r) \to \mathbb{R},$$

where $\mathcal{R}(V^r)$ is the range of V^r, such that

$$V(v) = \overline{V}(v^c, V^r(v^r)),$$

where $\overline{V}$ is nondecreasing in $V^r(v^r)$.

The algebraic requirement of indirect weak separability is that

$$\frac{\partial}{\partial v_k}\left(\frac{V_i(v)}{V_j(v)}\right) = 0, \quad \forall v \in \Omega^n,$$

or using Roy's identity (to be discussed in detail in the next chapter)

$$\frac{\partial}{\partial v_k}\left(\frac{x_i(v)}{x_j(v)}\right) = 0.$$

Also, since $V(v) = V(p, m)$, due to homogeneity of degree zero in p and m, the last equation can be rewritten as

$$\frac{\partial}{\partial p_k}\left(\frac{x_i(v)}{x_j(v)}\right) = 0,$$

which implies that the optimal asset ratios in I^r are independent of the kth price. Equivalently, the above can be written as

$$x_j(v)\left(\frac{\partial x_i(v)}{\partial p_k}\right) = x_i(v)\left(\frac{\partial x_j(v)}{\partial p_k}\right)$$

or

$$\eta_{ik} = \eta_{jk}, \tag{15.3}$$

where η_{ik} and η_{jk} are the cross price elasticities of assets i and j with respect to the kth price, respectively. Hence, indirect weak separability implies an equality restriction on the cross price elasticities.

15.6   Homothetic Separability

Separability is a characteristic of functional structure that does not necessarily carry over from direct to indirect utility functions. In particular, a separable direct utility function implies a different preference ordering than a separable indirect utility function. However, Lau (1970) has shown that if the direct utility function is homothetically separable, then the indirect utility function will have the same structure with respect to normalized prices. Hence, testing for homothetic separability is of considerable practical interest, since homothetic separability is a sufficient condition for simultaneous separability of $f(x)$ and $V(v)$.

Moreover, direct separability establishes only a necessary condition for aggregation in its simplest form. In particular, if we wish to measure the subaggregate $f^r(\boldsymbol{x}^r)$ using the most elementary method, we would require the additional assumption that $f^r(\boldsymbol{x}^r)$ be homothetic. In fact, homothetic weak separability is necessary and sufficient for the existence of the simplified form of subaggregation. Let us now define homothetic separability of the direct utility function.

DEFINITION 15.7 *I^r is homothetically weakly separable in $f(\boldsymbol{x})$ if and only if there exist functions*

$$f^r : \Omega^{(r)} \to \mathbb{R}$$

and

$$\overline{f} : \Omega^{(r)} \times \mathcal{R}(f^r) \to \mathbb{R},$$

where $\mathcal{R}(f^r)$ is the range of f^r, such that

$$f(\boldsymbol{x}) = \overline{f}(\boldsymbol{x}^c, f^r(\boldsymbol{x}^r)),$$

where $\overline{f}$ is nondecreasing in $f^r(\boldsymbol{x}^r)$ and $f^r(\boldsymbol{x}^r)$ is homothetic.

Varian (1983) provides the following theorem to test for direct homothetic separability, based on the Diewert and Celik Parkan (1978) suggested procedure.

THEOREM 15.4 *The following conditions are equivalent: (1) there exists a homothetically weakly separable, concave, monotonic, continuous, nonsatiated utility function that rationalizes the data; (2) the data $\left(\boldsymbol{p}^i, 1/W^i; \boldsymbol{x}^i, W^i\right)$ satisfy GARP for some choices of W^i that satisfies the homotheticity inequalities; (3) there exist numbers $U^i, W^i, \lambda^i > 0$, $i = 1, \cdots, T$ that satisfy*

$$U^i \leq U^j + \lambda^j \boldsymbol{p}^j (\boldsymbol{x}^i - \boldsymbol{x}^j) + \frac{\lambda^j}{W^j}(W^i - W^j),$$

$$W^i \leq W^j \boldsymbol{q}^j \boldsymbol{z}^j$$

for $i, j = 1, ..., T$.

15.7 NONPAR Tests of Consumer Behavior

GARP, homotheticity, direct separability, and direct homothetic separability are quite simple to test, using Varian's nonparametric (NONPAR) computational package. As we have argued, this approach to

Chapter 16

The Parametric Approach to the Demand for Monetary Assets

The parametric approach to applied demand analysis involves postulating parametric forms for the utility function and then fitting the resulting demand functions to a finite number of observations on consumer behavior. As we argued earlier, this approach will be satisfactory only when the postulated parametric forms are good approximations to the generating demand functions. Our approach in this chapter addresses the question of how to derive a set of demand functions for monetary assets from a framework in which the representative asset holder maximizes the monetary services utility function $f(x)$, subject to the budget constraint. We will state the problem first and then show why and how duality theory might be employed explicitly in the rationalization of estimable demand functions.

16.1 The Direct Utility Approach

In chapter 12 we saw that the neoclassical monetary problem is that of choosing a bundle of monetary services, given the utility function and the budget constraint. So the problem is

indirect utility function has prices exogenous in explaining consumer behavior. Moreover, we can easily derive the demand system by straightforward differentiation, without having to solve a system of simultaneous
equations (as is the case with the direct utility function approach).

In particular, a result known as *Roy's identity*

$$x_i = -\frac{\partial V(v)}{\partial p_i} \bigg/ \frac{\partial V(v)}{\partial m}, \quad i = 1, \dots, n,$$

allows us to derive the demand system, provided, of course, that $p_i > 0$
and $m > 0$. Alternatively, we can apply the 'logarithmic form' of Roy's
identity

$$s_i = -\frac{\partial \log V(v)}{\partial \log p_i} \bigg/ \frac{\partial \log V(v)}{\partial \log m}, \quad i = 1, \dots, n, \tag{16.5}$$

to derive the budget share equations, where $s_i = p_i x_i / m$ is the budget
share of the ith asset.

16.3   The HTL Demand System

As an example of how we can use the framework to get a set of equations that we can estimate, consider the *homothetic translog* (HTL) form
— the simplest member of the translog family of flexible functional forms
— for the indirect utility function $V(v)$. The homothetic translog indirect utility function is given by[3]

$$\log V(v) = \alpha_0 + \sum_{i=1}^{n} \alpha_i \log v_i + \frac{1}{2} \sum_{i=1}^{n} \sum_{j=1}^{n} \beta_{ij} \log v_i \log v_j,$$

---

[3] Recall that a homothetic function is a positive monotonic transformation of a linearly homogeneous (i.e., homogeneous of degree 1) function. That is, $f(x)$ is homothetic if and only
if we can write $f(x) = h(g(x))$, where $g(x)$ is linearly homogeneous and $h(\cdot)$ is a monotonic
function. Notice that since any monotonic transformation of a utility function implies the
same preference ordering, a homothetic preference ordering can be equivalently represented
by a linearly homogeneous utility function.

with the following restrictions (to be discussed in more detail later in this book) imposed

$$\beta_{ij} = \beta_{ji}, \quad \text{for all } i, j,$$

$$\sum_{i=1}^{n} \beta_{ij} = 0, \quad \text{for all } j,$$

$$\sum_{i=1}^{n} \alpha_i = 1.$$

This function is a generalization of the Cobb-Douglas function and reduces to it when all β_i are equal to zero.[4]

Application of Roy's identity in share form, equation (16.5) yields a set of share equations for the homothetic translog

$$s_i = \alpha_i + \sum_{j=1}^{n} \beta_{ij} \log v_j, \quad i = 1, ..., n,$$

With n assets, the n homothetic translog share equations have $n(n+3)/2$ parameters to be estimated. For example, let us assume that there are only three assets ($n = 3$). In this three-asset case the homothetic translog share equations become

$$s_1 = \alpha_1 + \beta_{11} \log v_1 + \beta_{12} \log v_2 + \beta_{13} \log v_3,$$

$$s_2 = \alpha_2 + \beta_{12} \log v_1 + \beta_{22} \log v_2 + \beta_{23} \log v_3,$$

$$s_3 = \alpha_1 + \beta_{13} \log v_1 + \beta_{23} \log v_2 + \beta_{33} \log v_3,$$

and have 9 parameters, α_1, α_2, α_3, β_{11}, β_{12}, β_{13}, β_{22}, β_{23}, and β_{33}.

Budget share equation systems, such as the above for the three-asset homothetic translog, are what are typically estimated. Once the parameters of the indirect utility function are estimated, we can move directly

---

[4] In fact, when all β_i are equal to zero, the homothetic translog decays to

$$\log V(v) = \alpha_0 + \sum_{i=1}^{n} \alpha_i \log v_i,$$

which is the Cobb-Douglas, written in logs.

to calculations of income and price elasticities and the elasticities of substitution. We will consider the empirical implementation of such systems later in this book.

16.4   Dimension Reduction

There is an immediate problem with the procedure just laid out. It is the difficult problem of estimating monetary asset demand systems when there is a large number of assets. In particular, if n is large, the estimation of a highly disaggregated demand system encompassing the full range of assets is econometrically intractable, because of computational difficulties in the large parameter space.[5]

In such cases, the number of variables can be reduced, in a large number of *ad hoc* ways, by assuming separability and using Divisia subaggregate indexes. We can assume, for example, in accordance with the Federal Reserve Board's *a priori* assignment of monetary assets to monetary aggregates, that the monetary services utility function $f(x)$ has the strongly recursive separable form[6]

$$f(x) = f^4(x^4, f^3(x^3, f^2(x^2, f^1(x^1)))),$$

where the components of x^1 are those that are included in the Fed's M1 monetary aggregate, the components of x^2 are those of the Board's M2 aggregate net of x^1, the components of x^3 are those of the Board's M3 aggregate net of x^1 and x^2, and the components of x^4 are those of the Boards L aggregate net of x^1, x^2, and x^3.

Each aggregator function f^r, $r = 1, ..., 4$, has two rather natural (mutually consistent) interpretations. On one hand it can be thought of as a (specific) category utility function; on the other hand, it may be interpreted as a subaggregate measure of monetary services. In the latter case, the aggregator functions f^r, $r = 1, ..., 4$ are the Board's functional monetary aggregates M1, M2, M3 and L, respectively. In particular, if

---

[5] In the United States, for example, the Federal Reserve Board's L monetary aggregate contains 26 monetary assets — see Anderson, Jones, and Nesmith (1997, Table 2) for details. If we were to deal with a homothetic translog demand system encompassing all 26 liquid assets, the share equations would contain $n(n+3)/2 = 377$ parameters. It is not feasible, for *degrees of freedom* reasons, to estimate that many parameters.

[6] The algebraic requirement of *strong recursive separability* is that

$$\frac{\partial}{\partial x_k} \left(\frac{f_i(x)}{f_j(x)} \right) = 0,$$

for every $i \in I^r$, $j \in I^s$, $k \in I^t$, $t > r, s$. This implies that the marginal rate of substitution between, say, an asset in x^1 and an asset in x^2 is independent of assets in x^3 and x^4.

Q_1 is the monetary aggregate for the components of M1, Q_2 for M2, Q_3 for M3, and Q_4 for L, then it follows that[7]

$$Q_1 = f^1(x^1);$$

$$Q_2 = f^2(x^2, f^1(x^1)) = f^2(x^2, Q_1);$$

$$Q_3 = f^3(x^3, f^2(x^2, f^1(x^1))) = f^3(x^3, Q_2);$$

$$Q_4 = f^4(x^4, f^3(x^3, f^2(x^2, f^1(x^1)))) = f^4(x^4, Q_3).$$

To focus on the details of demand for services of money and liquid assets at different levels of aggregation, one can assume a recursively decentralized decision-making process, reflected in the solution to the following optimizing problems,

$$\max_{x^r, Q_{r-1}} f^r(x^r, Q_{r-1}),$$

subject to

$$p^r x^r + P_{r-1}Q_{r-1} = P_r Q_r,$$

for $r = 4, 3, 2$, where P_r is the Divisia price aggregate corresponding to the Divisia quantity aggregate Q_r. Thus the allocation of expenditure between the assets within the rth group and the $(r-1)$th monetary aggregate may be carried out optimally knowing only the prices within the rth group, the price index of the $(r-1)$th monetary aggregate, and the optimal expenditure on Q_r (being passed down recursively from the previous stage constrained maximization).

This system of optimization problems reflects a sequential budgeting procedure, similar to the two-stage budgeting procedure discussed in Chapter 12. Although the consumer is making the decentralization decisions from the top of the tree down, one can estimate conditional money demand models at successive levels of aggregation recursively, from the bottom up. This approach to the recursive estimation of utility trees has been developed by Barnett (1977) and Ronald Anderson (1979), and has been applied to the demand for money problem by Serletis (1991a).

---

[7]Of course, the actual numbers produced by the official monetary aggregates require the restrictive assumptions that f^r, $r = 1, ..., 4$, and hence $f(x)$ itself, are all simple summations.

It should be obvious that strong recursive separability is a 'strong' assumption and that the the Fed's (and most other central banks') present practice of having this sort of structure is entirely unrealistic, and therefore not suitable for applied econometric work. In fact, one of the objectives of empirical demand analysis is to discover the structure of preferences. That is, instead of imposing a grouping pattern on the model, as is the case with most central banks' *a priori* assignment of monetary assets to monetary aggregates, the structure of preferences over monetary assets could be discovered by actually testing for weakly separable subgroups. We feel that separability-based modeling of the demand for liquid assets is an area for potentially productive future research. This matter is the subject of Chapter 20.

16.5   Duality and Functional Structure

There is another issue to be discussed, which is ultimately related to the uncertainty about the 'true structure' of preferences. We have argued that the structure of preferences can be represented by either a direct or an indirect utility function, with the latter being more easily approached because it simplifies the estimation considerably, since it has prices exogenous in explaining consumer behavior. However, a structural property of the direct utility function does not imply the same property on the indirect utility function, and in order to implement a model of demand based on the indirect function that satisfies properties of the direct function, a correspondence between direct and indirect properties is needed.

Although nonhomothetic direct and indirect separable utility functions are distinct structures, as we mentioned in Chapter 14, Lau (1970) showed that if the direct utility function is weakly separable with homothetic aggregator functions then the indirect utility function will have the same structure with respect to (expenditure-normalized) prices. Moreover, Blackorby, David Nissen, Primont, and Russell (1974) show that if the direct utility function is strongly recursively separable with homothetic aggregator functions then the indirect utility function will have the same structure with respect to normalized prices.[8]

The choice of homothetic indirect utility functions in some of the empirical work [such as, for example, Serletis (1991a, 1991b)] has been primarily motivated by these considerations. That is, it is motivated

---

[8] The above results also apply to *quasi-homothetic* (i.e., homothetic to a point other than the origin) preferences — see Gorman (1970) for an extensive treatment of quasi-homotheticity.

by the need to maintain a correspondence between direct and indirect utility function properties.

16.6   Conclusion

We have developed the systems approach to the demand for liquid assets, paying explicit attention to the increasingly obvious tradeoff that exists between theoretical purity and econometric simplicity. The reader should also note that the nonparametric and parametric approaches to applied demand analysis are not mutually exclusive. For example, one can test the data with GARP to find subsets that are consistent with utility maximization and then estimate parametric demand functions imposing the utility maximization restrictions (to be discussed in detail in Chapter 19).

Clearly, the use in recent years of the simple representative consumer paradigm in monetary economics has opened the door to the succeeding introduction into monetary economics of the entire microfoundations, aggregation theory, and micro-econometrics literatures. This new literature is actually an ongoing one and has only just begun to produce empirical results worthy of the effort required to understand it. In the following chapter we emphasize the contribution that can be made by using alternative functional forms for demand systems.

Chapter 17

Flexible Functional Forms and Demand Systems

For many years, econometricians used *globally regular functional* forms such as the Cobb-Douglas and the Constant Elasticity of Substitution (CES) forms to approximate the generating functions (such as, for example, direct utility, indirect utility, production, and cost functions) of neoclassical microeconomic theory. Such functional forms satisfy everywhere the theoretical regularity conditions for rational neoclassical economic behavior, but do not provide the capability to attain arbitrary elasticities of substitution.

In recent years a number of empirical studies have made use of the *flexible* functional forms method to approximate aggregator functions. A flexible functional form is an approximation to an arbitrary function, with parameters that can be chosen to make the value of the first and second derivatives of the approximation equal to the first and second derivatives of the true function at any point — see Diewert (1973a) for more details. In what follows we provide a theoretical comparison of a number of popular flexible functional forms by grouping them into three sets that have broadly similar characteristics. These are (i) *locally flexible* forms, (ii) *effectively globally regular* forms, and (iii) *asymptotically globally flexible* forms.

17.1   Locally Flexible Forms

We begin with three of the most popular flexible functional forms — the *generalized Leontief*, the *translog*, and the *almost ideal demand system*. These forms provide the capability to approximate systems resulting from a broad class of generating functions and also to attain arbitrary elasticities of substitution — although at only one point. They have, however, very small regions of theoretical regularity, as we shall discuss in the sequel.

17.1.1   The Generalized Leontief

The generalized Leontief (GL) model is based on the GL indirect utility function, due to Diewert (1971), which can be written as

$$h(\boldsymbol{v}) = \alpha_0 + \sum_{i=1}^{n} \alpha_i v_i^{1/2} + \frac{1}{2} \sum_{i=1}^{n} \sum_{j=1}^{n} \beta_{ij} v_i^{1/2} v_j^{1/2},$$

where v_i is the expenditure-normalized price for asset i. A sufficient condition for global regularity is that $\beta_{ij} > 0$, $\alpha_i > 0$ for all i and j — in this case the GL is a sum of concave functions. Douglas Caves and Laurits Christensen (1980) have shown that the GL has satisfactory local properties when preferences are nearly homothetic and substitution is low, implying that the GL can approximate Leontief preferences well. However, when preferences are not homothetic and substitution increases, they show that the GL has a rather small regularity region.

Application of Roy's identity allows us to obtain the GL demand system (in value share form),

$$s_i = \frac{\alpha_i + \sum_{i=1}^{n} \beta_{ij} v_i^{1/2} v_j^{1/2}}{\sum_{k=1}^{n} \sum_{m=1}^{n} \beta_{km} v_k^{1/2} v_m^{1/2}}, \quad i = 1, \ldots, n,$$

where s_i is the budget share of the ith asset. Notice that the symmetry restrictions, $\beta_{ij} = \beta_{ji}$, for all i and j, and that the adding up restriction, $\sum_{i=1}^{n} \alpha_i = 1$, are imposed in estimation.

17.1.2   The Translog

The second model we consider is the basic translog (BTL) introduced by Christensen, Jorgenson and Lau (1975), and which we already briefly discussed in Chapter 16.[1] The basic translog flexible form of an indirect utility function may be written as

$$\log V(\boldsymbol{v}) = \alpha_0 + \sum_{i=1}^{n} \alpha_i \log v_i + \frac{1}{2} \sum_{i=1}^{n} \sum_{j=1}^{n} \beta_{ij} \log v_i \log v_j,$$

with the symmetry restrictions, $\beta_{ij} = \beta_{ji}$, imposed. Wales (1977) investigated the approximation properties of the generalized Leontief and translog functional forms and found that the translog provides a better approximation to an arbitrary utility function for values of the elasticity of substitution around one. The opposite is true for very small values of the elasticity of substitution. Similarly, David Guilkey, Knox Lovell, and Robin Sickles (1983) showed that the translog is globally regular if and only if preferences are Cobb-Douglas, meaning that the translog performs very well if substitution between all commodities is close to unity. They also showed that the regularity properties deteriorate rapidly when substitution diverges from unity.

Applying the logarithmic form of Roy's identity allows us to derive the model's share equations

$$s_i = \frac{\alpha_i + \sum\limits_{j=1}^{n} \beta_{ij} \log v_j}{\sum\limits_{i=1}^{n} \alpha_i + \sum\limits_{j=1}^{n} \beta_{jM} \log v_j}, \quad i = 1, ..., n.$$

where $\beta_{jM} = \sum_{i=1}^{n} \beta_{ji}$. With n assets the BTL model's share equations contain $n(n+3)/2$ parameters. By imposing the restrictions

$$\sum_{i=1}^{n} \beta_{ij} = 0, \quad \text{for all } j,$$

on the BTL, the homothetic translog (HTL) model's share equations can also be obtained. These are (as we saw in Chapter 16)

$$s_i = \frac{\alpha_i + \sum\limits_{j=1}^{n} \beta_{ij} \log v_j}{\sum\limits_{i=1}^{n} \alpha_i}, \quad i = 1, \dots, n.$$

---

[1] The BTL is a special case of the generalized translog (GTL), due to Robert Pollak and Terence Wales (1980). See Serletis (1988) for a comparison of various translog flexible forms.

With n assets, the HTL model's share equations contain $n(n + 3)/2$ parameters. Notice that estimation of each model's share equations requires some parameter normalization, as the share equations are homogeneous of degree zero in the α's. Usually the normalization $\sum_{i=1}^{n} \alpha_i = 1$ is used.

17.1.3   The Almost Ideal Demand System

The almost ideal demand system (AIDS) model of Angus Deaton and John Muellbauer (1980) is a widely used flexible demand specification obtained from the following PIGLOG (price-independent generalized logarithmic) expenditure function

$$\log C(U, \boldsymbol{p}) = \alpha_0 + \sum_{i=1}^{n} \alpha_i \log p_i$$

$$+ \frac{1}{2} \sum_{i=1}^{n} \sum_{j=1}^{n} \gamma_{ij} \log p_i \log p_j + U^* \beta_0 \prod_{k=1}^{n} p_k^{\beta_k},$$

where C is the minimum level of expenditure that is necessary to achieve utility level U^*, at given prices.

The demand equations in budget share form appear as follows

$$s_i = \alpha_i + \sum_{j=1}^{n} \gamma_{ij} \log p_j + \beta_i \log \left(\frac{m}{P} \right), \quad i = 1, \ldots, n.$$

Here P is a translog price index defined by

$$\log P = \alpha_0 + \sum_{k=1}^{n} \alpha_k \log p_k + \frac{1}{2} \sum_{j=1}^{n} \sum_{k=1}^{n} \gamma_{jk} \log p_j \log p_k.$$

Adding up, symmetry, and homogeneity restrictions require that

$$\sum_{i=1}^{n} \alpha_i = 1, \sum_{i=1}^{n} \gamma_{ij} = 0, \sum_{i=1}^{n} \beta_i = 0, \text{ and } \gamma_{ij} = \gamma_{ji} \text{ for } i, j = 1, \ldots, n.$$

Since the estimation of the AIDS is difficult using the translog price index, Stone's price index P^* is often used instead of P, where

$$\log P^* = \sum_{k=1}^{n} w_k \log p_k,$$

with $w_k = p_k x_k / m$ being budget shares. However, results from Panos Pashardes (1993), Adolf Buse (1994), and Julian Alston, Kenneth Foster, and Richard Green (1994) show that using the Stone index approximation can severely bias the results.[2]

17.2   Effectively Globally Regular Forms

As argued earlier, models such as the GL, BTL, and AIDS are locally flexible but may have a relatively small regular region. In fact, Caves and Christensen (1980), Barnett and Yul Lee (1985), and Barnett, Lee, and Michael Wolfe (1985) show that the regularity regions of local flexible functional forms can be relatively small. Furthermore, the Monte Carlo analysis of Guilkey and Lovell (1980) finds that the generalized Leontief and the translog fail to provide a satisfactory approximation to the true data generating process for the moderate and even large elasticities of substitution that often arise in applications.

These problems led to the development of locally flexible functional forms that have larger regularity regions that Russel Cooper and Keith McLaren (1996) classify as 'effectively globally regular'. These functions typically have regular regions that include all data points in the sample. In addition, the regularity region increases as real expenditure levels grow, as is often the case with time series data. Furthermore, these functions provide more general Engel curve approximations, especially when income varies considerably.

Examples of these functions include the Minflex Laurent (ML) models introduced by Barnett (1983, 1985), Barnett and Lee (1985), and Barnett, Lee, and Wolfe (1985, 1987), based on the Laurent series expansion; the 'quadratic AIDS' (QUAIDS) model of James Banks, Richard Blundell and Arthur Lewbel (1996); and the 'general exponential form' (GEF) of Cooper and McLaren (1996). In what follows, we will consider two effectively globally regular flexible functional forms — the ML generalized Leontief and the ML translog.

17.2.1   The Minflex Laurent Generalized Leontief

Let $x = (x_1, \ldots, x_n)'$ and $p = (p_1, \ldots, p_n)'$ be the vectors of assets quantities and assets user costs, respectively. Let $m = p'x$ be total expenditure on monetary services and let $v = (v_1, \ldots, v_n)'$ be the vector of total expenditure-normalized user costs, $v_i = p_i / m$. Also, let the

---

[2] Julián Ramajo (1994) and James Chalfant (1987) show how to increase the approximation performance of the AIDS.

expenditure shares be $s = (s_1, \ldots, s_n)'$ where $s_i = x_i v_i$, and define the set of unequal subscript pairs $S = \{(i,j) : i \neq j;\ i,j = 1, \ldots, n\}$.

The ML generalized Leontief flexible form of an indirect utility function may be written as

$$V(v) = a_0 + 2\sum_{i=1}^{n} \alpha_i w_i + \sum_{i=1}^{n} \alpha_{ii} w_i^2$$

$$+ \sum\sum_{(i,j)\in S} \left(\alpha_{ij}^2 w_i w_j - b_{ij}^2 w_i^{-1} w_j^{-1} \right),$$

where $w_i = v_i^{1/2}$, a_0 is a scalar parameter, $\alpha = (\alpha_1, \ldots, \alpha_n)'$ is a vector of parameters and $[\alpha_{ij}]$ and $[b_{ij}]$ are symmetric (zero-diagonal) matrices of parameters.

Applying Roy's identity, we get the ML generalized Leontief model's share equations

$$s_i = \frac{A_i}{D}, \quad i = 1, \ldots, n, \tag{17.1}$$

where

$$A_i = \alpha_i w_i + \alpha_{ii} v_i + \sum_{j:j\neq i} \alpha_{ij}^2 w_i w_j + \sum_{j:j\neq i} b_{ij}^2 w_i^{-1} w_j^{-1},$$

and

$$D = \sum_{k=1}^{n} \alpha_k w_k + \sum_{k=1}^{n} \alpha_{kk} v_k$$

$$+ \sum\sum_{(k,j)\in S} \alpha_{kj}^2 w_k w_j + \sum\sum_{(k,j)\in S} b_{kj}^2 w_k^{-1} w_j^{-1}.$$

Estimation of (17.1) requires some normalization rule as (17.1) is homogeneous of degree zero in the parameters. Following Barnett (1985) one can use the normalization

$$\sum_{i=1}^{n} \alpha_{ii} + 2\sum_{i=1}^{n} \alpha_i + \sum_{(i,j)\in S} (\alpha_{ij}^2 - b_{ij}^2) = 1. \tag{17.2}$$

17.2.2   The Minflex Laurent Translog

Using the same notation as above, the ML translog flexible functional form of an indirect utility function may be written as

$$V(v) = a_0 + 2\sum_{i=1}^{n}\alpha_i w_i + \sum_{i=1}^{n}\alpha_{ii} w_i^2$$

$$- \sum\sum_{(i,j)\in S}\alpha_{ij}^2 w_i w_j + \sum\sum_{(i,j)\in S}b_{ij}^2 w_i^{-1} w_j^{-1},$$

where $w_i = \log \bar{v}_i$, $\bar{v}_i = v_i + \theta_i$ and θ_i is a constant.

Applying Roy's identity we get the ML translog model's share equations

$$s_i = \frac{B_i}{E}, \quad i - 1, ..., n, \tag{17.3}$$

where

$$B_i = \alpha_i v_i \bar{v}_i^{-1} + \alpha_{ii} v_i \bar{v}_i^{-1} w_i$$

$$- \sum_{j:j\neq i}\alpha_{ij}^2 v_i \bar{v}_i^{-1} w_j - \sum_{j:j\neq i}b_{ij}^2 v_i w_i^{-2} v_i^{-1} w_j^{-1},$$

and

$$E = \sum_{k=1}^{n}\alpha_k v_k \bar{v}_k^{-1} + \sum_{k=1}^{n}\alpha_{kk} v_k \bar{v}_k^{-1} w_k$$

$$- \sum\sum_{(k,j)\in S}\alpha_{kj}^2 v_k \bar{v}_k^{-1} w_j - \sum\sum_{(k,j)\in S}b_{kj}^2 v_k w_k^{-2} \bar{v}_k^{-1} w_j^{-1}.$$

Since (17.3) is homogeneous of degree zero, its estimation requires a normalization such as that in equation (17.2).

17.3   Globally Flexible Forms

As already pointed out, the functional forms considered so far are capable of approximating an arbitrary function locally at a single point

where

$$ss_1 = \sum_{k=1}^{K} \lambda(k) b_{1k} v_1^{\lambda(k)} + \sum_{k=1}^{K} \sum_{m=1}^{K} \left(\sum_{j=2}^{3} \lambda(k) b_{1jkm} v_1^{\lambda(k)} v_j^{\lambda(m)} \right)$$

$$+ \sum_{k=1}^{K} \sum_{m=1}^{K} \sum_{g=1}^{K} \lambda(k) b_{123kmg} v_1^{\lambda(k)} v_2^{\lambda(m)} v_3^{\lambda(g)},$$

$$ss_2 = \sum_{k=1}^{K} \lambda(k) b_{2k} v_2^{\lambda(k)} + \sum_{k=1}^{K} \sum_{m=1}^{K} \lambda(m) b_{12km} v_1^{\lambda(k)} v_2^{\lambda(m)}$$

$$+ \sum_{k=1}^{K} \sum_{m=1}^{K} \lambda(k) b_{23km} v_2^{\lambda(k)} v_3^{\lambda(m)}$$

$$+ \sum_{k=1}^{K} \sum_{m=1}^{K} \sum_{g=1}^{K} \lambda(m) b_{123kmg} v_1^{\lambda(k)} v_2^{\lambda(m)} v_3^{\lambda(g)},$$

$$ss_3 = \sum_{k=1}^{K} \lambda(k) b_{3k} v_3^{\lambda(k)} + \sum_{k=1}^{K} \sum_{m=1}^{K} \left(\sum_{i=1}^{2} \lambda(m) b_{i3km} v_i^{\lambda(k)} v_3^{\lambda(m)} \right)$$

$$+ \sum_{k=1}^{K} \sum_{m=1}^{K} \sum_{g=1}^{K} \lambda(g) b_{123kmg} v_1^{\lambda(k)} v_2^{\lambda(m)} v_3^{\lambda(g)}$$

$$ss = ss_1 + ss_2 + ss_3.$$

17.4   Conclusion

We have provided a theoretical discussion of a number of different flexible functional forms, by grouping them into three groups that have similar characteristics. Of course, there are many other possibilities, but we selected these functional forms because they provide a representation of the three groups of functional forms that are in the widest use in applied work based on the demand systems approach. We argued that the available flexible functional forms are either parametric or semi-nonparametric and differ in their specific parameterization and approximation properties. The reader should note that while the semi-nonparametric forms generally have more desirable asymptotic properties than the parametric functions, it does not follow that one is to be preferred to the other on particular data sets.[3]

We want to emphasize that it would be preferable if one could nest at least some flexible functional forms, so that the choice between them could be the subject of a statistical hypothesis test. This is currently possible for those flexible functional forms that have interpretations as Taylor series expansions. For example, Serletis (1988) uses likelihood ratio tests to choose between four nested translog demand systems — the generalized translog, the basic translog, the linear translog, and the homothetic translog. In general, however, given known estimation techniques, it is not possible to nest flexible functional forms with different approximation properties.

The systems of share equations presented in this chapter do not lend themselves easily to estimation. In the next chapter, we discuss a number of issues that are important in empirical demand analysis. These include stochastic specification for demand systems written in share form, time-series issues regarding the treatment of trends, and estimation and hypotheses testing.

---

[3]See Fisher, Fleissig, and Serletis (2001) for an interesting comparison of eight frequently used flexible functional forms, using consumption data for the United States.

Part 7:

Microeconometrics

and the Demand

for Money

Overview of Part 7

In Chapter 18, stochastic specifications of monetary asset budget share equations are discussed as well as income elasticities and own- and cross-price elasticities. These elasticities, along with the (Allen and Morishima) elasticities of substitution, are particularly useful in interpreting demand system parameter estimates. Attention is also focussed on the dynamic context in which policy operates. The 'Slutsky conditions' that every demand system should satisfy, irrespective of the form of the utility function, are also discussed.

Chapter 19 presents an econometrics digression emphasizing the contribution that can be made by using the demand-systems approach to the demand for money and monetary assets. We tackle the problem in three stages: (i) we apply revealed preference tests to determine the components of optimal monetary subaggregates; (ii) we employ the Divisia index to perform the aggregation of those components; and (iii) we estimate a system of share equations based on the basic translog flexible functional form.

The concluding chapter discusses a number of issues and presents a possible future research agenda that might flow out of this book.

Chapter 18

The Econometrics of Demand Systems

There are three main purposes to our investigations in the context of demand systems. First and foremost, we want to focus our attention on econometric techniques that can be used to analyze the interrelated demand for money and monetary assets in the context of share equation systems. Secondly, we want to analyze the properties of demand systems which result from the fact that demand systems are obtained by preference-maximizing behavior. Finally, we are interested in the substitutability/complementarity relationship between money and other monetary assets.

In this chapter we outline a standard stochastic specification for demand systems written in share form that forms the basis of our discussion in the rest of this book. Although our primary focus is the estimation of price and substitution elasticities, we also pay explicit attention to recent developments that have increased the usefulness of the demand-systems modeling approach for monetary studies. We attempt to clarify just what these developments are and how they are tending to reorganize a very traditional literature on an important topic.

where $\rho = [\rho_{ij}]$ is a matrix of unknown parameters and e_t is a non-autocorrelated vector disturbance term with constant covariance matrix. For example, in the three asset HTL case, we have

$$\rho = \begin{bmatrix} \rho_{11} & \rho_{12} & \rho_{13} \\ \rho_{21} & \rho_{22} & \rho_{23} \\ \rho_{31} & \rho_{32} & \rho_{33} \end{bmatrix} \quad \text{and} \quad e_t = \begin{bmatrix} e_{1t} \\ e_{2t} \\ e_{3t} \end{bmatrix},$$

and adding up of the budget shares implies the following restrictions on ρ,

$$\rho_{1i} + \rho_{2i} + \rho_{3i} = \kappa, \quad i = 1, 2, 3.$$

In this case, FIML estimates of the parameters can be obtained by using a result developed by Ernst Berndt and Eugene Savin (1975). They showed that if one assumes no autocorrelation across equations (i.e., ρ is diagonal), the autocorrelation coefficients for each equation must be identical, $\rho_{11} = \rho_{22} = \rho_{33} = \rho$. Consequently, by writing equation (18.1) for period $t - 1$, multiplying by ρ, and subtracting from (18.1), we can estimate (using FIML procedures) stochastic budget share equations given by

$$s_t = g(v_t, \boldsymbol{\theta}) + \rho s_{t-1} - \rho g(v_{t-1}, \boldsymbol{\theta}) + e_t. \tag{18.3}$$

As an example, the homothetic translog version of the problem, with symmetry imposed and the third equation deleted, can be set up as follows

$$s_{1t} = \alpha_1 + \beta_{11} \log v_{1t} + \beta_{12} \log v_{2t} + \beta_{13} \log v_{3t} + \rho s_{1t-1}$$
$$- \rho \left(\alpha_1 + \beta_{11} \log v_{1t-1} + \beta_{12} \log v_{2t-1} + \beta_{13} \log v_{3t-1} \right) + e_{1t},$$

$$s_{2t} = \alpha_2 + \beta_{12} \log v_{1t} + \beta_{22} \log v_{2t} + \beta_{23} \log v_{3t} + \rho s_{2t-1}$$
$$- \rho \left(\alpha_2 + \beta_{12} \log v_{1t-1} + \beta_{22} \log v_{2t-1} + \beta_{23} \log v_{3t-1} \right) + e_{2t},$$

Notice that imposing a common factor across the equations ensures the invariance of the FIML parameter estimates with respect to the equation deleted.

18.3   Expenditure and Price Elasticities

A system of budget share equations provides a complete characterization of consumer preferences over the services of monetary assets and can be used to estimate the income elasticities as well as the own- and cross-price elasticities. These elasticities are particularly useful in judging the validity of the parameter estimates and can be calculated directly from the estimated budget share equations by writing the left-hand side as

$$x_i = \frac{s_i m}{p_i}, \quad i = 1, \ldots, n,$$

or logarithmically

$$\log x_i = \log s_i + \log m - \log p_i.$$

In particular, the income elasticities can be calculated as

$$E_i = \frac{\partial \log x_i}{\partial \log m} = \frac{\partial \log s_i}{\partial \log m} + 1, \quad i = 1, \ldots, n.$$

Similarly, the own-price elasticities are given as

$$\eta_{ii} = \frac{\partial \log x_i}{\partial \log p_i} = \frac{\partial \log s_i}{\partial \log p_i} - 1, \quad i = 1, \ldots, n,$$

and the cross-price elasticities as

$$\eta_{ij} = \frac{\partial \log x_i}{\partial \log p_j} = \frac{\partial \log s_i}{\partial \log p_j}, \quad i, j = 1, \ldots, n, \quad i \neq j.$$

If $\eta_{ij} > 0$ the assets are gross substitutes, if $\eta_{ij} < 0$ they are gross complements, and if $\eta_{ij} = 0$ they are independent.

As an example, the elasticity formulas for the HTL are

$$E_i = 1, \quad \eta_{ii} = \frac{\beta_{ii}}{s_i} - 1, \quad \text{and} \quad \eta_{ij} = \frac{\beta_{ij}}{s_i}.$$

18.4   Elasticities of Substitution

We can also interpret the estimated parameter values by computing Allen and Morishima elasticities of substitution. One reason for our interest in these measures is that the degree of substitutability among monetary assets has been used — explicitly or implicitly — to provide a rationale for the appropriate definition of money, which as we have seen has been the focus of continuing controversy over the years. Moreover, knowledge of the substitutability between monetary assets is essential in order to understand the potential effects of monetary policy actions as well as the effects of the growth of financial intermediation.

$$\sum_{j=1}^{n} p_j \frac{\partial x_i}{\partial p_j} + m \frac{\partial x_i}{\partial m} = 0, \quad i = 1, ..., n.$$

Dividing all terms of the above expression by x_i we get the following reformulated restriction, in terms of price and income elasticities

$$\sum_{j=1}^{n} \eta_{ij} = -E_i, \quad i = 1, ..., n, \tag{18.8}$$

where η_{ij} is the elasticity of demand of asset i with respect to asset j and E_i is the income elasticity of demand for asset i.[2] Hence, the homogeneity condition (18.8) states that the sum of the own- and all cross-price elasticities of any asset i has to equal the negative of its income elasticity.

As already stated, homogeneity of degree zero in income and prices has to be exactly satisfied for our mathematical functions to be candidates for qualification as demand functions. Evidence that contradicts the homogeneity restriction has also important implications from a macroeconomics perspective. For example, homogeneity of degree zero with respect to prices and nominal income is an important assumption underlying classical macroeconomic theory, which requires the real side of the economy to be homogeneous of degree zero in the nominal variables.

18.5.2   Adding-Up (Summability)

Since the budget constraint has to be satisfied, the demand equations have to be such that the sum of the estimated expenditures on the different monetary assets equals total monetary asset expenditure in any period. Such a system is called *additive* — not to be confused with the additivity property of utility functions.

In the special case of homogeneity of degree zero ($\gamma = 0$), the above reduces to

$$\sum_{i=1}^{n} x_i \frac{\partial f(x_1, ..., x_n)}{\partial x_i} = 0.$$

[2] Note that

$$\eta_{ij} = \frac{p_j}{x_i} \frac{\partial x_i}{\partial p_j} \quad \text{and} \quad E_i = \frac{m}{x_i} \frac{\partial x_i}{\partial m}.$$

The adding-up restriction can also be expressed in terms of elasticities. In particular, partially differentiating (18.7) with respect to m we get

$$\sum_{i=1}^{n} p_i \frac{\partial x_i}{\partial m} = 1,$$

which implies that an increase in total expenditure is completely allocated to all monetary assets. Manipulating the above we obtain

$$\sum_{i=1}^{n} s_i E_i = 1, \tag{18.9}$$

where $s_i = p_i x_i / m$ is the budget share of asset i. Thus, the summability condition (18.9), often called the *Engel aggregation* condition in the terminology of Ragnar Frisch (1959), states that the sum of the income elasticities weighted by their respective expenditure proportions has to equal unity.

18.5.3   Symmetry of the Slutsky Matrix

Total differentiation of the first order conditions for utility maximization, conditions (18.4) and (18.5), gives

$$\left[\begin{array}{cc} \mathbf{F} & \mathbf{p} \\ \mathbf{p}' & 0 \end{array} \right] \left[\begin{array}{c} d\mathbf{x} \\ -d\lambda \end{array} \right] = \left[\begin{array}{cc} 0 & \lambda\mathbf{I} \\ 1 & -\mathbf{x}' \end{array} \right] \left[\begin{array}{c} dm \\ d\mathbf{p} \end{array} \right] \tag{18.10}$$

where $\mathbf{F}$ is the $n \times n$ Hessian matrix of the utility function,

$$\mathbf{F} = \left[\begin{array}{ccc} \dfrac{\partial^2 f(\mathbf{x})}{\partial x_1^2} & \cdots & \dfrac{\partial^2 f(\mathbf{x})}{\partial x_1 \partial x_n} \\ \vdots & \ddots & \vdots \\ \dfrac{\partial^2 f(\mathbf{x})}{\partial x_n \partial x_1} & \cdots & \dfrac{\partial^2 f(\mathbf{x})}{\partial x_n^2} \end{array} \right].$$

As already noted in Chapter 16, the solution to (18.4) and (18.5) is the demand system

$$x_i = x_i(\mathbf{p}, m), \quad i = 1, ..., n,$$

$$\lambda = \lambda(\mathbf{p}, m).$$

Total differentiation of this demand system yields

$$\left[\begin{array}{c} d\mathbf{x} \\ -d\lambda \end{array} \right] = \left[\begin{array}{cc} \mathbf{x}_m & \mathbf{X}_p \\ -\lambda_m & -\lambda_p' \end{array} \right] \left[\begin{array}{c} dm \\ d\mathbf{p} \end{array} \right] \tag{18.11}$$

where

$$
\lambda_p = \begin{bmatrix} \dfrac{\partial \lambda}{\partial p_1} \\ \vdots \\ \dfrac{\partial \lambda}{\partial p_n} \end{bmatrix}, \quad
x_m = \begin{bmatrix} \dfrac{\partial x_1}{\partial m} \\ \vdots \\ \dfrac{\partial x_n}{\partial m} \end{bmatrix}, \quad
\mathbf{X}_p = \begin{bmatrix} \dfrac{\partial x_1}{\partial p_1} & \cdots & \dfrac{\partial x_1}{\partial p_n} \\ \vdots & \ddots & \vdots \\ \dfrac{\partial x_n}{\partial p_1} & \cdots & \dfrac{\partial x_n}{\partial p_n} \end{bmatrix},
$$

and $\lambda_m = \partial \lambda / \partial m$.

Substitution of (18.11) into (18.10) leads to

$$
\begin{bmatrix} \mathbf{F} & p \\ p' & 0 \end{bmatrix} \begin{bmatrix} x_m & \mathbf{X}_p \\ -\lambda_m & -\lambda_p' \end{bmatrix} = \begin{bmatrix} 0 & \lambda \mathbf{I} \\ 1 & -x' \end{bmatrix} \tag{18.12}
$$

the solution of which can be written in the form

$$
\begin{bmatrix} x_m & \mathbf{X}_p \\ -\lambda_m & -\lambda_p' \end{bmatrix} = \begin{bmatrix} \mathbf{F} & p \\ p' & 0 \end{bmatrix}^{-1} \begin{bmatrix} 0 & \lambda \mathbf{I} \\ 1 & -x' \end{bmatrix} \tag{18.13}
$$

Equation (18.13) implies [see Barten (1964) or Louis Phlips (1974) for details]

$$
x_m = \lambda_m \mathbf{F}^{-1} p
$$

$$
\mathbf{X}_p = \lambda \mathbf{F}^{-1} - (\lambda/\lambda_m) x_m x_m' - x_m x' \tag{18.14}
$$

Equation (18.14) is known as the *Slutsky equation* — the fundamental equation of value theory. It can be written as

$$
\mathbf{X}_p = \mathbf{K} - x_m x' \tag{18.15}
$$

where $\mathbf{K} = \lambda \mathbf{F}^{-1} - (\lambda/\lambda_m) x_m x_m'$ is the *substitution matrix* (also known as the *Slutsky matrix*) of income compensated price responses and $x_m x'$ is the *matrix of income effects*. Notice that the i, j element of (18.15) is

$$
\frac{\partial x_i}{\partial p_j} = k_{ij} - \frac{\partial x_i}{\partial m} x_j \tag{18.16}
$$

where $\partial x_i / \partial p_j$ is the *total effect* of a price change on demand, k_{ij} (i.e., the i, j element of $\mathbf{K}$) is the *substitution effect* of a compensated price change on demand, and $(-\partial x_i / \partial m) x_j$ is the *income effect*, resulting from a change in price (not in income).

Notice that, in the absence of a particular specification of the utility function, economic theory has nothing to say about the sign of the income effect. It is an empirical question to determine the sign of the income effect. In the case, for example, of normal goods (also known as superior goods), $\partial x_i/\partial m > 0$ and the income effect is negative; in the case of inferior goods, $\partial x_i/\partial m < 0$ and the income effect is positive

The Slutsky decomposition is not a restriction in itself. Its importance lies in the fact that the Slutsky matrix $\boldsymbol{K}$ is an $n \times n$ symmetric matrix, since $\lambda \mathbf{F}^{-1} - (\lambda/\lambda_m)\boldsymbol{x}_m \boldsymbol{x}_m'$ is symmetric. Hence,

$$k_{ij} = k_{ji}.$$

This symmetry restriction of the Slutsky matrix may also be written in elasticity terms, making use of equation (18.16), as follows

$$\frac{\eta_{ij}}{s_j} + E_i = \frac{\eta_{ji}}{s_i} + E_j,$$

where η_{ij} is the elasticity of demand of asset i with respect to the price of asset j, E_i is the income elasticity of demand of asset i, and $s_j = p_j x_j/m$ is the proportion of total expenditure devoted to asset j. Clearly, the symmetrical terms are the Allen elasticities of substitution

$$\sigma_{ij}^a = \frac{\eta_{ij}}{s_j} + E_i = \frac{\eta_{ji}}{s_i} + E_j = \sigma_{ji}^a, \tag{18.17}$$

where σ_{ij}^a is the Allen elasticity of substitution between assets i and j. Hence, the Allen elasticities of substitution are equivalent to compensated price elasticities.

As with the sign of the income effect, the sign of the cross substitution effect, k_{ij}, is not determined, in the absence of a particular specification of the utility function. This sign is to be determined empirically. If $\sigma_{ij}^a < 0$, assets are said to be Allen complements, in the sense that an increase in the price of asset j causes a decreased consumption of asset i; if $\sigma_{ij}^a > 0$, assets are said to be Allen substitutes.

18.5.4 Negativity of the Own Substitution Effect

Finally, the most important restriction of all is the negativity of the own substitution effect[3]

$$k_{ii} < 0, \quad i = 1, ..., n. \tag{18.18}$$

This restriction establishes the negative relationship between quantity and price (i.e., the negativity of the slope of the demand curves), for those assets that are not inferior (i.e., assets for which the income elasticity is positive or zero).

---

[3]See Phlips (1974, p. 52-53) for a proof of the negativity property.

Equations (18.8), (18.9), (18.17), and (18.18) are the Slutsky conditions that each system of demand equations should satisfy, irrespective of the choice of a particular utility function. These conditions, together with the usual neoclassical monotonicity requirement that the direct utility function should be an increasing function of each good consumed, are also known as the *integrability conditions*. If they hold, then the demand system is integrable in the sense that it can be generated by utility maximization subject to a budget constraint. As Fisher (1989, p. 87) puts it

> "[t]he importance of this is clear: if the integrability conditions
> are valid, then the theory of individual consumer behavior is ap-
> plicable to the analysis of aggregate consumer demand functions
> in *per capita* form ... ."

18.6   Conclusion

In this chapter we have illustrated some basic aspects of demand system specification that will provide context and motivation for the discussion in Chapters 19. One of the possible ways of improving on the foregoing is to pay explicit attention to the time series properties of the data. A recent finding in the econometrics literature, as we discussed in Chapters 9, 10, and 11, is that estimation and hypotheses testing critically depend on the integration and cointegration properties of the variables. For example, in the context of linear demand systems such as the homothetic translog and the AIDS, Serena Ng (1995) and C. Attfield (1997) test the null hypothesis of homogeneity (with respect to prices and nominal income) and show that this cannot be rejected once the time series properties of the data are imposed in estimation.

This implies that testing for cointegration [in the spirit of Engle and Granger (1987)], and constructing a form of the error correction model is appropriate. Most demand systems, however, have share equations that are nonlinear and, as Granger (1995) points out, nonlinear modeling of nonstationary variables is a new, complicated, and largely undeveloped area. We generally ignore this issue in this book, keeping in mind that this is an area for potentially productive future research.

Chapter 19

Applied Monetary Demand
Analysis

In this chapter we consider and illustrate a solution to the inter-related problems of monetary aggregation and estimation of money demand functions. In doing so, we use quarterly U.S. data and take a demand systems approach. We handle the problem in three stages: (i) we apply revealed preference tests to determine admissible and separable components; (ii) we aggregate these components using a superlative index — the Divisia index; and (iii) we use the basic translog demand system to deal with the problem of money demand.

We cannot establish weakly separable groupings for the traditional Federal Reserve definitions of M1, M2, M3, and MZM, meaning that these aggregates are not consistent with preference-maximizing behavior. Moreover, we think the results of this chapter underscore the inefficiency of both simple-sum monetary aggregation and the estimation of single-equation, log linear money-demand functions.

19.1   The Revealed Preference Approach

As we have seen in Chapter 16, Varian's NONPAR procedure can be used to determine the components of optimal (in a revealed-preference sense) monetary aggregates. To see how Varian's tests might look in practice, consider the set of thirteen U.S. liquid assets shown in Table 19.1. Notice that M1 consists of assets 1-4, M2 of assets 1-9, M3 of assets

Table 19.3.   Weak Separability Tests for the Fed's M1, M2, M3, and MZM Aggregates

Separability hypothesis	1975:1- 1982:2	1981:4- 1991:2	1991:4- 1999:4
$f\left(f_1(x_1, x_2, x_3, x_4), x_5, x_6, x_7, x_8, x_9, x_{10}, x_{11}, x_{12}, x_{13})\right)$	X	X	X
$f\left(f_1(x_1, x_2, x_3, x_4, x_5), x_6, x_7, x_8, x_9, x_{10}, x_{11}, x_{12}, x_{13})\right)$	X	X	N
$f\left(f_1(x_1, x_2, x_3, x_4, x_5, x_6), x_7, x_8, x_9, x_{10}, x_{11}, x_{12}, x_{13})\right)$	X	X	X
$f\left(f_1(x_1, x_2, x_3, x_4, x_5, x_6, x_7), x_8, x_9, x_{10}, x_{11}, x_{12}, x_{13})\right)$	X	X	X
$f\left(f_1(x_1, x_2, x_3, x_4, x_5, x_6, x_7, x_8), x_9, x_{10}, x_{11}, x_{12}, x_{13})\right)$	N	X	X
$f\left(f_1(x_1, x_2, x_3, x_4, x_5, x_6, x_7, x_8, x_9), x_{10}, x_{11}, x_{12}, x_{13})\right)$	X	X	X
$f\left(f_1(x_1, x_2, x_3, x_4, x_5, x_6, x_7, x_8, x_9, x_{10}), x_{11}, x_{12}, x_{13})\right)$	N	X	X
$f\left(f_1(x_1, x_2, x_3, x_4, x_5, x_6, x_7, x_8, x_9, x_{10}, x_{11}), x_{12}, x_{13})\right)$	N	X	X
$f\left(f_1(x_1, x_2, x_3, x_4, x_5, x_6, x_7, x_8, x_9, x_{10}, x_{11}, x_{12}), x_{13})\right)$	N	X	X

Notes: N: passes necessary condition, N&S: passes necessary condition and a sufficient condition, X: fails both necessary and sufficient conditions.

rable groupings could be established for the traditional Federal Reserve definitions of M1, M2, M3, and MZM. The results are reported in Table 19.3. Clearly, the Fed's groupings of assets fail separability tests in each of the three subperiods, suggesting that entities such as the Fed's measures of M1, M2, M3, and MZM are inconsistent with rational consumer behavior. As Fisher and Fleissig (1997, p. 464) put it, "[t]hese measures include items that are held for different reasons by different economic agents (businesses and consumers) who may react differently to the same (or even to different) variables."

Considering that the Fed's monetary aggregates are inconsistent with a representative economic agent maximizing a separable utility function, we search for some alternative weakly separable groupings of assets. After much testing, we found that the structures in Table 19.4 satisfy

Table 19.4. Structures Satisfying the Necessary and Sufficient Conditions for Weak Separability Over the 1991:4–1999:4 Subperiod

$$f\left(f_1(x_1, x_2), f_2(x_3, x_4, x_5, x_6), x_7, f_3(x_8, x_9, x_{10}, x_{11}, x_{12}, x_{13})\right)$$

$$f\left(f_1(x_1), f_2(x_2, x_3, x_4, x_5, x_6), x_7, f_3(x_8, x_9, x_{10}, x_{11}, x_{12}, x_{13})\right)$$

$$f\left(f_1(x_1, x_3, x_4), f_2(x_2, x_5, x_6), x_7, f_3(x_8, x_9, x_{10}, x_{11}, x_{12}, x_{13})\right)$$

$$f\left(f_1(x_1, x_3, x_4), f_2(x_2, x_5, x_6, x_7), f_3(x_8, x_9, x_{10}, x_{11}, x_{12}, x_{13})\right)$$

the necessary and sufficient conditions for weak separability over the 1991:4-1999:4 subsample. Looking at the test results, it is clear that money market mutual funds (series x_7), in most cases, forms a group by itself. This exclusion of money market funds from other separable groupings makes economic sense, and is consistent with the evidence in Fisher and Fleissig (1997) and Swofford and Whitney (1987, 1988). It also points up a major reason as to why bond and stock mutual funds should not be added to traditional money measures, thereby adding to the debate initiated by Sean Collins and Cheryl Edwards (1994).

One further property of the results in Table 19.4 which deserves comment is their uniformity. It is clear that a number of different grouping patterns are available and we have the problem of the choice of the grouping pattern to be imposed on the model. Of course there is no usable model which yields all of these groupings through the imposition of parameter restrictions, so classical hypothesis tests are powerless to provide a direction. Although the choice of the grouping pattern seems to be arbitrary at this stage, out of the four plausible separable structures presented in Table 19.4, we choose the first one, because of its intuitive appeal. In what follows we are concerned with the resulting budgeting of consumer decisions.

19.2   The Divisia Aggregator

The preference structure we are suggesting is

$$f(\boldsymbol{x}) = f\left(f_1(x_1, x_2), f_2(x_3, x_4, x_5, x_6), x_7, f_3(x_8, x_9, x_{10}, x_{11}, x_{12}, x_{13})\right),$$

where the aggregator functions, f_i $(i = 1, 2, 3)$, are treated as subaggregate measures of monetary services. The Federal Reserve Board, and most central banks around the world, calculate such monetary aggregates using simple summation. Simple-sum aggregation, however, implies that all of the assets are perfect substitutes for each other. This is unlikely to be the case and therefore an aggregation method that allows for less than perfect substitution should be used.

Here the subaggregates, f_i $(i = 1, 2, 3)$, are thought of as Divisia quantity indexes, corresponding to which there exist Divisia price indexes, P_i $(i = 1, 2, 3)$. Hence, using monetary asset quantity and user cost data, we reduce the structure of the representative agent's utility function to

$$f(x) = f(Q_1, Q_2, x_7, Q_3),$$

where

$$Q_1 \ = \ f_1(x_1, x_2)$$

$$Q_2 \ = \ f_2(x_3, x_4, x_5, x_6)$$

$$Q_3 \ = \ f_3(x_8, x_9, x_{10}, x_{11}, x_{12}, x_{13}).$$

The demand system in the next section is estimated using data on Q_1, Q_2, x_7, and Q_3, and the corresponding Divisia price indexes. For Q_1, Q_2, and Q_3, these Divisia price indexes are computed making use of Fisher's weak factor reversal test. The test states that the product of the values of the price and quantity indexes should be equal to the ratio of total expenditure in the two periods.

19.3   The Demand Systems Approach

Our objective is to estimate income, price, and elasticities of substitution, by estimating (over the GARP-consistent subsample, 1991:4-1999:4) a system of demand equations derived from the indirect utility function. In order to do so, we need to choose a functional form that will accurately approximate both the true indirect utility function and its partial derivatives. As already noted, parametric functions (such as, for example, the Cobb-Douglas) fail to accurately approximate the data generating function and often restrict the substitutability/complementarity relationship between assets.

Here, we use the basic translog functional form to approximate the unknown indirect utility function. As we argued in Chapter 17, however, the translog is capable of approximating an arbitrary function only locally (at a point), and that a more constructive approach would be based on the use of flexible functional forms that possess global properties. Thus, the results in this chapter are not definitive in any sense, but are meant to demonstrate the demand systems methodology described in the discussion thus far.

19.3.1   The Basic Translog

We will begin with the basic translog functional form, discussed in Chapter 17, with the symmetry restrictions, $\beta_{ij} = \beta_{ji}$, imposed. We reproduce it here for the four-asset case,

$$\log V(\boldsymbol{v}) = \alpha_0 + \sum_{i=1}^{4} \alpha_i \log v_i + \frac{1}{2} \sum_{i=1}^{4} \sum_{j=1}^{4} \beta_{ij} \log v_i \log v_j.$$

Applying the logarithmic form of Roy's identity allows us to derive the model's share equations

$$s_i = \frac{\alpha_i + \sum_{j=1}^{4} \beta_{ij} \log v_j}{\sum_{i=1}^{4} \alpha_i + \sum_{j=1}^{4} \beta_{jM} \log v_j} + e_i, \quad i = 1, ..., 4,$$

where $\beta_{jM} = \sum_{i=1}^{4} \beta_{ji}$. The disturbance terms e_i $(i = 1, ..., 4)$ have been added to capture deviations of the observed shares from the true shares. As we argued in Chapter 18, the errors are assumed to be additive, jointly normally distributed with zero means, and with constant but unknown variances and covariances. This distributional assumption on the errors is standard and is fundamental in the derivation of the FIML estimator.

Since demand theory provides that the budget shares sum to 1, it follows that the disturbance covariance matrix is singular. If autocorrelation in the disturbances is absent (as assumed here), Barten (1969) showed that FIML estimates of the parameters can be obtained by arbitrarily deleting an equation in such a system and that the estimation results are invariant with respect to the equation deleted. Thus, with four shares one equation must be dropped, and only three equations are estimated. Here, we drop the third equation and estimate the remaining three equations. Notice also that estimation of this system requires some parameter normalization, as the share equations are homogeneous of degree zero in the α's. Usually the normalization $\sum_{i=1}^{4} \alpha_i = 1$ is used. Thus, in terms of the variables defined above, we estimate

$$s_1 = \frac{\alpha_1 + \beta_{11} \log v_1 + \beta_{12} \log v_2 + \beta_{13} \log v_3 + \beta_{14} \log v_4}{1 + \sum_{j=1}^{4} \sum_{i=1}^{4} \beta_{ji} \log v_j} + e_1$$

$$s_2 = \frac{\alpha_2 + \beta_{12} \log v_1 + \beta_{22} \log v_2 + \beta_{23} \log v_3 + \beta_{24} \log v_4}{1 + \sum_{j=1}^{4} \sum_{i=1}^{4} \beta_{ji} \log v_j} + e_2$$

$$s_4 = \frac{\alpha_4 + \beta_{14} \log v_1 + \beta_{24} \log v_2 + \beta_{34} \log v_3 + \beta_{44} \log v_4}{1 + \sum_{j=1}^{4} \sum_{i=1}^{4} \beta_{ji} \log v_j} + e_4.$$

This system has 13 free parameters — that is, 13 parameters estimated directly. These parameters are: α_1, α_2, α_4, β_{11}, β_{12}, β_{13}, β_{14}, β_{22}, β_{23}, β_{24}, β_{33}, and β_{34}.

Prior to estimation (and the logarithmic transformation of the data), the income-normalized prices were normalized again by dividing each v_i by its mean in order to place the Taylor's expansion around the point $v^* = 1$. The system was estimated using the seemingly unrelated regression procedure in TSP International (version 4.5) — convergence is set at 0.00001. As with vector autoregressions and other time series models, there are many parameters to be estimated and it does not matter if all the parameters are statistically significant or not — what is important is for the model to fit the data well. We initially estimated the model as shown above. The results, however, led us to believe that the disturbances were serially correlated — the computed equation-by-equation Durbin-Watson statistics were very low.

Autocorrelation in money demand systems is a common result and may be caused by institutional constraints which prevent people from adjusting their asset holdings within one period. As discussed in Chapter 18, Berndt and Savin (1975) show that a satisfactory way of dealing with the problem is to estimate the system with an AR(1) correction, and restricting the autocorrelation parameter to be the same for each of the equations in the system. Consequently, this is what we assume, and by writing the share equations for period $t - 1$, multiplying by ρ, and subtracting, we estimate stochastic budget share equations given by

$$s_t = g(v_t, \boldsymbol{\theta}) + \rho s_{t-1} - \rho g(v_{t-1}, \boldsymbol{\theta}) + e_t,$$

to put it in the notation of Chapter 18.

Imposing a common factor across the equations ensures that the elasticities of substitution are invariant to which equation is omitted from the system during estimation. However, David Hendry and Grayham Mizon (1978) show that autocorrelation may be due to dynamic misspecification and by imposing an AR(1) correction may bias parameter estimations. An alternative is to estimate an unrestricted autoregressive distributed lag specification, but the drawback of such an approach is that the elasticities of substitution are sensitive to which equation is omitted during estimation. Thus there is a trade-off between the possibility of biased estimates, which may be small, from imposing a common restriction across equations to estimating an unrestricted model where the results can be quite sensitive to which equation is omitted.

The estimation results are presented in Table 19.5. The results were checked for global convergence by estimating the model more than once, deleting a different equation each time. The parameters are reasonably

Table 19.5.   Parameter Estimates for the Basic Translog

Parameter	Estimate	t-statistic
α_1	.2162	36.6
α_2	.3758	18.5
α_4	.3276	14.4
β_{11}	.1770	11.3
β_{12}	−.1638	− 4.5
β_{13}	−.0288	− 4.4
β_{14}	−.0166	− 0.6
β_{22}	−.1854	− 2.6
β_{23}	−.0978	− 7.8
β_{24}	−.1894	− 4.2
β_{33}	.0449	11.8
β_{34}	−.0446	− 3.8
β_{44}	.2617	5.5
ρ	.9354	68.1

Log likelihood = 479.729
$R_1^2 = .998$, $R_2^2 = .971$, $R_4^2 = .991$,
$\text{DW}_1 = .748$, $\text{DW}_2 = .595$, $\text{DW}_4 = .553$.

well determined, with 13 out of the 14 estimated parameters being statistically significant — achieving t-values in excess of 2. Also, the R^2
statistics are quite high, indicating that the model fits the data well.
However, the computed equation-by-equation Durbin-Watson statistics
are still low, suggesting that the model is perhaps dynamically mispec-
ified, an issue that we will not explore in this chapter — see Serletis
(1991b), Fleissig and Swofford (1996, 1997), Fleissig (1997), Fisher and
Fleissig (1997), Drake, Fleissig, and Mullineaux (1999), and Fleissig and
Serletis (2001) for work along these lines.

19.3.2   The Regularity Tests

Before trying to interpret the results, it is useful to perform tests
to establish whether the parameter estimates are consistent with the
utility maximization hypothesis underlying the model. Since we have
restricted the parameters, as part of the maintained hypothesis, to satisfy
adding up and symmetry, we test, at each data point, the theoretical
restrictions that are not part of the maintained hypothesis — that is,
nonnegativity, monotonicity, and the curvature condition on the indirect
utility function.

The nonnegativity restriction requires that the values of the fitted
demand functions be nonnegative ($x_i \geq 0$, for every i), and can be easily
checked by direct computation of the values of the estimated budget
shares. The usual neoclassical monotonicity requirement is that the
direct utility function should be an increasing function of each good
consumed, that is

$$\frac{\partial f(\boldsymbol{x})}{\partial x_i} > 0, \quad \text{for } i = 1, ..., n.$$

In terms of the indirect utility function, the monotonicity conditions
require that the indirect utility function should be a decreasing function
of each income-normalized price. That is,

$$\frac{\partial \log V(\boldsymbol{v})}{\partial \log v_i} < 0 \quad \text{for } i = 1, ..., n.$$

The monotonicity conditions, like the nonnegativity conditions, can also
be checked by direct computation of the values of the gradient vector of
the estimated indirect utility function.

Finally, the curvature condition requires quasi-convexity of the indirect utility function, and it can be checked, provided the monotonicity
conditions hold, by direct computation of the matrix of the Allen partial

elasticities of substitution. This matrix must be negative semidefinite. This requires that (i) all own four σ_{ii}^a are negative at each (quarterly) observation, (ii) each of the six possible 2×2 matrices

$$\begin{bmatrix} \sigma_{ii}^a & \sigma_{ij}^a \\ \sigma_{ij}^a & \sigma_{jj}^a \end{bmatrix}$$

for $i, j = 1, 2, 3, 4$ but $i \neq j$, has a positive determinant at every observation, (iii) each of the four possible 3×3 matrices

$$\begin{bmatrix} \sigma_{ii}^a & \sigma_{ij}^a & \sigma_{ik}^a \\ \sigma_{ij}^a & \sigma_{jj}^a & \sigma_{jk}^a \\ \sigma_{ik}^a & \sigma_{jk}^a & \sigma_{kk}^a \end{bmatrix}$$

for $i, j, k = 1, 2, 3, 4$ but $i \neq j$, $i \neq k$, $j \neq k$, has a negative determinant at every observation, and (iv) the 4×4 matrix consisting of all the σ_{ij}^a, $i, j = 1, 2, 3, 4$,

$$\begin{bmatrix} \sigma_{11}^a & \sigma_{12}^a & \sigma_{13}^a & \sigma_{14}^a \\ \sigma_{12}^a & \sigma_{22}^a & \sigma_{23}^a & \sigma_{24}^a \\ \sigma_{13}^a & \sigma_{23}^a & \sigma_{33}^a & \sigma_{34}^a \\ \sigma_{14}^a & \sigma_{24}^a & \sigma_{34}^a & \sigma_{44}^a \end{bmatrix}$$

has a determinant whose value is zero (or near zero).

The results of the regularity tests indicate that nonnegativity and monotonicity hold at every observation. However, the curvature condition is only satisfied at 65.6% of the observations. This suggests, as we argued before, that we should be using flexible functional forms that possess global properties, such as Barnett's asymptotically ideal model or Gallant's Fourier form that we discussed in Chapter 17. With this in mind, at this point we will evaluate the parameter estimates from Table 19.5 by calculating income and price elasticities and the elasticities of substitution.

19.3.3   The Elasticities

Following Serletis (1988), the formula for the income elasticities for the basic translog model is

$$E_i = 1 + \frac{-\sum_j \beta_{ij}/s_i + \sum_i \sum_j \beta_{ij}}{1 + \sum_i \sum_j \beta_{ij} \log v_j}, \quad i = 1, ..., 4,$$

Table 19.6.   Income and Price Elasticities

Asset	E_i	Price elasticities			
		η_{i1}	η_{i2}	η_{i3}	η_{i4}
Q_1	0.362 (4.3)	−0.143 (4.3)	−0.123 (2.3)	−0.007 (0.4)	−0.088 (2.4)
Q_2	1.907 (10.8)	−0.403 (7.5)	−0.854 (13.3)	−0.133 (6.1)	−0.515 (7.0)
x_7	1.802 (7.7)	−0.330 (5.1)	−0.591 (5.0)	−0.307 (6.8)	−0.572 (6.1)
Q_3	0.178 (1.1)	−0.018 (0.4)	0.057 (0.7)	−0.010 (0.5)	−0.207 (2.8)

NOTE: Numbers in parentheses are absolute t-statistics.

while that for the own-price elasticities is

$$\eta_{ii} = -1 + \frac{\beta_{ii}/s_i + \sum_j \beta_{ij}}{1 + \sum_i \sum_j \beta_{ij} \log v_j}, \quad i = 1, ..., 4,$$

and that for the cross-price elasticities is

$$\eta_{ij} = \frac{\beta_{ij}/s_i - \sum_i \beta_{ij}}{1 + \sum_i \sum_j \beta_{ij} \log v_j}, \quad i, j = 1, ..., 4, \quad \text{but } i \neq j.$$

These elasticities, calculated at the mean of the data, are presented in Table 19.6. Numbers in parentheses are t-statistics computed by linearizing the elasticity formulas around the estimated parameter values and then by using the standard formulas for the variance of linear functions of random variables. This was carried out in a somewhat automatic fashion by using the ANALYZ command in TSP. Such an approximation technique has been recommended for translog aggregator functions by Toers (1980, 1982), and as Green, Hahn, and Rocke (1987, p. 148) conclude, "it appears that demand analysts can have a certain amount of confidence in the asymptotic standard errors that are obtained from using Taylor series approximations."

Turning to the elasticity estimates in Table 19.6, it is interesting to note that almost all estimated elasticities are significant at conventional significance levels and that they reveal a pattern consistent with demand theory. In particular, the income elasticities are all positive ($E_i > 0$)

Table 19.7.   Allen and Morishima Elasticities of Substitution

| Asset | Elasticities of substitution | | | |
	σ_{i1}	σ_{i2}	σ_{i3}	σ_{i4}
	A. Allen elasticities of substitution			
Q_1	−0.301 (2.1)	0.036 (0.3)	0.270 (1.4)	0.091 (1.4)
Q_2	—	−0.357 (2.9)	0.234 (1.4)	0.331 (2.6)
x_7	—	—	−2.049 (3.6)	0.051 (0.2)
Q_3	—	—	—	−0.454 (3.3)
	B. Morishima elasticities of substitution			
Q_1	—	0.072 (1.4)	0.123 (2.1)	0.084 (2.6)
Q_2	0.148 (2.3)	—	0.223 (2.8)	0.259 (3.0)
x_7	0.185 (3.3)	0.182 (3.5)	—	0.167 (2.9)
Q_3	0.178 (3.0)	0.257 (2.7)	0.165 (1.8)	—

NOTE: Numbers in parentheses are absolute t-statistics.

with Q_2 and x_7 being 'luxury assets,' ($E_2 = 1.907$ and $E_3 = 1.802$). The own-price elasticities are all negative ($\eta_{ii} < 0$), with the own-price elasticity for Q_2 being particularly high ($\eta_{22} = -0.854$). Looking now at the cross-price elasticities, we see that all are negative ($\eta_{ij} < 0$), except for η_{42}, suggesting that Q_1, Q_2, x_7, and Q_3 are gross complements.

Finally, diagonal and upper off-diagonal Allen elasticities of substitution are reported in Panel A of Table 19.7 (since these elasticities are symmetric) and the Morishima elasticities of substitution are reported in Panel B. As already noted in Chapter 18, the Allen elasticities of substitution are computed from the income and price elasticities, using the Slutsky equation

$$\sigma_{ij}^a = E_i + \eta_{ij}/s_j,$$

and the Morishima elasticities of substitution are defined as

$$\sigma_{ij}^m = s_i \left(\sigma_{ji}^a - \sigma_{ii}^a \right).$$

All own Allen elasticities of substitution are negative ($\sigma_{ii}^a < 0$), while the assets appear to be net substitutes, irrespective of whether the Allen or the Morishima elasticities of substitution are used. Based on the Morishima elasticities of substitution — the correct measures of substitution — the degree of substitutability between Q_1, Q_2, x_7, and Q_3 is low, a finding that corroborates previous results using other consumer demand models. This is also consistent with the nonparametric weak separability test results of the previous section.

19.4   Conclusion

We have provided a solution to the inter-related problems of monetary aggregation and estimation of money demand, using revealed preference theory and demand systems analysis. As Fisher (1989, p. xiii) puts it,

> "[t]his work represents a literature that has developed in the monetary context over the last 15 or so years and one that now offers theoretical and empirical insights on both the nature of what we might call 'the monetary problem' and on most of the major issues involving monetary policy."

We have also addressed several other matters that we haven't simultaneously examined. A discussion of these matters is the subject of the next, final, chapter of this book.

Chapter 20

Future Research Agenda

Clearly many unsolved problems exist in what Barnett (1997) calls the 'high road' literature regarding the inter-related problems of monetary aggregation and estimation of money demand. These problems continue to be the subject of expanding research. In fact, as Barnett (1997, p. 1182) puts it,

> "[t]he high road builds on the foundation of existing microeconomic theory, including the theory of the firm, consumer theory, and the implied microeconomic aggregation and index number theory. Advances in those areas are accepted and absorbed in a coherent manner as research proceeds up the high road. Constructive criticism of the high road is based upon recognition of the existence of unsolved problems in the supporting areas of economic research and the need for further development in those areas to permit the high road to climb even higher."

With this in mind, in this concluding chapter of the book we address a number of issues and point particular directions (not necessarily in order of importance) that high road research could take.

20.1   Outstanding Credit

The monetary aggregates currently available (either simple-sum, Divisia, or currency equivalent) exclude unused credit, potentially generating spurious instability of money demand. Given that a conceptually more appropriate measure of the quantity of the medium of exchange should assign a nonzero weight to outstanding credit, the current monetary aggregation literature should be extended to include in the definition of the medium of exchange some measure of outstanding credit available to the public.

Outstanding credit is a very useful asset. The problem is how to price assets such as, for example, overdraft facilities of firms and individuals and approved credit lines available to the public, in order to be explicitly included in microeconomic- and aggregation-theoretic monetary aggregates. The gains remain to be seen, of course, but we suggest that many of the anomalies in the literature on monetary topics will be eliminated when theoretically designed index numbers are employed.

20.2   Monetary Policy

An exposition is needed of what the usefulness of the estimated elasticities of substitution and, more importantly, the underlying demand equations would be in practice. That is, to what extent are higher or lower elasticities of substitution important for the conduct of effective monetary policy? To what use would the central bank put this information in its actions? What are the practical implications of using the wrong elasticities?

A breakthrough from the current state of 'interest target' monetary policy back to the correct control of monetary quantities will be through demand systems. The research agenda is clear, and it starts with getting across the procedures and showing that elasticities make sense and that the properties of the models are nicely neoclassical. Since this has been done, the next step is to analyze actual policies, using actual demand system estimates, compared to the other ways of guiding policy.

20.3   Dynamics

We should note that most of the early studies of demand systems directly applied data to static models, implicitly assuming that the pattern of demand adjusts to a change in exogenous variables instantaneously. No attention had been paid to the dynamic structure of the models used, although many studies reported results with serially correlated residuals suggesting that the underlying models are perhaps dynamically misspecified. In fact, most of the early money demand studies tended to ignore dynamic issues, although the issue of dynamic adjustment has been considerably addressed in the 'traditional' log-levels money demand specification by considering different, short-run adjustment processes. In particular, in Chapter 8 we considered three fundamentally different, short-run dynamic adjustment processes in the traditional approach — the 'real' adjustment specification, the 'price' adjustment specification, and the 'nominal' adjustment specification.

Recently, however, a number of demand studies have focussed attention on the development of dynamic generalizations of the traditional static models that allow a test of the static model itself, as well as the theoretical restrictions and simplifications from demand theory. For example, Serletis (1991a) develops microtheoretic dynamic generalizations of four static translog models, by appealing to the habit *hysteresis* theory and assuming that consumers' current preferences depend on their past consumption pattern so that lagged variables will influence current demand. Also, Gordon Anderson and Richard Blundell (1982) motivated from the lack of accord between the postulates of demand theory and empirical static demand functions estimated on time series data, develop an unrestricted dynamic formulation to accommodate short-run disequilibrium situations, by including lagged endogenous and exogenous variables as regressors.

To illustrate the Anderson and Blundell (1982) approach, let's consider the share equation system of the HTL, equation (18.2). The dynamics are introduced by replacing the usual static assumption of instantaneous adjustment by a more general one that the static model holds only asymptotically. Under this assumption it is possible to specify the dynamic structure (data generation process) by a general stationary stochastic process. In particular, following Anderson and Blundell (1982), we replace s in (18.2) by a vector autoregressive process in s of order 1 and v by a vector autoregressive process in v of order 1. After some manipulation and consideration of the adding up restrictions — see Anderson and Blundell (1982, p. 1560-66) — a general first-order dynamic model may be written as

$$\Delta s_t = \mathbf{D}\Delta \tilde{v}_t - \mathbf{A}(s_{t-1}^n - \Pi^n v_{t-1}) + u_t \qquad (20.1)$$

where Δ represents the first difference operator, $\tilde{v}$ refers to v with the first element excluded, superscript n on a matrix or a vector denotes the deletion of the nth row and $\mathbf{D}$ and $\mathbf{A}$ are appropriately dimensioned short-run coefficient matrices. Note that the adding-up restrictions associated with (18.2) require certain additional restrictions on the elements of $\mathbf{D}$ and $\mathbf{A}$ in (20.1). These imply that the column sums of $\mathbf{D}$ and $\mathbf{A}$ in (20.1) are all zero.

The advantage of estimating in the context of (20.1) is that equation (20.1) is the alternative hypothesis against which a number of hypotheses can be tested. For example, if $\mathbf{D} = \Pi_1$, where Π_1 denotes Π with the first column corresponding to the intercept term deleted, equation (20.1) reduces to the static model with AR(1) error term,

$$s_t = \Pi v_t + u_t, \quad u_t = \rho u_{t-1} + e_t$$

If $\mathbf{D} = \mathbf{A}\Pi_1$, equation (20.1) reduces to the partial adjustment model considered by Ishag Nadiri and Sherwin Rosen (1969). Finally, if $\mathbf{D} = \Pi_1$, and $\mathbf{A} = \mathbf{I}$, equation (20.1) reduces to the static model (18.2).

Notice that the Anderson and Blundell approach to dynamic specification, adopted in the money demand literature by Serletis (1991b), follows in the spirit of the error correction models and stands in contrast to the theoretical approaches that maintain specific theories of dynamic adjustment. It is, however, intuitively appealing as it seems that no theoretical approach is likely to deal with the actual dynamics of a demand system, which are likely to be a complicated amalgam of effects, including habit persistence, adjustment costs, the formation of expectations, and misinterpretation of real price changes.

More recently, Fisher and Fleissig (1994) produce two versions of the dynamic Fourier demand system — one is a 'dynamic utility function approach,' following the lead of Serletis (1991a), and the other is a 'time series approach,' following the lead of Anderson and Blundell (1982, 1983) and Serletis (1991b). For other interesting follow-up papers that utilize some of the flexible functional forms that we discussed in Chapter 17, see Fleissig and Swofford (1996, 1997), Fleissig (1997), Fisher and Fleissig (1997), Leigh Drake , Fleissig, and Andy Mullineaux (1999), and Fleissig and Serletis (2001).

Those works are interesting and attractive; they include estimates of the degree of substitutability using some constrained flexible functional forms or unconstrained versions used to test for theoretical and functional form restrictions. Yet Serletis (1991b), in addition to modeling the demand for aggreagte Divisia money measures, systematically tests for the appropriateness of the weak separability (aggregation) conditions using flexible functional form interpretations of the translog functional form. All these specifications, however, simply add lagged variables to the system. There is no explicit dynamic optimization framework under consideration. We believe that a particularly constructive approach will be based on the use of dynamic models.

Moreover, high autocorrelation in demand systems estimated with per capita data could also be due to either the effects of nonstationarity of prices — see, for example, Arthur Lewbel (1996) — and/or aggregation across consumers — see, for example, Thomas Stoker (1986). None of these potential biases to the models have been successfully considered in the existing monetary demand literature. Of course, dealing with these issues is not easy. The combination, for example, of nonstationary data and nonlinear estimation in fairly large models is an extremely difficult problem.

20.4 Risk Matters

In this book we haven't dealt with the extension of riskless models to situations where the economic agent makes decisions under uncertainty. In fact, in the theory of microeconomic quantity and price aggregation reviewed in this book, the theoretical existence of exact aggregates is proved through the use of nested two-stage budgeting and duality theory. Under risk, however, two-stage budgeting theorems do not work, and most duality theory does not apply.

Recently, however, Barnett (1995), and Barnett, Yi Liu, and Mark Jensen (1997) have extended aggregation theory to the case of risk and derived the 'generalized Divisia index.' This work is very interesting and innovative and we briefly review it here in the context of an optimal growth model, similar to those we dealt with in Chapters 3 and 4. Our objective is to show the process by which the generalized Divisia index may be derived, its connection to optimal growth theory and capital asset pricing models, and to also discuss a possible future research agenda that might flow out of this work.

Assume an infinitely lived economic agent having expected utility

$$E_0 \sum_{t=0}^{\infty} \beta^t u\left(c_t, \boldsymbol{x}_t\right), \qquad (20.2)$$

where E_0 is the mathematical expectation operator conditional on all information at time 0, β is the discount factor, c is aggregate real consumption of goods and services, and $\boldsymbol{x}$ is an n-dimensional vector of real balances of monetary assets. It is assumed that the one-period utility function, $u(\cdot)$ is weakly separable in $\boldsymbol{x}$. That is, it must be possible to write it as $u = u\left(c_t, f(\boldsymbol{x}_t)\right)$, in which $f(\boldsymbol{x})$ defines the monetary subutiltiy function.

The objective (20.2) is maximized with respect to $\{c_t, \boldsymbol{x}_t, A_t\}_{t=0}^{\infty}$, where A_t denotes holdings of the benchmark asset during period t, subject to a sequence of one period budget constraints

$$q_t c_t \quad = \quad \sum_{i=1}^{n} \left[(1 + r_{i,t-1}) p_{t-1}^* x_{i,t-1} - p_t^* x_{it}\right]$$

$$+ (1 + R_{t-1}) p_{t-1}^* A_{t-1} - p_t^* A_t + I_t, \qquad (20.3)$$

for $t = 0, 1, \ldots$. In equation (20.3), q is the exact price aggregate that is dual to the consumer goods quantity aggregate c; r_i is the nominal holding period yield on assets i; R is the holding-period yield on the benchmark asset; p^* is the true cost of living index, $p^* = p^*(q)$; and I_t is the sum of all other sources of income during period t. To rule out perpetual borrowing on the part of the consumer, we impose the condition

$$\lim_{t \to \infty} d_t A_t = 0, \tag{20.4}$$

where the present value factor d_t is defined by $d_t = d_{t-1}/(1 + R_{t-1})$, with $d_{t-1} = 1$.

Solving the difference equation (20.3) forward, using (20.4) as the terminal condition, we obtain the following intertemporal version of the budget constraint

$$\sum_{t=0}^{\infty} d_t q_t c_t = p_{t-1}^* A_{t-1} + \sum_{t=0}^{\infty} d_t I_t$$

$$\tag{20.5}$$

$$+ \sum_{t=0}^{\infty} \sum_{i=1}^{n} d_t \left[(1 + r_{i,t-1}) p_{t-1}^* x_{i,t-1} - p_t^* x_{it} \right].$$

The Euler equations for monetary assets and the consumer goods aggregate are

$$\frac{\partial u}{\partial x_{it}} = \beta E_t \frac{p_t^* (R_t - r_{it})}{p_{t+1}^*} \frac{\partial u}{\partial c_{t+1}}, \quad i = 1, \ldots, n \tag{20.6}$$

$$\frac{\partial u}{\partial c_t} = \beta E_t \frac{p_t^* (1 + R_t)}{p_{t+1}^*} \frac{\partial u}{\partial c_{t+1}}. \tag{20.7}$$

For notational convenience, we convert the nominal rates of return, R_t and r_{it}, into real rates, R_t^* and r_{it}^*, such that

$$(1 + R_t^*) = p_t^* \frac{(1 + R_t)}{p_{t+1}^*} \quad \text{and} \quad (1 + r_{it}^*) = p_t^* \frac{(1 + r_{it})}{p_{t+1}^*}.$$

Under this new notation (20.6) and (20.7) can be written as

$$\frac{\partial u}{\partial x_{it}} = \beta E_t \left[(R_t^* - r_{it}^*) \frac{\partial u}{\partial c_{t+1}} \right], \quad i = 1, ..., n \qquad (20.8)$$

$$\frac{\partial u}{\partial c_t} = \beta E_t \left[(1 + R_t^*) \frac{\partial u}{\partial c_{t+1}} \right]. \qquad (20.9)$$

Under risk aversion, the marginal utility of consumption and the interest rates in the expectation on the right-hand side of each of (20.8) and (20.9) are correlated. Hence, these equations can be written as

$$\frac{\partial u}{\partial x_{it}} = \beta E_t \left[\frac{\partial u}{\partial c_{t+1}} \right] (E_t R_t^* - E_t r_{it}^*) + \beta \mathrm{Cov} \left(R_t^*, \frac{\partial u}{\partial c_{t+1}} \right)$$
$$- \beta \mathrm{Cov} \left(r_{it}^*, \frac{\partial u}{\partial c_{t+1}} \right), \quad \text{for all } i \qquad (20.10)$$

$$\frac{\partial u}{\partial c_t} = \beta E_t \left[\frac{\partial u}{\partial c_{t+1}} \right] + \beta E_t \left[R_t^* \right] E_t \left[\frac{\partial u}{\partial c_{t+1}} \right]$$
$$+ \beta \mathrm{Cov} \left(R_t^*, \frac{\partial u}{\partial c_{t+1}} \right). \qquad (20.11)$$

Solving (20.11) for $\beta E_t \left[\partial u / \partial c_{t+1} \right]$ and substituting into (20.10) yields

$$\frac{\partial u}{\partial x_{it}} = (p_{it} + \psi_{it}) \frac{\partial u}{\partial c_t} \quad i = 1, ..., n, \qquad (20.12)$$

where $(p_{it} + \psi_{it})$ is the risk-adjusted user cost of holding asset i, with

$$p_{it} = \frac{E_t R_t^* - E_t r_{it}^*}{1 + R_t^*},$$

or in nominal terms

$$p_{it} = \frac{E_t R_t - E_t r_{it}}{1 + R_t},$$

and

$$\psi_{it} = \beta \left(1 - p_{it}\right) \frac{\mathrm{Cov}\left(R_t^*, \dfrac{\partial u}{\partial c_{t+1}}\right)}{\dfrac{\partial u}{\partial c_t}} - \beta \frac{\mathrm{Cov}\left(r_{it}^*, \dfrac{\partial u}{\partial c_{t+1}}\right)}{\dfrac{\partial u}{\partial c_t}}.$$

To derive the Divisia index under risk aversion, let us return to the consumer's utility function as defined above, this was $u = u\left(c_t, f(\boldsymbol{x}_t)\right)$. Because of the weak separability assumption of $u(\cdot)$, we have

$$\frac{\partial u}{\partial x_{it}} = \frac{\partial u}{\partial f(\boldsymbol{x}_t)} \frac{\partial f(\boldsymbol{x}_t)}{\partial x_{it}}, \quad i = 1, ..., n,$$

which because of (20.12) becomes

$$\frac{\partial f(\boldsymbol{x}_t)}{\partial x_{it}} = (p_{it} + \psi_{it}) \frac{\partial u/\partial c_t}{\partial u/\partial f(\boldsymbol{x}_t)}. \tag{20.13}$$

Since the total differential of $f(\boldsymbol{x})$ is

$$df(\boldsymbol{x}_t) = \sum_{i=1}^{n} \left(\frac{\partial f(\boldsymbol{x}_t)}{\partial x_{it}}\right) dx_{it}, \tag{20.14}$$

substitution of (20.13) into (20.14) yields

$$df(\boldsymbol{x}_t) = \frac{\partial u/\partial c_t}{\partial u/\partial f(\boldsymbol{x}_t)} \sum_{i=1}^{n} (p_{it} + \psi_{it}) dx_{it}. \tag{20.15}$$

Also, since linear homogeneity of $f(\boldsymbol{x})$ implies

$$f(\boldsymbol{x}_t) = \sum_{i=1}^{n} \left(\frac{\partial f(\boldsymbol{x}_t)}{\partial x_{it}}\right) x_{it}, \tag{20.16}$$

substitution of (20.13) into (20.16) yields

$$f(\boldsymbol{x}_t) = \frac{\partial u/\partial c_t}{\partial u/\partial f(\boldsymbol{x}_t)} \sum_{i=1}^{n} (p_{it} + \psi_{it}) x_{it}. \tag{20.17}$$

Finally, dividing (20.15) by (20.17) and rearranging yields the *generalized Divisia index*

$$d\log f(\boldsymbol{x}_t) = \sum_{i=1}^{n} w_{it}^* d\log x_{it}, \qquad (20.18)$$

where

$$w_{it}^* = \frac{(p_{it} + \psi_{it})\, x_{it}}{\sum_{k=1}^{n} (p_{kt} + \psi_{kt})\, x_{kt}},$$

is the risk-adjusted share of asset i. Of course, under risk neutrality, the marginal utility of consumption and the interest rates in the expectations on the right-hand sides of (20.10) and (20.11) are uncorrelated. Hence, ψ_{it} would be zero, for all i, and the generalized Divisia index (20.18) reduces to the Divisia index in the perfect-certainty (or risk neutrality) case that we studied in this book.

This extension of the theory of microeconomic quantity and price aggregation under perfect certainty to situations under risk is interesting and innovative . However, there is a need for the expected utility approach to be extended to a nonexpected utility approach. As Diewert (2000, p. xxvi) puts it, in his introduction to Barnett and Serletis (2000a),

"[s]tarting with Allais (1953), various researchers, including for example, Machina (1982), Mehra and Prescott (1985), and Chew and Epstein (1989), have noted various paradoxes associated with the use of the expected utility approach. Using the state contingent commodity approach to choice under risk that was pioneered by Blackorby, Davidson, and Donaldson (1977), Diewert (1993) tried to show that the expected utility framework led to a relatively inflexible class of functional forms to model preferences over uncertain alternatives. Diewert showed that a much more flexible class of functional forms can be obtained by moving to nonexpected utility models that are counterparts to the choice over lotteries models of the type pioneered by Dekel (1986), Chew (1989), Epstein and Zin (1990, 1991), and Gul (1991). Epstein and Zin (1990), Epstein (1992), and Diewert (1993, 1995) showed that these more flexible models can explain many of the choice under uncertainty paradoxes, including the equity premium puzzle of Mehra and Prescott (1985)."

20.5   Conclusion

Until fairly recently most money demand studies were based on the use of simple-sum measures of money and log-linear demand for money functions. The subject was, as Barnett (1987, p. 1184) puts it, " ... the unstable non-demand function for a non-variable regressed on other non-variables through non-theory." This book has focused attention on the gains that can be achieved by a rigorous use of microeconomic theory, index number theory, aggregation theory, and related econometric approaches to the study of the inter-related problems of monetary aggregation and estimation of money demand. Of course, many unsolved problems exist in this literature. The investigation of those problems, however, is likely to be significantly useful and productive.

References

Afriat, S., 1967. "The Construction of a Utility Function from Expenditure Data," *International Economic Review* 8, 67-77.

Ahmad, S., 1977. "Transactions Demand for Money and the Quantity Theory," *Quarterly Journal of Economics* 91, 327-335.

Allais, M., 1953. "Le comportement de l'homme rationnel devant le risque: critique de postulats et axiomes de l'école américaines," *Econometrica* 21, 503-546.

Alston, J. M., K. A. Foster, and R. D. Green, 1994. "Estimating Elasticities with the Linear Approximate Ideal Demand System: Some Monte Carlo Results," *Review of Economics and Statistics* 76, 351-356.

Anderson, G. J. and R. W. Blundell, 1982. "Estimation and Hypothesis Testing in Dynamic Singular Equation Systems," *Econometrica* 50, 1559-1571.

Anderson, G. J. and R. W. Blundell, 1983. "Testing Restrictions in a Flexible Dynamic Demand System: An Application to Consumers' Expenditure in Canada," *Review of Economic Studies* 50, 397-410.

Anderson, R. G., B. E. Jones, and T. D. Nesmith, 1997. "Building New Monetary Services Indexes: Concepts, Data and Methods," The Federal Reserve Bank of St. Louis *Review* 79, 53-82.

Anderson, R. W., 1979. "Perfect Price Aggregation and Empirical Demand Analysis," *Econometrica* 47, 1209-1230.

Attfield, C. L. F., 1997. "Estimating a Cointegrating Demand System," *European Economic Review* 41, 61-73.

Azariadis, C., 1993. *Intertemporal Macroeconomics*, Oxford: Blackwell.

Backus, D. K. and P. J. Kehoe, 1992. "International Evidence on the Historical Properties of Business Cycles," *American Economic Review* 82, 864-888.

Banerjee, A., R. L. Lumsdaine, and J. H. Stock, 1992. "Recursive and Sequential Tests of the Unit-Root and Trend-Break Hypotheses: Theory and International Evidence," *Journal of Business and Economic Statistics* 10, 271-287.

Banks, J., R. Blundell, and A. Lewbel, 1997. "Quadratic Engel Curves and Consumer Demand," *Review of Economics and Statistics* 79, 527-539.

Barnett, W. A., 1977. "Recursive Subaggregation and a Generalized Hypocycloidal Demand Model," *Econometrica* 45, 1117-1136.

Barnett, W. A., 1978. "The User Cost of Money," *Economics Letters* 1, 145-14.

Barnett, W. A., 1980. "Economic Monetary Aggregates: An Application of Aggregation and Index Number Theory," *Journal of Econometrics* 14, 11-48.

Barnett, W. A., 1982. "The Optimal Level of Monetary Aggregation," *Journal of Money, Credit, and Banking* 14, 687-710.

Barnett, W. A., 1983. "New Indices of Money Supply and the Flexible Laurent Demand System," *Journal of Business and Economic Statistics* 1, 7-23.

Barnett, W. A., 1984. "Recent Monetary Policy and the Divisia Monetary Aggregates," *American Statistician* 38, 165-172.

Barnett, W. A., 1985. "The Minflex Laurent Translog Flexible Functional Form," *Journal of Econometrics* 30, 33-44.

Barnett, W. A., 1995. "Exact Aggregation Under Risk." In *Social Choice, Welfare, and Ethics,* W. A. Barnett, H. Moulin, M. Salles, and N. Schofield (eds.), Cambridge: Cambridge University Press, 353-374.

Barnett, W. A., 1997. "Which Road Leads to a Stable Money Demand?" *The Economic Journal* 107, 1171-1185.

Barnett, W. A. and P. Chen, 1988. "The Aggregation Theoretic Monetary Aggregates are Chaotic and Have Strange Attractors: An Economic Application of Mathematical Chaos." In *Dynamic Econometric Modeling,* W. A. Barnett, E. Berndt, and H. White (eds.), Cambridge: Cambridge University Press, 199-245.

Barnett, W. A. and S. Choi, 1989. "A Monte Carlo Study of Tests of Blockwise Weak Separability," *Journal of Business and Economic Statistics* 7, 363-377.

Barnett, W. A. and A. Jonas, 1983. "The Muntz-Szatz Demand System: An Application of a Globally Well Behaved Series Expansion," *Economics Letters* 11, 337-342.

Barnett, W. A. and Y. W. Lee, 1985. "The Global Properties of the Minflex Laurent, Generalized Leontief, and Translog Flexible Functional Forms," *Econometrica* 53, 1421-1437.

Barnett, W. A. and A. Serletis, 1990. "A Dispersion-Dependency Diagnostic Test for Aggregation Error: With Applications to Monetary Economics and Income Distribution," *Journal of Econometrics* 43, 5-34.

Barnett, W. A. and A. Serletis, 2000a. *The Theory of Monetary Aggregation*, Amsterdam: North-Holland.

Barnett, W. A. and A. Serletis, 2000b. "Martingales, Nonlinearity, and Chaos," *Journal of Economic Dynamics and Control* 24, 703-724.

Barnett, W. A. and P. Yue, 1988. "Seminonparametric Estimation of the Asymptotically Ideal Model: The AIM Demand System." In *Nonparametric and Robust Inference: Advances in Econometrics,* Vol. 7, G. F. Rhodes and T. B. Fomby (eds.), Greenwich, CT : JAI Press, 229-251.

Barnett, W. A., D. Fisher, and A. Serletis, 1992. "Consumer Theory and the Demand for Money," *Journal of Economic Literature* 30, 2086-2119.

Barnett, W. A., M. J. Hinich, and P. Yue, 2000. "The Exact Theoretical Rational Expectations Monetary Aggregates," *Macroeconomic Dynamics* 4, 197-221.

Barnett, W. A., Y. W. Lee, and M. D. Wolfe, 1985. "The Three-Dimensional Global Properties of the Minflex Laurent, Generalized Leontief, and Translog Flexible Functional Forms," *Journal of Econometrics* 30, 3-31.

Barnett, W. A., Y. Liu, and M. J. Jensen, 1997. "CAPM Risk Adjustment for Exact Aggregation over Financial Assets," *Macroeconomic Dynamics* 1, 485-512.

Barnett, W. A., E. K. Offenbacher, and P. A. Spindt, 1984. "The New Divisia Monetary Aggregates," *Journal of Political Economy* 92, 1049-1085.

Barro, R. J., 1976. "Rational Expectations and the Role of Monetary Policy," *Journal of Monetary Economics* 2, 1-32.

Barro, R. J., 1977. "Unanticipated Money Growth and Unemployment in the United States," *American Economic Review* 67, 101-115.

Barro, R. J., 1978. "Unanticipated Money, Output, and the Price Level in the United States," *Journal of Political Economy* 86, 548-580.

Barro, R. J., 1997. *Macroeconomics*, 5th ed., Cambridge: The MIT Press.

Barro, R. J. and X. Sala-i-Martin, 1995. *Economic Growth*, New York: McGraw-Hill.

Barro, R. J. and H. I. Grossman, 1976. *Money, Employment, and Inflation*, Cambridge: Cambridge University Press.

Barten, A. P., 1964. "Consumer Demand Functions under Conditions of Almost Additive Preferences," *Econometrica* 32, 1-38.

Barten, A. P., 1967. "Evidence on the Slutsky Conditions for Demand Equations," *Review of Economics and Statistics* 49, 77-84.

Barten, A. P., 1969. "Maximum Likelihood Estimation of a Complete System of Demand Equations," *European Economic Review* 1, 7-73.

Baumol, W. J., 1952. "The Transactions Demand for Cash: An Inventory Theoretic Approach," *Quarterly Journal of Economics* 66, 545-556.

Baxter, M. and R. G. King, 1999. "Measuring Business Cycles: Approximate Band-Pass Filters for Economic Time Series," *Review of Economics and Statistics* 81, 573-593.

Belongia, M. T., 1996. "Measurement Matters: Recent Results from Monetary Economics Reexamined," *Journal of Political Economy* 104, 1065-1083.

Berndt, E. R. and N. E. Savin, 1975. "Estimation and Hypothesis Testing in Singular Equation Systems with Autoregressive Disturbances," *Econometrica* 43, 937-957.

Blackorby, C. and R. R. Russell, 1981. "The Morishima Elasticity of Substitution, Symmetry, Constancy, Separability, and its Relationship to the Hicks and Allen Elasticities," *Review of Economic Studies* 48, 147-158.

Blackorby, C. and R. R. Russell, 1989. "Will the Real Elasticity of Substitution Please Stand Up?" *American Economic Review* 79, 882-888.

Blackorby, C., R. Davidson, and D. Donaldson, 1977. "A Homiletic Exposition of the Expected Utility Hypothesis," *Economica* 44, 351-358.

Blackorby, C., D. Primont, and R. R. Russell, 1978. *Duality, Separability, and Functional Structure*, Amsterdam: North-Holland.

Blackorby, C., D. Nissen, D. Primont, and R. R. Russell, 1974. "Recursively Decentralized Decision Making," *Econometrica* 42, 487-496.

Blanchard, O. J. and S. Fischer, 1989. *Lectures in Macroeconomics*, Cambridge, MA: The MIT Press.

Brock, W. A., 1974. "Money and Growth: The Case of Long-Run Perfect Foresight," *International Economic Review* 15, 750-777.

Brock, W. A. and C. Sayers, 1988. "Is the Business Cycle Characterized by Deterministic Chaos?" *Journal of Monetary Economics* 22, 71-90.

Brunner, K. and A. H. Meltzer, 1967. "Economies of Scale in Cash Balances Reconsidered," *Quarterly Journal of Economics* 81, 422-436.

Buse, A., 1994. "Evaluating the Linearized Almost Ideal Demand System," *American Journal of Agricultural Economics* 76, 781-793.

Bullard, J. B., 1999. "Testing Long-Run Monetary Neutrality Propositions: Lessons from the Recent Research," Federal Reserve Bank of St. Louis *Review* 81, 57-77.

Burns, A. F. and W. C. Mitchell, 1946. *Measuring Business Cycles*, New York: National Bureau of Economic Research.

Cagan, P., 1956. "The Monetary Dynamics of Hyperinflation." In *Studies in the Quantity Theory of Money*, M. Friedman (ed.), Chicago: University of Chicago Press.

Campbell, J. Y. and P. Perron, 1991. "Pitfalls and Opportunities: What Macroeconomists Should Know about Unit Roots," *NBER Macroeconomics Annual,* 141-200.

Campbell, J. Y., A. W. Lo, and A. C. MacKinlay, 1997. *The Econometrics of Financial Markets*, Princeton, NJ: Princeton University Press.

Cass, D., 1965. "Optimum Growth in an Aggregative Model of Capital Accumulation," *Review of Economic Studies* 32, 233-240.

Caves, D. W. and L. R. Christensen, 1980. "Global Properties of Flexible Functional Forms," *American Economic Review* 70, 422-432.

Chadha, B. and E. Prasad, 1994. "Are Prices Countercyclical? Evidence from the G7," *Journal of Monetary Economics* 34, 239-257.

Chalfant, J. A., 1987. "A Globally Flexible Almost Ideal System," *Journal of Business and Economic Statistics* 5, 233-242.

Chalfant, J. A. and A. R. Gallant, 1985. "Estimating Substitution Elasticities with the Fourier Cost Function: Some Monte Carlo Results," *Journal of Econometrics* 28, 205-222.

Champ, B. and S. Freeman, 1994. *Modeling Monetary Economies*, New York: John Wiley & Sons, Inc.

Chetty, K. V., 1969. "On Measuring the Nearness of Near-Moneys," *American Economic Review* 59, 270-281.

Chew, S. H., 1989. "Axiomatic Utility Theories with the Betweenness Property," *Annals of Operations Research* 19, 273-298.

Chew, S. H. and L. G. Epstein, 1989. "A Unifying Approach to Axiomatic Non-Expected Utility Theories," *Journal of Economic Theory* 49, 207-240.

Chow, G. C., 1960. "Tests of Equality Between Sets of Coefficients in Two Linear Regressions," *Econometrica* 28, 591-605.

Chow, G. C., 1966. "On the Long-Run and Short-Run Demand for Money," *Journal of Political Economy* 74, 111-131.

Christensen, L. R., D. W. Jorgenson, and L. J. Lau, 1975. "Transcendental Logarithmic Utility Functions," *American Economic Review* 65, 367-383.

Christiano, L. J., 1986. "Money and the U.S. Economy in the 1980s: A Break from the Past?" Federal Reserve Bank of Minneapolis *Quarterly Review* 10, 2-13.

Christiano, L. J., 1992. "Searching for a Break in GNP," *Journal of Business and Economic Statistics* 10, 237-250.

Clower, R. W., 1967. "A Reconsideration of the Microeconomic Foundations of Monetary Theory," *Western Economic Journal* 6, 1-8.

Coe, P. and A. Serletis, 2001. "Bounds Tests of the Theory of Purchasing Power Parity," *Journal of International Money and Finance* forthcoming.

Cogley, T. and J. M. Nason, 1995. "Effects of the Hodrick-Prescott Filter on Trend and Difference Stationary Time Series: Implications for Business Cycle Research," *Journal of Economic Dynamics and Control* 19, 253-278.

Collins, S. and C. L. Edwards, 1994. "An Alternative Monetary Aggregate: M2 Plus Household Holdings of Bond and Equity Mutual Funds," *Federal Reserve Bank of St. Louis Review* 76, 7-29.

Cooley, T. F. and G. D. Hansen, 1989. "The Inflation Tax in a Real Business Cycle Model," *American Economic Review* 79, 733-748.

Cooley, T. F. and L. E. Ohanian, 1991. "The Cyclical Behavior of Prices," *Journal of Monetary Economics* 28, 25-60.

Cooper, R. J. and K. R. McLaren, 1996. "A System of Demand Equations Satisfying Effectively Global Regularity Conditions," *Review of Economics and Statistics* 78, 359-364.

Deaton, A. and J. N. Muellbauer, 1980. "An Almost Ideal Demand System," *American Economic Review* 70, 312-326.

Dekel, E., 1986. "An Axiomatic Characterization of Preferences Under Uncertainty: Weakening the Independence Axiom," *Journal of Economic Theory* 40, 304-314.

Diamond, P. A., 1965. "National Debt in a Neoclassical Growth Model," *American Economic Review* 55, 1126-1150.

Dickey, D. A. and W. A. Fuller, 1979. "Distribution of the Estimates for Autoregressive Time Series with a Unit Root," *Journal of the American Statistical Association* 74, 427-431.

Dickey, D. A. and W. A. Fuller, 1981. "Likelihood Ratio Tests for Autoregressive Time Series with a Unit Root," *Econometrica* 49, 1057-1072.

Diebold, F. X. and M. Nerlove, 1990. "Unit Roots in Economic Time Series: A Selective Survey." In *Advances in Econometrics: Co-Integration, Spurious Regressions, and Unit Roots*, Vol. 8, T. B. Fomby and G. F. Rhodes Jr. (eds.), Greenwich, CT: JAI Press, 3-69.

Diewert, W. E., 1971. "An Application of the Shephard Duality Theorem: A Generalized Leontief Production Function," *Journal of Political Economy* 79, 481-507.

Diewert, W. E., 1973a. "Functional Forms for Profit and Transformation Functions," *Journal of Economic Theory* 6, 284-316.

Diewert, W. E., 1973b. "Afriat and Revealed Preference Theory," *Review of Economic Studies* 40, 419-426.

Diewert, W. E., 1976. "Exact and Superlative Index Numbers," *Journal of Econometrics* 4, 115-145.

Diewert, W. E., 1993. "Symmetric Means and Choice Under Uncertainty." In *Essays in Index Number Theory,* Vol. 1, W. E. Diewert and A. O. Nakamura (eds.), Amsterdam: North-Holland, 355-433.

Diewert, W. E., 1995. "Functional Form Problems in Modeling Insurance and Gambling," *Geneva Papers on Risk and Insurance Theory* 20, 135-150.

Diewert, W. E., 2000. "Preface to *The Theory of Monetary Aggregation.*" In *Theory of Monetary Aggregation,* W. A. Barnett and A. Serletis (eds.), Amsterdam: North-Holland, xxiii-xxviii.

Diewert, W. E. and C. Parkan, 1978. "Test for Consistency of Consumer Data and Nonparametric Index Numbers," Discussion Paper #78-27. Department of Economics, University of British Columbia.

Donovan, D. J., 1978. "Modeling the Demand for Liquid Assets: An Application to Canada," International Monetary Fund *Staff Papers* 25, 676-704.

Dowd, K., 1990. "The Value of Time and the Transactions Demand for Money," *Journal Money, Credit, and Banking* 22, 51-64.

Drake, L., A. Fleissig, and A. Mullineaux, 1999. "Are 'Risky' Assets Substitutes for 'Monetary Assets'? Evidence from an AIM Demand System," *Economic Inquiry* 37, 510-526.

Eichhorn, W., 1976. "Fisher's Tests Revisited," *Econometrica* 44, 247-256.

Eichhorn, W., 1978. *Functional Equations in Economics*, Reading, MA: Addison-Wesley.

Enders, W., 1995. *Applied Econometric Time Series*, New York: John Wiley & Sons, Inc.

Engle, R. F., 1982. "Autoregressive Conditional Heteroskedasticity with Estimates of the Variance of United Kingdom Inflation," *Econometrica* 50, 987-1008.

Engle, R. F. and C. W. Granger, 1987. "Cointegration and Error Correction: Representation, Estimation and Testing," *Econometrica* 55, 251-276.

Engle, R. F. and B. S. Yoo, 1987. "Forecasting and Testing in Cointegrated Systems," *Journal of Econometrics* 35, 143-159.

Epstein, L. G., 1992. "Behavior Under Risk: Recent Developments in Theory and Applications." In *Advances in Economic Theory*, J. J. Laffont (ed.), New York: Cambridge University Press.

Epstein, L. G. and S. E. Zin, 1990. "First Order Risk Aversion and the Equity Premium Puzzle," *Journal of Monetary Economics* 26, 387-407.

Epstein, L. G. and S. E. Zin, 1991. "The Independence Axiom and Asset Returns," NBER Working Paper #109. Cambridge, Mass.

Feenstra, R. C., 1986. "Functional Equivalence Between Liquidity Costs and the Utility of Money," *Journal of Monetary Economics* 17, 271-291.

Feige, E. L. and D. K. Pearce, 1977. "The Substitutability of Money and Near-Monies: A Survey of the Time-Series Evidence," *Journal of Economic Literature* 15, 439-469.

Fiorito, R. and T. Kollintzas, 1994. "Stylized Facts of Business Cycles in the G7 from a Real Business Cycles Perspective," *European Economic Review* 38, 235-269.

Fisher, D., 1989. *Money Demand and Monetary Policy*, Ann Arbor: The University of Michigan Press.

Fisher, D. and A. R. Fleissig, 1994. "Money Demand in a Flexible Dynamic Fourier Expenditure System," Federal Reserve Bank of St. Louis *Review* 76, 117-128.

Fisher, D. and A. R. Fleissig, 1997. "Monetary Aggregation and the Demand for Assets," *Journal of Money, Credit and Banking* 29, 458-475.

Fisher, D. and A. Serletis, 1989. "Velocity and the Growth of Money in the United States, 1970-1985," *Journal of Macroeconomics* 11, 323-332.

Fisher, D., A. R. Fleissig, and A. Serletis, 2001. "An Empirical Comparison of Flexible Demand System Functional Forms," *Journal of Applied Econometrics* forthcoming.

Fisher, M. and J. J. Seater, 1993. "Long-Run Neutrality and Superneutrality in an ARIMA Framework," *American Economic Review* 83, 402-415.

Fisher, I., 1911. *The Purchasing Power of Money*, London: Macmillan.

Fisher, I., 1922. *The Making of Index Numbers: A Study of Their Varieties, Tests, and Reliability*, Boston: Houghton Mifflin.

Fleissig, A. R., 1997. "The Dynamic Laurent Flexible Form and Long-Run Analysis," *Journal of Applied Econometrics* 12, 687-699.

Fleissig, A. R. and A. Serletis, 2001. "Semi-Nonparametric Estimates of Substitution for Canadian Monetary Assets," *Canadian Journal of Economics* forthcoming.

Fleissig, A. R. and J. L. Swofford, 1996. "A Dynamic Asymptotically Ideal Model of Money Demand," *Journal of Monetary Economics* 37, 371-380.

Fleissig, A. R. and J. L. Swofford, 1997. "Dynamic Asymptotically Ideal Models and Finite Approximation," *Journal of Business and Economic Statistics* 15, 482-492.

Fleissig, A. R., A. R. Hall, and J. J. Seater, 2000. "GARP, Separability, and the Representative Agent," *Macroeconomic Dynamics* 4, 324-342.

Fleissig, A. R., T. Kastens, and D. Terrell, 1997. "Semi-Nonparametric Estimates of Substitution Elasticities," *Economics Letters* 54, 209-215.

Friedman, M., 1956. "The Quantity Theory of Money: A Restatement." In *Studies in the Quantity Theory of Money*, M. Friedman (ed.), Chicago: University of Chicago Press.

Friedman, M. and A. J. Schwartz, 1970. *Monetary Statistics of the United States: Estimates, Sources, Methods, and Data*, New York: Columbia University Press (for the NBER).

Frisch, R., 1959. "A Complete Scheme for Computing All Direct and Cross Demand Elasticities in a Model with Many Sectors," *Econometrica* 27, 177-196.

Fuller, W. A., 1976. *Introduction to Statistical Time Series*, New York: John Wiley & Sons, Inc.

Gallant, A. R., 1981. "On the Bias in Flexible Functional Forms and an Essentially Unbiased Form: The Fourier Flexible Form," *Journal of Econometrics* 15, 211-245.

Gallant, A. R. and H. White, 1992. "On Learning the Derivatives of an Unknown Mapping with Multilayer Feedforward Networks," *Neural Networks* 5, 129-138.

Gencay, R. and W. D. Dechert, 1992. "An Algorithm for the n-Lyapunov Exponents of an n-Dimensional Unknown Dynamical System," *Physica D* 59, 142-157.

Goldfeld, S. M., 1973. "The Demand for Money Revisited," *Brookings Papers on Economic Activity* 3, 577-638.

Goldfeld, S. M., 1976. "The Case of the Missing Money," *Brookings Papers on Economic Activity* 3, 683-730.

Goldfeld, S. M. and D. Sichel, 1990. "The Demand for Money." In *Handbook of Monetary Economics*, Vol. 1, B. M. Friedman and F. H. Hahn (eds.), Amsterdam: North-Holland, 299-356.

Gonzalo, J., 1994. "Five Alternative Methods of Estimating Long-Run Equilibrium Relationships," *Journal of Econometrics* 60, 203-233.

Gordon, R. J., 1984. "The Short-Run Demand for Money: A Reconsideration," *Journal of Money, Credit, and Banking* 16, 403-434.

Gorman, W. M., 1959. "Separable Utility and Aggregation," *Econometrica* 27, 469-481.

Gorman, W. M., 1970. "Tricks with Utility Functions." In *Essays in Economic Analysis*, M. J. Artis and A. R. Nobay (eds.), Cambridge: Cambridge University Press, 211-243.

Granger, C. W. J., 1995. "Modelling Nonlinear Relationships Between Extended-Memory Variables," *Econometrica* 63, 265-279.

Green, H. A. J., 1964. *Aggregation in Economic Analysis: An Introductory Survey*, Princeton, N.J.: Princeton University Press.

Green, R., D. Rocke, and W. Hahn, 1987. "Standard Errors for Elasticities: A Comparison of Bootstrap and Asymptotic Standard Errors," *Journal of Business and Economic Statistics* 5, 145-149.

Guilkey, D. K. and C. A. K. Lovell, 1980. "On the Flexibility of the Translog Approximation," *International Economic Review* 21, 137-147.

Guilkey, D. K., C. A. K. Lovell, and R. C. Sickles, 1983. "A Comparison of the Performance of Three Flexible Functional Forms," *International Economic Review* 24, 591-616.

Gul, F., 1991. "A Theory of Disappointment Aversion," *Econometrica* 59, 667-686.

Hendry, D. and G. E. Mizon, 1978. "Serial Correlation as a Convenient Simplification, not a Nuisance: A Comment of a Study of the Demand for Money by the Bank of England," *Economic Journal* 88, 549-563.

Hicks, J. R., 1937. "Mr. Keynes and the 'Classics'," *Econometrica* 5, 147-159.

Hodrick, R. J. and E. C. Prescott, 1980. "Post War U.S. Business Cycles: An Empirical Investigation," Mimeo. Carnegie-Mellon University, Pittsburgh, PA.

Hoffman, D. L. and R. H. Rasche, 1996. *Aggregate Money Demand Functions*, Boston: Kluwer Academic.

Jarque, C. M. and A. K. Bera, 1980. "Efficient Tests for Normality, Homoscedasticity, and Serial Independence of Regression Residuals," *Economics Letters* 6, 255-259.

Johansen, S., 1988. "Statistical Analysis of Cointegrated Vectors," *Journal of Economic Dynamics and Control* 12, 231-254.

Johansen, S., 1991. "The Power Function for the Likelihood Ratio Test for Cointegration." In *Econometric Decision Models: New Methods of Modelling and Applications*, J. Gruber (ed.), New York: Springer Verlag, 323-335.

Johansen, S. and K. Juselius, 1992. "Testing Structural Hypotheses in a Multivariate Cointegration Analysis of the PPP and UIP for the UK," *Journal of Econometrics* 53, 211-244.

Judd, J. P. and J. L. Scadding, 1982. "The Search for a Stable Money Demand Function," *Journal of Economic Literature* 20, 993-1023.

Keynes, J. M., 1936. *The General Theory of Employment, Interest, and Money*, London and New York: Macmillan.

King, R. G. and S. T. Rebelo, 1993. "Low Frequency Filtering and Real Business Cycles," *Journal of Economic Dynamics and Control* 17, 207-232.

King, R. G. and M. W. Watson, 1997. "Testing Long-Run Neutrality," Federal Reserve Bank of Richmond *Economic Quarterly* 83, 69-101.

King, R. G., C. I. Plosser, J. H. Stock, and M. W. Watson, 1991. "Stochastic Trends and Economic Fluctuations," *American Economic Review* 81, 819-840.

King, R. G., C. I. Plosser, and S. T. Rebelo, 1988. "Production, Growth and Business Cycles: I. The Basic Neoclassical Model," *Journal of Monetary Economics* 21, 195-232.

Klein, B., 1974. "Competitive Interest Payments on Bank Deposits and the Long-Run Demand for Money," *American Economic Review* 64, 931-949.

Koopmans, T. C., 1947. "Measurement Without Theory," *Review of Economics and Statistics* 29, 161-172.

Koopmans, T. C., 1965. "On the Concept of Optimal Economic Growth." In *The Econometric Approach to Development Planning*, Chicago: Rand-McNally.

Koustas, Z. and A. Serletis, 1999. "On the Fisher Effect," *Journal of Monetary Economics* 44, 105-130.

Kunst, R. and K. Neusser, 1990. "Cointegration in a Macroeconomic System," *Journal of Applied Econometrics* 5, 351-365.

Kydland, F. E. and E. C. Prescott, 1990. "Business Cycles: Real Facts and a Monetary Myth," Federal Reserve Bank of Minneapolis *Quarterly Review*, 3-18.

Kwiatkowski, D., P. C. B. Phillips, P. Schmidt, and Y. Shin, 1992. "Testing the Null Hypothesis of Stationarity Against the Alternative of a Unit Root," *Journal of Econometrics* 54, 159-178.

Laidler, D. E. W., 1993. *The Demand for Money: Theories, Evidence, and Problems*, 4th ed., New York: HarperCollins College Publishers.

Lau, L. J., 1970. "Duality and the Structure of Utility Functions," *Journal of Economic Theory* 1, 374-396.

Lau, L. J., 1978. "On Exact Index Numbers," *Review of Economics and Statistics* 61, 73-82.

Leontief, W. W., 1947. "An Introduction to a Theory of the Internal Structure of Functional Relationships," *Econometrica* 15, 361-373.

Lewbel, A., 1996. "Aggregation without Separability: A Generalized Composite Commodity Theorem," *American Economic Review* 86, 524-543.

Ljung, G. M. and G. E. P. Box, 1978. "On a Measure of Lack of Fit in Time Series Models," *Biometrica* 65, 297-303.

Lucas, R. E., Jr., 1972. "Expectations and the Neutrality of Money," *Journal of Economic Theory* 4, 103-124.

Lucas, R. E., Jr., 1973. "Some International Evidence on Output-Inflation Tradeoffs," *American Economic Review* 63, 326-334.

Lucas, R. E., Jr., 1977. "Understanding Business Cycles." In *Stabilization of the Domestic and International Economy*, K. Brunner and A. H. Meltzer (eds.), Carnegie-Rochester Series on Public Policy 5, 7-29.

Lucas, R. E., Jr., 1988. "On the Mechanics of Economic Development," *Journal of Monetary Economics* 22, 3-42.

Lucas, R. E., Jr., 1996. "Nobel Lecture: Monetary Neutrality," *Journal of Political Economy* 104, 661-682.

Lucas, R. E., Jr. and N. L. Stockey, 1987. "Money and Interest in a Cash-in-Advance Economy," *Econometrica* 55, 491-513.

Machina, M., 1982. " 'Expected Utility' Analysis without the Independence Axiom," *Econometrica* 50, 277-323.

MacKinnon J. G., 1994. "Approximate Asymptotic Distribution Functions for Unit-Root and Cointegration Tests," *Journal of Business and Economic Statistics* 12, 167-176.

Mankiw, N. G., and L. H. Summers, 1986. "Money Demand and the Effects of Fiscal Policies," *Journal of Money, Credit, and Banking* 18, 415-429.

Mas-Colell, A., M. D. Whinston, and J. R. Green, 1995. *Microeconomic Theory*, New York: Oxford University Press.

McCaffrey, D., S. Ellner, R. Gallant, and D. Nychka, 1992. "Estimating the Lyapunov Exponent of a Chaotic System with Nonparametric Regression," *Journal of the American Statistical Association* 87, 682-695.

McCallum, B. T., 1989. *Monetary Economics: Theory and Policy,* New York: Macmillan.

McCallum, B. T., 1990. "Inflation: Theory and Evidence." In *Handbook of Monetary Economics*, Vol. 2, B. M. Friedman and F. H. Hahn (eds.), Amsterdam: North-Holland, 963-1012.

McCallum, B. T. and M. S. Goodfriend, 1987. "Demand for Money: Theoretical Studies." In *The New Palgrave: A Dictionary of Economics,* J. Eatwell, M. Millgate, and P. Newman (eds.), London: Macmillan, 117-130.

Mehra, R. and E. C. Prescott, 1985. "The Equity Premium: A Puzzle," *Journal of Monetary Economics* 15, 145-161.

Muth, J. F., 1961. "Rational Expectations and the Theory of Price Movements," *Econometrica* 29, 315-335.

Nadiri, I. I. and S. Rosen, 1969. "Interrelated Factor Demand Functions," *American Economic Review* 59, 457-471.

Nelson, C. R. and C. I. Plosser, 1982. "Trends and Random Walks in Macroeconomic Time Series," *Journal of Monetary Economics* 10, 139-162.

Neusser, K., 1991. "Testing the Long-Run Implications of the Neoclassical Growth Model," *Journal of Monetary Economics* 27, 3-37.

Newey, W. K. and K. D. West, 1987. "A Simple, Positive Semi-Definite, Heteroskedasticity and Autocorrelation Consistent Covariance Matrix," *Econometrica* 55, 703-708.

Ng, S., 1995. "Testing for Homogeneity in Demand Systems when the Regressors are Nonstationary," *Journal of Applied Econometrics* 10, 147-163.

Ng, S. and P. Perron, 1997. "Estimation and Inference in Nearly Unbalanced Nearly Cointegrated Systems," *Journal of Econometrics* 79, 53-81.

Nychka, D., S. Ellner, R. Gallant, and D. McCaffrey, 1992. "Finding Chaos in Noisy Systems," *Journal of the Royal Statistical Society B* 54, 399-426.

Orphanides, A. and R. Solow, 1990. "Money, Inflation and Growth." In *Handbook of Monetary Economics*, Vol. 1, B. M. Friedman and F. H. Hahn (eds.), Amsterdam: North-Holland, 223-261.

Pantula, S. G., G. Gonsalez-Farias, and W. A. Fuller, 1994. "A Comparison of Unit-Root Test Criteria," *Journal of Business and Economics Statistics* 12, 449-459.

Pashardes, P., 1993. "Bias in Estimating the Almost Ideal Demand System with the Stone Index Approximation," *Economic Journal* 103, 908-915.

Patinkin, D., 1965. *Money, Interest, and Prices*, 2nd ed., New York: Harper & Row Publishers.

Perron, P., 1989. "The Great Crash, the Oil Price Shosk, and the Unit Root Hypothesis," *Econometrica* 57, 1361-1401.

Perron, P. and T. J. Vogelsang, 1992a. "Nonstationarity and Level Shifts with an Application to Purchasing Power Parity," *Journal of Business and Economic Statistics* 10, 301-320.

Perron, P. and T. J. Vogelsang, 1992b. "Testing for a Unit Root in a Time Series with a Changing Mean: Corrections and Extensions," *Journal of Business and Economic Statistics* 10, 467-470.

Pesaran, M. H., Y. Shin, and R. J. Smith, 1999. "Bounds Testing Approaches to the Analysis of Long-Run Relationships," Working Paper #9907. Department of Applied Economics, University of Cambridge.

Author Index

Afriat, S., 203
Ahmad, S., 70
Allais, M., 271
Alston, J. M., 227
Anderson, G. J., 265–266
Anderson, R. G., xxiv, 89, 157, 180, 218
Anderson, R. W., 219
Andreadis, I., 124
Andrews, D. W. K., 119
Attfield, C. L. F., 248
Azariadis, C., 25, 40

Backus, D. K., 194
Banerjee, A., 119
Banks, J., 227
Barnett, W. A., xvii, xxiv, 93, 122, 124,
    157, 159–160, 162, 171, 176–178, 180,
    219, 227–228, 231, 259, 263, 267,
    271–272
Barro, R. J., 5, 13–14, 19, 22, 31, 39, 96
Barten, A. P., 239, 243, 246, 255
Baumol, W. J., 53, 67–68, 73
Baxter, M., 196
Belongia, M. T., 181, 194
Bera, A. K., 98–99, 106, 112
Berndt, E. R., 240, 256
Blackorby, C., 164, 205, 220, 242, 271
Blanchard, O. J., 38, 40, 82
Blundell, R. W., 227, 265–266
Box, G. E. P., 98–99, 106, 112, 124
Brock, W. A., 48, 122
Brunner, K., 69–70
Bullard, J. B., 51
Burns, A. F., 187, 196
Buse, A., 227

Cagan, P., 95
Campbell, J. Y., 116, 121, 131
Cass, D., 27
Caves, D. W., 224, 227

Chadha, B., 194
Chalfant, J. A., 227, 230
Champ, B., 82
Chen, P., 124
Chetty, K. V., 160
Chew, S. H., 271
Chow, G. C., 98 100, 106, 112
Christensen, L. R., 166, 224, 227
Christiano, L. J., 119
Clower, R., 73
Coe, P., 138
Cogley, T., 196
Collins, S., 253
Cooley, T. F., 77, 194
Cooper, R. J., 227

Davidson, R., 271
Deaton, A., 226
Dechert, W. D., 122
Dekel, E., 271
Diamond, P. A., 27, 32
Dickey, D. A., 117, 143
Diebold, F. X., 116
Diewert, W. E., xvii, xxiv, 93, 168–171,
    203, 209, 223–224, 271
Donaldson, D., 271
Donovan, D. J., 162
Dowd, K., 70
Drake, L., 258, 266
Driscoll, J. C., xxiv, 94, 179–180

Edwards, C., 253
Eichhorn, W., 167
Ellner, S., 122–123
Enders, W., 116, 131
Engle, R. F., 50, 98–99, 106, 108, 112, 125,
    128, 130–133, 136, 141–142, 248
Epstein, L. G., 271

Feige, E. L., xxiii, 92

Topic Index